C000125835

Stuarts' Field Guide to

NATIONAL PARKS
& GAME RESERVES
of East Africa

**Chris &
Mathilde Stuart**

Published by Struik Nature (an imprint of
Penguin Random House South Africa
(Pty) Ltd
Reg. No. 1953/000441/07
The Estuaries No. 4, Oxbow Crescent,
Century Avenue, Century City, 7441
PO Box 1144, Cape Town, 8000 South Africa

Visit **www.penguinrandomhouse.co.za**
and join the Struik Nature Club for
updates, news, events and special offers.

First published in 2018

10 9 8 7 6 5 4 3 2 1

Copyright © in text, 2018: Chris and
Mathilde Stuart
Copyright © in photographs, 2018: Chris
and Mathilde Stuart and individual
photographers as listed on pp 247–248
Copyright © in maps, 2018: Chris and
Mathilde Stuart and Penguin Random
House South Africa (Pty) Ltd
Copyright © in published edition, 2018:
Penguin Random House South Africa
(Pty) Ltd

Print: 978 1 77584 062 6
ePUB: 978 1 77584 625 3

Publisher: Pippa Parker
Managing editor: Helen de Villiers
Editor: Colette Alves
Designer: Gillian Black
Cartographer: Liezel Bohdanowicz
Proofreader: Emsie du Plessis
Picture researcher: Colette Stott

Reproduction by Hirt & Carter Cape
(Pty) Ltd
Printed and bound in China by Leo Paper
Products Ltd

MIX
Paper from
responsible sources
FSC
www.fsc.org   FSC® C020056

All rights reserved. No part of this
publication may be reproduced, stored in a
retrieval system or transmitted in any form
or by any means, electronic, mechanical,
photocopying, recording or otherwise,
without the prior written permission of
the publishers and copyright holders.

Front cover: Lioness attack on Grant's Zebra (GUDKOV ANDREY/Shutterstock.com)
Spine: Southern Carmine Bee-eater (Nigel Dennis/Images of Africa)
Back cover: Savanna Elephant (Ariadne van Zandbergen/Africa Image Library)
Title page: Ugandan Red Colobus (Charlesjsharp/Sharp Photography/WC, CC BY-SA 4.0)
Page 4 (top to bottom): Sitatunga (Ariadne van Zandbergen/Africa Image Library);
Grey-crowned Crane (Roger de la Harpe/Images of Africa); Savanna Elephants
(kyslynskyyhal/Shutterstock)
Page 5 (top to bottom): Maasai Giraffe (mbrand85/Shutterstock); Jackson's Three-horned
Chameleon (Mark Dudley Photography/Shutterstock); Mountain Gorilla (GUDKOV
ANDREY/Shutterstock)

Visit Chris and Mathilde Stuart on **www.stuartonnature.com**

ACKNOWLEDGEMENTS

We would like to acknowledge the late Pat and Mo Frere for first introducing us to Kenya many years ago and whetting our appetites for more visits. Lis and Tony Farrell of Kimbla-Mantana Safaris are also thanked for their advice over the years.

Thanks also go to the many researchers, wardens, rangers and staff of East Africa's parks and reserves that we have been in contact with over the years and who put out the scientific reports, management plans and unpublished reports that hold invaluable information.

And last, but not least, of course, thanks to the great Struik Nature team of Pippa Parker, Helen de Villiers, Colette Alves, Gillian Black and Colette Stott, for guiding yet another of our books.

Hakuna matata!

MAP KEY

■	Capital city	$\iiint$	Waterfall
●	Town	•	Point of interest
○	Village	——	Major road
⊠	Park gate	——	Secondary road
⚑	Headquarters	----------	4x4 track
ⓘ	Visitor centre	···🚶···	Walking trail
👀	Viewpoint	----------	Railway line
⊼	Picnic site	——	River
⬆	Lodge	⊓⊓⊓⊓⊓⊓	Crater rim/Escarpment
⬆	Hut	——	Gorge
⋀	Public campsite		Lake
⋀	Tented camp		National Park
⋀	Special campsite		Game Reserve (country maps)
▪	Ranger post		Forest/Montane
▲	Peak		Wetland/Marsh
▲	Ash cone (Arusha)		Mangrove
•	Waterhole		Plain

CONTENTS

INTRODUCTION

A herd of Savanna Elephant in Amboseli, with Mount Kilimanjaro in the background

This field guide has two main aims: to outline the natural history of the best conservation areas that East Africa has to offer, and to assist the reader in identifying the more common mammals, birds, reptiles, amphibians and plants in their national parks and other conservation areas.

The first of this field guide's two sections, and by far the bigger of the two, deals with each conservation area's natural history – the landscapes, geology, vegetation, climate and those animals that survive and thrive. The second takes the form of an image gallery, helping the reader to identify the more common mammals, birds, reptiles, amphibians, trees and flowers that may be encountered in the region.

East Africa is probably best known for its great savanna grasslands with scattered umbrella thorn trees – a distinctive landscape that is home to vast herds of hoofed mammals and within which many of the principal parks lie. Yet the region is comprised of many different habitats, from high mountains to rainforests, great lakes and rivers to coastline, all providing living space for a vast range of species.

Politically, East Africa consists of Tanzania, Kenya, Uganda, Burundi and Rwanda. Unfortunately, Burundi and Rwanda have only a few national parks and conservation areas, which are largely depleted of much of their animal and plant life and are under increasing threat from an ever-growing human population.

To the east of the region lies the Indian Ocean and to the west are the four great lakes – Edward, Victoria, Tanganyika and Nyasa (Malawi). Here are the legendary Rwenzoris, or

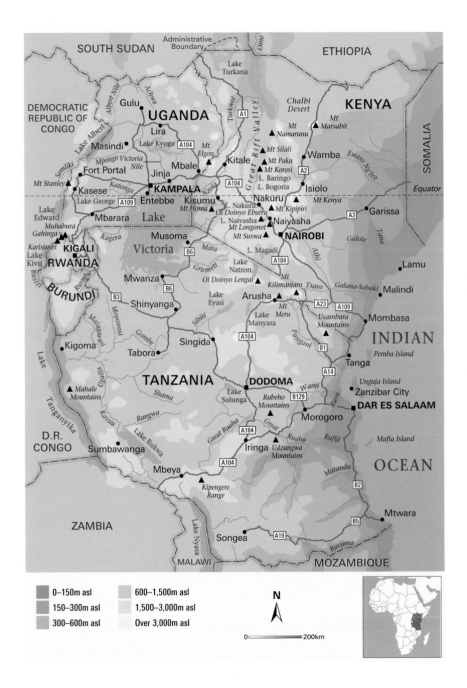

SOUTH SUDAN

ETHIOPIA

Administrative Boundary

Omo

Lake Turkana

DEMOCRATIC REPUBLIC OF CONGO

Gulu

UGANDA

Lira

Achwa

Albert Nile

Turkwel

Chalbi Desert

KENYA

Mt Marsabit ▲

Mt Namarunu ▲

Masindi

Lake Albert

Fort Portal

Semliki

Mpongo

Victoria Nile

Lake Kyoga

A104

Mt Elgon ▲

Kitale

Mt Silali ▲

Mt Paka ▲

Mt Korosi ▲

L. Baringo

L. Bogoria

Wamba

Ewaso Ng'iro

SOMALIA

Mt Stanley ▲

Kasese

Katonga

Mbale

Jinja

KAMPALA

A104

Nzoia

Isiolo

A2

Equator

Lake George

A109

Entebbe

Kisumu

Nakuru

Mt Kipipiri ▲

Mt Kenya ▲

A3

Garissa

Lake Edward

Muhabura

Gahinga ▲

Mbarara

Mt Homa ▲

Ol Doinyo Eburru

L. Nakuru

L. Naivasha

Mt Longonot ▲

Mt Suswa ▲

Naivasha

Lake

Kagera

Karisimbi ▲

KIGALI

Lake Kivu

RWANDA

Ruhwa

Rusizi

BURUNDI

Musoma

Victoria

Mara

B6

L. Magadi

A104

NAIROBI

Galole

Athi

Tana

Lamu

Mwanza

Grumeti

Ol Doinyo Lengai ▲

Lake Natron

Mt Kilimanjaro ▲

Tsavo

Galana-Sabaki

Malindi

B3

Shinyanga

B6

Lake Eyasi

Sibiti

Arusha

Mt Meru ▲

A23

A109

Mombasa

INDIAN

Kigoma

Tabora

Gombe

Singida

Lake Manyara

A104

Usambara Mountains

B1

Tanga

Pemba Island

Moyowosi

Malagarasi

▲ Mahale Mountains

TANZANIA

Shama

DODOMA

A14

Unguja Island

Zanzibar City

Lake Tanganyika

Ugalla

Kavuu

Rungwa

Lake Sulunga

Rubeho Mountains ▲

B129

Wami

Ruvu

DAR ES SALAAM

Morogoro

D.R. CONGO

Sumbawanga

Lake Rukwa

Great Ruaha

A104

Iringa

Great Ruaha

Ruaha

Rufiji

Mafia Island

OCEAN

Udzungwa Mountains

Matandu

B2

Mbeya

Kipengere Range ▲

B5

Mtwara

ZAMBIA

Lake Nyasa

Songea

A19

Ruvuma

MALAWI

MOZAMBIQUE

0–150m asl	600–1,500m asl
150–300m asl	1,500–3,000m asl
300–600m asl	Over 3,000m asl

N

0 ▬▬▬▬ 200km

WOODLAND DESTRUCTION

Vast tracts of woodland are cleared every year in the region to produce charcoal (which is used by many people for heating and cooking). This harvesting of a resource that is valuable to both humans and the biota that depend on the woodland is unsustainable. Hundreds of thousands of hectares of woodland are lost every year, up to 60% to charcoal production alone. In Kenya 80% of urban dwellers and 30% of rural people rely on charcoal for their energy needs. Urban dwellers in Dar es Salaam consume 70% of all charcoal produced in Tanzania, causing a loss of over 150,000ha each year. Once the forest is gone so is its diverse biota. In East Africa charcoal is viewed as 'black gold', a quick-return cash crop. Charcoal kilns are usually built close to where trees are felled in order to reduce transport costs. Timber harvesting and charcoal production also encroaches not only on unprotected areas, but on conservation areas too.

Mountains of the Moon, and the mighty peaks of Kilimanjaro, Kenya and Elgon, as well as those biota-rich mountain blocks that form the Eastern Arc (including the Usambaras, Udzungwas, Rungwe and Uluguru). A chain of soda lakes, with their primordial brew, runs like an uneven necklace down the floor of the Great Rift Valley. Where the mighty Blue Nile River rises there are active, dormant and long-dead volcanoes. The region is topographically diverse and home to a range of vegetation types.

Outside the national parks and other conservation areas, much of the landscape has been modified by the actions of growing human populations. Large tracts of natural bushland have been cleared for agriculture, both subsistence and commercial, and numerous trees have been converted to charcoal to feed the growing urban demand for cooking fuel. Human settlements have increased and existing ones have expanded. Poaching has resulted in decreasing game animal diversity and populations. When the first Arabs and Europeans penetrated into the East African interior they did not find the

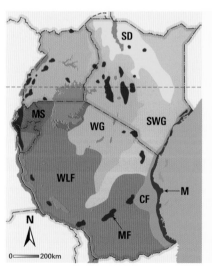

MAJOR BIOTIC ZONES

SD – Semi-desert

SWG – Savanna woodland/grassland

WLF – Savanna woodland/dry forest (Miombo)

WG – Wooded and open grassland

MS – Moist savanna/forest mosaic

MF – Montane forest and grassland

CF – Coastal forest/grassland mosaic

M – Mangroves

FLAMINGOS AND THE PRIMORDIAL SOUP

Flamingos gather in great numbers at soda lakes, such as Lake Bogoria in Kenya.

Along a stretch of the eastern arm of the Great Rift Valley lies a 'necklace' of small to medium-sized lakes. A few, such as lakes Baringo and Naivasha, are filled with sweet waters, but most are fed by volcanic springs. It is those lakes, filled with their caustic brew, that concern us here: from the north, Bogoria, Nakuru, Elmenteita, Magadi and the largest, Natron. These lakes are home to the world's greatest gatherings of flamingos. Their waters can scald and scar the flesh on the feet and legs of almost all species, but not those of the Greater and Lesser flamingos. These strange, long-legged and -necked birds find their principal strongholds in these lakes. The most abundant is the Lesser Flamingo, with 2–3 million birds present.

Lake Natron is the only location in the world where large numbers of these birds breed with considerable success. They establish their colonies and build their nests surrounded by a slushy mix of water and soda, protected from land-based predators. Lesser Flamingos feed on or near the surface, taking mainly blue-green algae and diatoms filtered from the water. In just one day, a million Lesser Flamingos can consume 180 tons of blue-green algae. These are thus some of the most 'fertile pastures' on Earth. Sadly, all is not well with these waters, as some suffer from pollution, such as lakes Nakuru and Bogoria, and others, such as Lake Natron, are threatened by disturbance and proposed mining of soda ash.

Poaching in the 1970s and 1980s resulted in the near eradication of the Hook-lipped Rhinoceros in East Africa.

AFRICA, THE FIRE CONTINENT

On a visit to East Africa, your scenic images will more often than not be blighted by a smoke haze. Humans have been burning African forest, woodland and savanna for many thousands of years to aid new plant growth for their livestock, to clear land for cultivation and while driving game during hunts. Not all fires are caused by humans but most are! If managed properly, fire is not always a bad thing. However, problems arise when there are too many people, making too many fires, too often and sometimes for the wrong reasons. Many plant and animal species are adapted to regular burns – such as birds that regularly nest on recently burned patches and antelope that give birth shortly after fire, when there is a green flush and milk production by females can be maximized. Without seasonal fires the African savanna parks and reserves would undoubtedly turn to thicket and woodland and the grazers would be greatly reduced or would disappear.

pristine environment that is often portrayed in much of the popular media. The area had been settled by humans for thousands of years and many changes had already been wrought on the landscape due to the use of fire, livestock grazing and other activities. However, human numbers were relatively low at that time and it is only in the past 50 years that populations have exploded. With the arrival of Arabs and Europeans, firearms were introduced to the continent and the slaughter of game began. Land was needed for cultivation and grazing, and railways and roads improved access to previously hard-to-reach areas. More positively, during the course of the 20th century large tracts of land were set aside for conservation purposes, such as the world-famous Selous and Serengeti. In some cases local people were moved out of the areas, causing resentment and bitterness, which in some cases persists to this day.

But the real slaughter began in the 1970s and 1980s, with the Hook-lipped Rhinoceros being almost eradicated in East Africa for its horns – which were desired for dagger handles in Yemen and to meet the insatiable demand of the traditional pharmacopeia of the East. Elephant fell by the thousands for their ivory, a killing that was unprecedented in the region. During the 1990s the killing was greatly reduced but in

EASTERN ARC MOUNTAINS

The Eastern Arc Mountains consist of 13 isolated blocks that run from the Taita Hills in south-east Kenya into eastern Tanzania. From north to south, these include the North Pare, South Pare, West Usambara, East Usambara, Nguu, Ukaguru, Uluguru, Rubeho, Malundwe, Udzungwa and the Mahenge mountains. Unlike younger mountains, such as Kilimanjaro and Meru that were formed just one million years before present, the blocks of the Eastern Arc were formed as flat-topped mountains between 290 and 180 million years before present and were further modified by faulting some seven million years before present. All the Eastern Arc Mountains have forests, to a greater or lesser extent. Their age is the reason these fascinating 'islands' have such an incredibly rich biodiversity and so many endemic species, often found on a single 'sky island'. The climate in these mountains has probably remained relatively stable over time, in contrast to the surrounding lowlands, and these constant conditions have served as a refugium for those species dependent on forest. Consider that these small areas support over 120 vertebrates and 800 plant species that occur nowhere else, including three monkey species, more than 50 reptiles and at least 50 amphibians, several birds and unknown numbers of invertebrates. The Udzungwa Forest Partridge is found only in the Rubeho and Udzungwa mountains and its closest relatives reside in Asia, not Africa. These mountain blocks are considered to be among the most important areas for conserving biological biodiversity in the world. Despite their importance, an estimated 70% of the forests have been lost to fire and unsustainable timber harvesting and most receive minimal protection. They have become true 'sky islands' surrounded by agricultural settlements and a burgeoning human population.

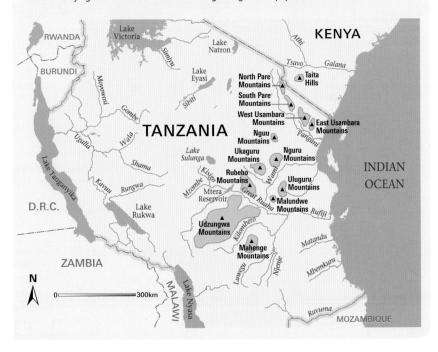

East Africa is known for its extraordinary landscapes and diverse fauna, such as the zebra, wildebeest and flamingos here gathering in the Ngorongoro Crater in Tanzania.

TSETSE FLY

The Tsetse is present in many of East Africa's conservation areas, and a bite from one of these flies is painful. *Tsetse* is the Tswana name for fly, hence it is nowadays just referred to as Tsetse. The principal savanna species is *Glossina morsitans*, and has been called Africa's greatest conservationist for a very good reason. It transmits sleeping sickness (trypanosomiasis) to humans and their livestock when sucking their blood, thereby preventing encroachment into game areas. Although some game species are carriers of the parasites, they have a natural immunity and do not develop sleeping sickness. This unpleasant regional drawback has nevertheless had a positive spin-off – enabling us to view game where it has prevented habitat encroachment. With the advent of modern insecticides some areas have been cleared of Tsetse, enabling herders to move in with their cattle, and causing game numbers to dwindle and disappear.

recent years the 'killing fields' have been revisited. Consider that in 1976 there were some 110,000 Savanna Elephant in the Selous ecosystem, but by 2013 just 13,000 remained!

Poaching has resulted in the continuing reduction of diversity and populations, largely outside conservation areas but also within them. Nevertheless, those interested in wildlife still have much to look forward to in the parks and wildlife sanctuaries of East Africa. In this guide we hope to offer you a broad overview of these critical conservation areas, their landscapes and inhabitants, and provide you with a better understanding of why they need continued protection.

The conservation areas in East Africa fall into several different categories: national parks, national reserves (Kenya), game reserves and nature reserves. In broad definition, national parks and their plant and animal life are completely protected and human utilization, other than tourism, is precluded, whereas in the Kenyan national reserves and in game reserves (especially in Tanzania) some level of human activity is often permitted, such as cattle grazing, honey harvesting or trophy hunting, the latter principally in Tanzania. A game reserve such as the Selous is divided into numerous hunting blocks where controlled trophy hunting is permitted. Ngorongoro in northern Tanzania is designated as a conservation area where the Maasai people continue to live. Unfortunately, poaching, timber extraction and other illegal activities continue in some conservation areas. This is unlikely to change, as many of the people living around these protected lands live in extreme poverty; desperate for resources that are depleted beyond the boundaries of the parks and reserves, they are therefore easily tempted by the money offered to them by the poaching middlemen.

As well as protecting the natural environment and the organisms that rely on them, conservation areas promote an understanding of the natural processes and an awareness of the need for conservation.

GAME-VIEWING GUIDELINES

- Do not feed any animal, no matter how appealing it may seem; by doing so you are probably signing its death warrant. Such an animal comes to rely on hand-outs and, more seriously, becomes a nuisance or even a threat to other visitors.
- In conservation areas where visitors are requested to stay in the vehicle, do so, both for your own safety and to avoid disturbance.
- Drive only on public roads or designated tracks. Taking shortcuts damages the vegetation and soil, and driving too close to animals disturbs them and can create dangerous situations. This also applies if you are not on a self-drive safari, so ensure that your driver/guide adheres to the rules.
- Build fires only in designated areas, and take care to extinguish the coals properly after you are done.
- Remember that many camps, lodges and viewing sites are not fenced in most East African conservation areas, so always be alert and aware of your surroundings. You would be surprised at how rapidly and silently large game such as Savanna Elephant, Hippopotamus, Savanna Buffalo and Lion can move.
- Malaria and bilharzia are a factor in virtually all East African conservation areas. Although rare, sleeping sickness is a potential hazard wherever tsetse fly occur.
- You should always be aware of safety and security risks in any given region by checking with your embassy, or the local authorities. Areas of concern at the time of writing are in north-eastern Kenya and parts of northern Uganda. Circumstances change!

For safety's sake, do not drive too close to animals and remain in the vehicle.

TANZANIA

Lions occur throughout the Serengeti, here a lioness and her cubs near the Grumeti River.

Tanzania is the largest country in East Africa, covering a total of 947,303km². It borders the Indian Ocean (the coastline extends for 1,424km) to the east, Mozambique, Malawi and Zambia in the south, Burundi, Rwanda and Democratic Republic of Congo in the west, and Uganda and Kenya in the north. It also includes the Zanzibar Archipelago of Unguja, Pemba and Mafia islands. Tanzania borders on three of the Great Lakes – Victoria, Tanganyika and Nyasa (Malawi) – and hosts the continent's tallest peak, Kilimanjaro, which towers 5,895m asl, and the active volcano Ol Doinyo Lengai.

Tanzania has two major rainfall periods, October to April in the south, central and western parts of the country, and October to December and March to May in the north, between Lake Victoria and the coast. Temperatures are at their highest between November and February (25–31˚C) and coolest May to August (15–20˚C), except in the highland regions, where temperatures are in the range of 10–20˚C throughout the year.

Indigenous peoples in Tanzania are believed to be the Hadza and Sandawe hunter-gatherers, with movement of the ancestral Iraqw, Gorowa and Burunge from present-day Ethiopia between 4,000 and 2,000 years before present. A further wave from the north arrived in present-day Tanzania between 2,900 and 2,400 years before present. At about the same time Mashariki Bantu migrated into the area from western Africa. The Maasai were relatively recent immigrants, arriving in East Africa from about 1,500 to 500 years before present.

The first non-Africans, the Omanis and Indians, traded and later settled along the coast during the course of the first thousand years A.D. Europeans began exploring the coast in the late 15th century, with the Portuguese holding sway until the end of the 17th century, when they were ousted by the Omani Arabs. During the latter period of the 'Scramble for Africa', late

in the 19th century, Germany conquered the region they called Tanganyika, but were ousted by the British at the end of the First World War. Tanganyika gained independence in 1961, and took the name Tanzania when it absorbed Zanzibar. Tanzania's first land set aside for conservation later formed the core of the mighty **Selous Game Reserve** and was a gift by the German Kaiser to his wife. During the British colonial era more areas were set aside, including the famous **Serengeti**. Today some 38% of Tanzania's land surface is set aside for conservation, including 16 national parks. There are a number of large game reserves, apart from Selous, including **Moyowosi**, **Kigosi**, **Ugalla River**, **Uwanda** and **Rungwa**, but these are not geared for tourism, with several catering for hunters. There are 15 marine reserves and three marine parks, mostly associated with offshore islands, and several are popular diving destinations.

Biodiversity is considerable in Tanzania, with about 1,100 bird species, 340 mammals, 335 reptiles, 130 amphibians, well over 800 freshwater fish and more than 10,000 species of plant. Unlike the case in many southern African conservation areas, biodiversity inventories for parks and reserves in Tanzania are far from complete, especially for smaller mammals, reptiles, amphibians and fish.

THE SERENGETI MIGRATION

The great migration that takes place annually in the Serengeti is a major drawcard for visitors. However, in recent years it has become increasingly difficult to predict the timing of the migration of the large herds, largely due to climate change and unpredictable rainfall patterns. Rainfall is the motivator for the greatest large-mammal migration on Earth, as herds move to feed on the fresh grass that results from these falls. Apart from the million or more Western White-bearded Wildebeest that participate in this annual event, there are vast numbers of Plains Zebra and Thomson's Gazelles. With the onset of the short rains usually in November, the massed herds start moving southwards away from the Maasai Mara in Kenya down to the Serengeti plains in the south and the adjacent Ngorongoro Conservation Area in December. From January into March they remain on these short-grass plains and it is during this time the wildebeest calves are born. By April the southern plains begin drying out and the lack of grazing and water forces the great herds to move towards central and western Serengeti. During the migration in May and June mating gets into full swing, with bulls trying to control and breed with the receptive cows. In this month most herds have reached the central Serengeti, especially into the Seronera Valley. By July the grass and water are depleted and the massive herds continue moving northwards. The herds follow two routes to the north during August and September: the larger group moves into the Western Corridor, crosses the Grumeti River and moves northwards across the area crossing the Mara River, where they can access fresh grazing and abundant water; a smaller group heads nearly due north on to the northern Serengeti plains and into the Maasai Mara without the risks of major river crossings. Large numbers of those that cross the rivers drown or are taken by Nile Crocodiles. Once the short rains start in the south in November the herds return on their long journey to the short-grass plains and the breeding cycle is repeated.

Crossings of the Grumeti and Mara rivers expose the game to accidental drownings and attacks by Nile Crocodiles.

Wildebeest move away from the short-grass plains as grazing and water disappear.

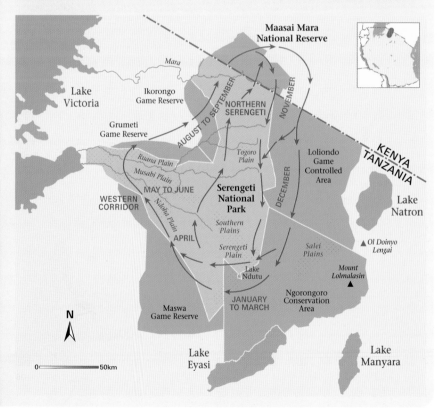

Maasai Mara National Reserve

Mara

Lake Victoria

Ikorongo Game Reserve

Grumeti Game Reserve

AUGUST TO SEPTEMBER

NORTHERN SERENGETI

NOVEMBER

Togoro Plain

Loliondo Game Controlled Area

KENYA
TANZANIA

Ruana Plain

Musabi Plain

Serengeti National Park

DECEMBER

Lake Natron

WESTERN CORRIDOR

Ndutu plain

APRIL

MAY TO JUNE

Southern Plains

Serengeti Plain

Salei Plains

▲ Ol Doinyo Lengai

Lake Ndutu

Mount Lolmalasin ▲

Maswa Game Reserve

JANUARY TO MARCH

Ngorongoro Conservation Area

N

0 ——— 50km

Lake Eyasi

Lake Manyara

ARUSHA NATIONAL PARK

A group of Maasai Giraffe in thornveld

Lie of the land

Arusha is a small park, just 552km² (including Mount Meru), and lies on the northern safari circuit between Kilimanjaro and the Serengeti. It is located 25km east of the town of Arusha, which derives its name from the Warusha people. There are three distinct areas within the park, the Ngurdoto Crater, Momella lakes and Mount Meru, which dominates the area. The altitudinal range is 1,500m to 4,565m at the summit of Mount Meru. The cluster of seven Momella lakes are alkaline, as with many others in the Rift Valley, but there are also several freshwater lakes in the east. The park is flanked by the Mount Meru Forest Reserve in the west and the Ngurdoto Forest Reserve in the east. Surrounding areas are heavily settled by people, and the extent of this development can be clearly seen from higher altitude sectors of the park.

Brief history

Much of the Arusha Region, an administrative division of Tanzania, was Maasai pastoral land at the time of the arrival of the first Europeans. The Maasai are still dominant in the area and many of the place names within Arusha National Park have their origins in their language. The first European known to visit the area of the present-day park was Count Teleki, a Hungarian, in 1876. In 1907 the Trappe family moved into the area to farm, and in 1960 the property was incorporated into the newly established park. The original name was Ngurdoto Crater National Park but this was changed to its current name when Mount Meru was incorporated into the park.

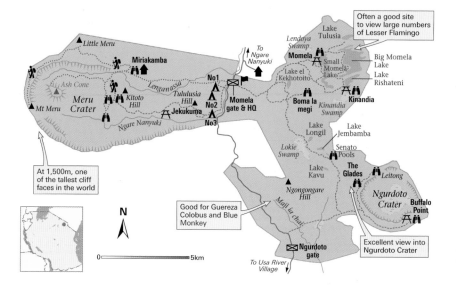

Arusha is one of the best localities in Tanzania to see Guereza.

Geology and landscape

Arusha National Park is situated on the eastern edge of the Great Rift Valley, which formed some 20 million years before present. Both the Ngurdoto Crater (actually a caldera) and Mount Meru are of volcanic origin, the former now extinct but Meru is classified as a dormant volcano and its crater wall was ruptured about 250,000 years before present. Massive explosions caused the eastern wall to collapse and the water, mud, rock, ash and lava spread across the surrounding area. The Momella lakes formed in depressions in the drying mud and ash. Meru has had periodic eruptions, the most recent occurred about 130 years before present and resulted in a small lava flow on the north-west flank of the ash cone. Mount Meru is the second-highest peak in Tanzania,

HIGHLIGHTS

- Diverse scenery, including Mount Meru and Mount Kilimanjaro.
- Numerous observation points and picnic sites.
- One of the tallest cliff faces in the world, at over 1,500m, from the open floor of Mount Meru Crater.
- Ngurdoto Forest is rich in tree and bird species.
- A good location to view the Guereza (Black and White Colobus).
- Close proximity to the town of Arusha, making day visits feasible.

Roads in Arusha are dirt roads and can be difficult to negotiate during heavy rains.

Mount Kilimanjaro being the highest. The terrain is hilly to mountainous, with small scattered alkaline (Momella lakes) and freshwater lakes (such as Jembamba and Longil).

Climate

Being a highland park, weather may be unpredictable. Although there are two rainy seasons, March to May (peaks in April and averages 368mm) and October to December, some rain may fall in the other months but rarely to the same extent. For Arusha town the average annual rainfall is 1,237mm but in the vicinity of the lakes it is about 1,000mm and in the dry grasslands and savanna 250–500mm. Despite being close to the equator, Arusha town lies at an altitude of 1,400m with maximum temperatures of between 13° and 30°C (average 21°–25°C) throughout the year. Cool, dry air occurs throughout much of the year. The hottest months are October to March, and the coolest May to August. Increases in altitude result in decreases in temperature.

Vegetation

This hill and mountain terrain is largely dominated by montane forest divided into several altitudinal strata, acacia grassland and semi-aquatic vegetation associated with the lakes. At the lower altitudes (1,400–1,700m) there is a mix of shrub, thicket and dry evergreen forest with species such as **East African Olive** (**Black Ironwood**) (*Olea hochstetteri*) and **Giant Diospyros** (*Diospyros abyssinica*) dominating. Also look

Strangler Fig on host

in this zone for the distinctive **Strangler Fig** (*Ficus thonningii*) with its smooth grey bark and numerous aerial roots. Other trees here include the **Wild Mango** (*Tabernaemontana usambarensis*) with its long, slender leaves and distinctive fruit and **Mwerere** (**Quinine Tree**) (*Rauvolfia caffra*). In the vicinity of Kambi ya Fisi in the east the forest thins and two tree species dominate, the **Broad-leaved Croton** (*Croton macrostachyus*) and the **Croton** (*Croton megalocarpus*). As one climbs to higher altitudes, above 1,800m, one enters the realm of the giants, the **African Pencil Cedar** (*Juniperus procera*) that can reach 40m in height and the **East African Yellowwood** (*Afrocarpus gracilior*) that rises to 35m. Once above the tree line you will find **giant lobelias** and **giant senecios**, as well as the extensive areas covered by the coarse tussock grasses. Stratification of vegetation is similar to that on Mount Kilimanjaro but there is a belt of **African Alpine Bamboo** (*Yushania alpina*) on the south slope with a scattering of **Yellowwood** (*Podocarpus milanjianus*) between 2,300 and 2,700m. **Reedmace** (bulrush) and **Papyrus** (*Cyperus papyrus*) grow in the vicinity of the freshwater lakes.

Quinine Tree fruits

Wildlife
Mammals

This is not a park to visit if you only have eyes for the big five, although **Plains Zebra, Common Hippopotamus, Common Warthog, Bushpig, Maasai** race of the **Giraffe, Common Waterbuck, Bohor Reedbuck, Bushbuck (Imbabala), Ugogo (Naivasha) Dik-dik, Suni, Klipspringer, Harvey's Red Duiker** and **Common Duiker** occur. **Savanna Elephant** is also present in small numbers. Four species of primate are commonly seen, **Olive Baboon, Vervet Monkey, Sykes's Monkey** and the **Guereza (Black and White Colobus)**. The **Guereza** is one of the most impressive of the East African forest monkeys, with its long white mantle and bushy white tail contrasting with its black coat, and Arusha is one of the best locations in the country to observe it.

Naivasha Dik-dik occur on the forest edges.

> **!**
> - If you intend climbing Mount Meru, or walking, you must be accompanied by a ranger.
> - Always be aware of your surroundings as potentially dangerous game, such as Buffalo, are present in the park.
> - The public road that cuts through the park is in bad condition and is used by many lorries and buses.
> - After heavy rain roads become muddy and often difficult to negotiate.
> - Arusha lies within a malaria zone.

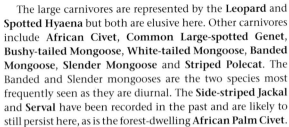
- The official mammal list is just 40 species, but at least 70 species occur.
- A top birding destination, with more than 400 species in the area.
- Some 35 reptile species, including five species of chameleon.
- Ten species of amphibian.
- Tree diversity is great (includes African Pencil Cedar and Yellowwood species).

The large carnivores are represented by the **Leopard** and **Spotted Hyaena** but both are elusive here. Other carnivores include **African Civet, Common Large-spotted Genet, Bushy-tailed Mongoose, White-tailed Mongoose, Banded Mongoose, Slender Mongoose** and **Striped Polecat**. The Banded and Slender mongooses are the two species most frequently seen as they are diurnal. The **Side-striped Jackal** and **Serval** have been recorded in the past and are likely to still persist here, as is the forest-dwelling **African Palm Civet**.

Although only 40 species of mammal have been recorded in the park, it is expected that this total is considerably higher, given that no systematic survey of rodents, bats (10 species known) and shrews (six species known from Arusha) has been undertaken. Several species of fruit-eating bat are present but are heard more frequently than seen, including **Wahlberg's Epauletted Fruit Bat** with its distinctive 'hammer on anvil' call. A few of the smaller species known from museum collections or direct observations in Arusha include **Southern Tree Hyrax, Yellow-spotted Rock Hyrax, Crested Porcupine** and **Ochre Bush Squirrel**.

Birds

Despite its relatively small size, more than 400 bird species have been recorded in this national park and surrounding areas. The mix of montane forest, acacia and grassland savanna, lakes and marshes contributes to this diversity. Generally, birding is considered to be good throughout the year, especially from November to April when many migratory species are present. At certain times of year the alkaline lakes attract thousands of **Lesser** and **Greater** flamingos, as well as a great diversity of waterfowl (11 species). The park is home to several pairs of **African Crowned Eagle**, with **African Fish Eagle** frequenting the lakes, and **Verreaux's Eagle** at the higher altitudes in areas of exposed rock where hyraxes (their main prey) live. This eagle and the **Bearded Vulture**, or **Lammergeier**, nest on the Red Crescent cliffs on Mount Meru.

No less than 30 species of raptor have been recorded here, including **Ayres's Hawk-Eagle, Mountain Buzzard** and **Augur Buzzard**. Other species to watch for include **African Green Pigeon, Narina Trogon** and **Bar-tailed Trogon** (the trogons are more commonly heard than seen), **Cinnamon-chested Bee-eater, Silvery-cheeked Hornbill, Spot-flanked Barbet, White-headed Barbet,**

Silvery-cheeked Hornbill female

- Two lodges on park fringes, Hatari Lodge and Momella Wildlife Lodge; three campgrounds, mainly concentrated in the vicinity of the Momella and Ngurdoto gates. Numerous accommodation options in Arusha and surrounds; two huts for climbers tackling Mount Meru.
- Picnic sites and viewpoints, mainly concentrated around the Ngurdoto Crater, the Momella lakes and approach to Mount Meru.
- Guided walks accompanied by an armed ranger. Unaccompanied walking is not permitted.
- The 3–4-day climb of Mount Meru is good acclimatization for those intending to tackle Mount Kilimanjaro. Best climbed between June and February.
- Fairly extensive dirt road network, best tackled with a 4x4 as roads become slippery after rain.
- No fuel available in the park.
- One safari operator offers canoeing; many offer day trips into the park.
- Makoa Farm, outside the park, offers horse riding within the park boundary.

Red-fronted Parrot, Fischer's Lovebird, Red-throated Tit and **Golden-winged Sunbird**. Also watch for the localized **Taveta Golden Weaver** around the edge of Lake Longil and **Hartlaub's Turaco** and the **Abyssinian Crimsonwing** in the higher forest areas.

Reptiles and amphibians

Of the 13 species of snake known to occur in the park by far the largest is the **Southern African Rock Python**, which is said to be particularly common in the vicinity of the lakes. Other species include the **Puff Adder, Egyptian Cobra, Green Mamba, Savanna Vine Snake** and the **Common Egg-eater**. Of the 14 lizard species the five species of chameleon are of interest; the large (to 38cm) **Jackson's Chameleon**, with males 'armed' with three long horns on the head, is a particularly sought-after subject for the camera. Most lizards here are cryptic and difficult to spot, with the exception of the **Mwanza Flat-headed Agama**, especially the brightly coloured male, as they often sit on top of rocks in the drier upland areas of the park. They are said to be quite common near the Momella gate, along with the **Striped Skink**. Although just 10 amphibian species have been recorded from the park, it is highly likely that the list could be longer. Most visitors are unlikely to encounter any frogs or toads, although during the rainy season their calls will be heard. The more common species include **Guttural Toad, Mueller's Clawed Frog, Mascarene Rocket Frog, Angolan River Frog** and the **Painted Reed Frog**.

Common Egg-eater striking

GOMBE STREAM NATIONAL PARK

The waters of Lake Tanganyika do not fall within Gombe Stream National Park.

Lie of the land

At just 52km², Gombe is one of Tanzania's smallest conservation areas. It lies just 16km north of Kigoma and can be accessed only by boat. Its western boundary is marked by the eastern shore of Lake Tanganyika, although the actual lake shore is excluded from the park. Its eastern boundary is marked by the ridge of the eastern Rift Valley escarpment. It is a narrow strip of land incorporating 13 steep-sided valleys, carved by fast-flowing streams that flow into Lake Tanganyika. The altitudinal range is from 773m at the lake shore to 1,500m at the top of the escarpment. To the north, east and south it is flanked by subsistence farmland.

Brief history

The local people, the Ha, have their ancestral roots in Bantu migrations from West Africa more than 2,000 years before present. The first non-Africans to enter the area were the coastal Arab slave traders in the early part of the 19th century and they established their base at Ujiji, south of Kigoma. The slave routes stretched from this eastern shore of Lake Tanganyika to the island of Unguja, within the Zanzibar Archipelago. British explorers Richard Burton and John Speke were the first Europeans to reach the shore of Lake Tanganyika in their search for the source of the Nile River in 1858. In 1866 the explorer-missionary David Livingstone started his exploration in the vicinity of the lake, also searching for the Nile's source. Gombe Stream Game Reserve was gazetted by the British colonial authorities in 1943 to conserve the last remnant of forest in the region and its Chimpanzees. In 1968 Gombe was raised to national park status. It was during the 1960s that the park rose to prominence as a result of Jane Goodall's research into the wild Chimpanzees, one of the longest-running studies of any wild mammal population.

Geology and landscape

Gombe is located on the shore of Lake Tanganyika, a rift lake that formed in the Albertine Rift on the western arm of the Great Rift Valley. Lake Tanganyika is the oldest of the Rift Valley lakes and is the world's second-deepest lake, with an average depth of 570m and a maximum of 1,470m. The lake is 50km wide on average and 676km long, its waters flowing into the Congo River system and ultimately into the Atlantic Ocean. The rocks underlying the park are ancient gneisses with quartzites on the upper slopes. At a few locations there are exposed down-faulted sandstones of more recent origin.

Climate

The wet season here is relatively long, beginning mid-October and running to mid-May, with the remaining period largely dry. Although most years receive about 1,600mm of rain, precipitation can exceed 2,600mm in some years. Temperatures during the rains average 21˚–27˚C, and 18˚–32˚C in the dry season. Strong winds are typical for April to May and August to September.

Vegetation

In its broadest sense the vegetation in Gombe falls within the miombo woodland zone but can be further divided into five types within the park. As one moves eastwards from the lake shore one finds wooded grassland, dry forest on the valley slopes flanking the evergreen forest situated along the streams and valley bottoms, then open woodlands before it opens to grassland along the high ridges. Of special interest is that the evergreen forest here is more closely allied to those of Central and West Africa than it is to the forests elsewhere in Tanzania.

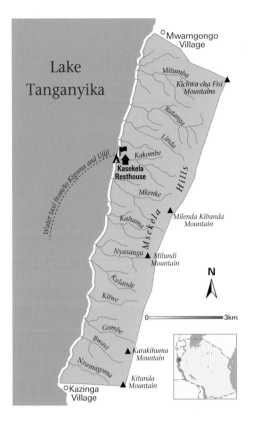

HIGHLIGHTS

- Opportunity to observe a wild but habituated Chimpanzee population.
- Great diversity of birds, butterflies and plants.
- Abundance of cichlid fish in the lake.

Fruits of the Sugar Plum (*Uapaca kirkiana*) are favoured by humans, other primates and fruit-eating bats.

Typical forest trees include **African Nutmeg (mSululu)** (*Pycnanthus angolensis*), **Waterberry (muGege)** (*Syzygium guineense*), **Common Wild Fig (muManda)** (*Ficus thonningii*) and **False Thorn (mSebei)** (*Albizia glaberrima*). **Newtonia** (*Piptadenia buchananii*) is a tall tree with a straight trunk and a rather flat-topped appearance, somewhat feathery leaves and pods 15–30cm in length. The fig *Ficus vallis-choudae* has very large, rounded leaves and grows along the streams. *Anthocleista schweinfurthii*, sometimes called the **Forest Fever Tree**, is distinguished by its exceptionally large leaves and slender trunk. Exotic trees here include **African Oil Palm** (*Elaeis guineensis*) and **Mango** (*Mangifera indica*).

In contrast, the dry forest and woodland has lower-growing trees and bushes that are more typical of the miombo. Some of the easier to identify trees here include **Wild Teak** (*Pterocarpus angolensis*), with its slender, pinnate leaves, spikes of yellow, pea-like flowers and its large (to 10cm) disc-winged seed; the **Mobola Plum (mBula)** (*Parinari curatellifolia*) grows mainly along the ridges and produces a tasty, brown plum-like fruit that is eagerly sought after by humans and Chimpanzees; and *Antidesma venosum*, a small tree or shrub, which also has edible fruits hanging in tight elongated clusters. The more open woodland areas have such species as **African Custard Apple (mTopetope)** (*Annona senegalensis*), several species of *Terminalia*, including **muHongoro** (*T. mollis*) and **muHenya** (*T. kaiserana*), and *Combretum*. **Monkey Orange (muKomme)** (*Strychnos madagascariensis*) produces distinctive dark green, hard-shelled, cricket ball-sized fruits that are sought after by Chimpanzees for the bitter but juicy seed pulp. The **Flame Tree** (*Erythrina abyssinica*) only stands out just before the onset of the rains, when it is usually bare of leaves and produces copious quantities of orange-red blossoms. At the highest woodland levels, fringing the grassland, are some trees familiar from lower levels but also typical miombo members of the genus *Brachystegia*, with fern-like leaves and woody pods.

FACILITIES AND ACTIVITIES

- Chimpanzee viewing.
- Accommodation at Gombe Forest Lodge; Kasekela Resthouse, run by park authorities; camping on the beach at a fee; advisable to take your own food. Variety of accommodation in Kigoma and Ujiji.
- Walking in the park is by guide only, at a fee.
- Access only by boat (local water taxi or more expensive speed boat).
- Swimming in the lake is permitted.

Wildlife
Mammals

The vast majority of people visiting Gombe are there to see the habituated **Common Chimpanzee** population. Much of our understanding of Chimpanzee behaviour has its origins in this small national park. Here, they utilize all habitat types with some seasonal variations as they move to those areas with the most sought-after and abundant foods. Fruits make up a large percentage of their intake but their diet also includes leaves, seeds, flowers and resin. They are also adept predators, especially the adult males, and often hunt cooperatively. In Gombe chimps commonly target **Eastern Red Colobus** but will also take **Blue Monkey**, **Red-tail Monkey**, young **Olive Baboon**, **Bushpig** piglets and **Bushbuck** fawns. There are several troops of **Olive Baboons**, which can be a nuisance to campers. **Vervet Monkeys** are also common in Gombe, ranging through all habitats. Although these primates are diurnal, at least two (possibly three) species of nocturnal galagos are present in the area, the **Brown Thick-tailed Galago**, as well as the **Southern Lesser** and **Northern Lesser galagos**. In the case of the last two it is not clear whether just one or both species occur in the park. The call of the thick-tailed galago is distinctive and can be unnerving to those not used to its screaming. Nocturnal carnivores are well represented with **African Civet**, **African Palm Civet**, **Common Large-spotted Genet**, **White-tailed Mongoose** and **Water Mongoose**. You are more likely to see **Egyptian Mongoose** and **Slender Mongoose**, as they are active during daylight hours. **Cape Porcupine** is also present but you are more likely to see their droppings and black and white banded quills along the trails. One small denizen of the forest floor that you may encounter is the **Giant Chequered Sengi** as it forages for insects during the day. Along the lake edge both the **Cape Clawless Otter** and the **Spotted-necked Otter** are occasionally sighted.

Gombe protects a small population of Common Chimpanzee.

Birds

To date, 267 bird species have been listed from Gombe, with a mix of lake, forest and miombo species. Birdwatching here is good throughout the year, but particularly from November to April, when northern migrants are present. Diversity along the lake is not great due to lack of sand- and mudbanks and inadequate aquatic vegetation but the **African Fish Eagle** is

Olive Baboons, here an adult male, are frequently seen, especially at the lake shore.

Pied Kingfisher

frequently sighted, with the **Palmnut Vulture** occasionally observed. Twenty seven species of raptor have been noted here. The **African Crowned Eagle** can be frequently seen circling over the forest canopy. **Giant** and **Pied kingfishers** are common, as are **African Pied Wagtails**. **White-winged Black Terns** are present during summer. Forest birds here are diverse and abundant, but are more likely to be heard than seen. There are two species of **turaco** here, **Livingstone's** and **Ross's**, both fruit eaters, as are many other forest birds. Other species to watch for in the forest are **Double-toothed Barbet**, **Golden-rumped Tinker Barbet**, **Red-capped Robin-Chat**, **White-browed Robin-Chat**, **Tropical Boubou**, **White-browed Coucal**, **African Broadbill** and **Peters's Twinspot**. Eight species of pigeon and dove occur, including **Afep Pigeon**, **African Green Pigeon** and **Blue-spotted Wood Dove**. Kingfishers are well represented and include the **Blue-breasted**, **Pied**, **Half-collared** and **Woodland kingfishers**. There are eight species of **sunbird**, and no less than 13 **weaver** species.

Reptiles and amphibians

It is likely that reptile and amphibian diversity is quite high but no detailed survey has been undertaken on these groups. Snakes include **Southern African Rock Python**, **Banded Water Cobra**, **Forest Cobra**, four species of adder (including the large **Puff Adder**), **Great Lakes Bush Viper**, **Boomslang** and the **Savanna Vine Snake**. The **Serrated Hinged Terrapin** is the only terrapin species known from the Gombe area. Two gecko species are recorded here: the **Tropical House Gecko** and the **Cape Dwarf Gecko**. It is likely that several species of skink occur, including the **Striped Skink** and **Speckle-lipped Skink**. The **Flap-necked Chameleon** occurs and **Montane Side-striped Chameleon** and **Smooth Chameleon** may be present. It is also likely that one of the **pygmy chameleons** is present on the forest floor. The largest lizard known to occur is the **Nile (Water) Monitor**, which may occasionally be seen along the edge of the lake. Both the **Nile** and **Slender-snouted crocodiles** occur in the lake, but are rarely spotted.

WILDLIFE FACTS

- 30 species of mammal; smaller species not listed may occur.
- 267 bird species.
- At least 14 snakes and 6 lizards recorded; 18 species of amphibian could occur.
- Approximately 250 species of cichlid fish in Lake Tanganyika but numbers occurring off Gombe unrecorded.
- At least 250 species of butterfly.
- 510 species of plant, including 112 tree species.

- **Malaria area; tsetse flies are present but sleeping sickness is not recorded.**
- **Water should be boiled before drinking.**
- **When viewing Chimpanzees, adhere to the rules for your own safety and that of the animal.**
- **Olive Baboons can be destructive and dangerous.**

JOZANI CHWAKA BAY NATIONAL PARK

The rare Zanzibar Red Colobus is commonly seen here; several groups are habituated.

Lie of the land

The 50km² Jozani Chwaka Bay National Park is the only park on the island of Unguja, in the Zanzibar Archipelago. It is located in the south-central part of the island, about 35km to the south-east of Zanzibar town (Stone Town). It lies between Chwaka Bay and Uzi Bay and extends over flat terrain, rising from sea level to just 31m in the west. Jozani forest is located in the lowest- lying part of the island.

Brief history

Microlithic tools found on the island indicate that humans have been on Unguja for at least 20,000 years. The western part of the Jozani forest, Unguja Ukuu, was apparently the first area on the island to be settled by Kisiju immigrants from the mainland and from here they spread across Unguja. Persian traders, among others, used the island as a trading base, followed by the Portuguese, until 1698 when they were displaced by Omani Arabs and in 1890 it became a protectorate of Britain. Jozani Forest Reserve was established and gazetted in 1960 and covered just 194ha, expanding to 590ha in 1965 and increasing to 2,512ha in 1980. Harvesting within the forest was banned in 1992 but extraction and poaching is an ongoing problem. The area was proclaimed a national park in 2004.

- Largest remaining stand of near-natural forest on the island.
- Site of the only remaining natural mangrove forest on the island.
- Excellent viewing of the endemic Zanzibar Red Colobus Monkey and Blue Monkey.
- A chance to see the seriously endangered Aders' Duiker.
- Easy access from main tourist centres.

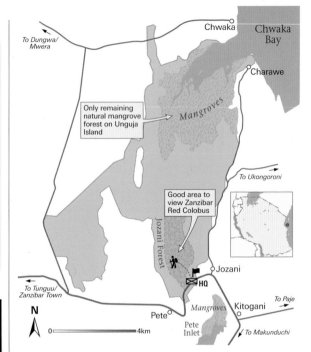

Only remaining natural mangrove forest on Unguja Island

Good area to view Zanzibar Red Colobus

Stilt roots of *Pandanus*

FACILITIES AND ACTIVITIES

- Self-guided, or guided, walking trails.
- No accommodation in the park but much available in Stone Town and around the coast.
- Easy access by road.

Geology and landscape

The island of Unguja has been separated from the mainland for between 10,000 and 15,000 years. The area lies predominantly on coral rag limestone, or reef limestone marine terrace, that was laid down during the Quaternary period, extending to the Miocene, although Jozani forest is mainly the former. The coral rag ranges from 25–35m in thickness. Miocene deposits are much thicker, consist of limestone, sandstones and clays derived from materials flushed out of the Rufiji River delta on the mainland. Soils are shallow and in many areas the coral rag is exposed on the surface. General topography is flat and without any prominent landform features.

Climate

Rain can be expected in all months of the year, with an annual average of 1,565mm. The period March to May sees the heaviest falls, with a second peak October to December. The north-west monsoon (Kaskazi) from November to February brings high temperatures and light winds, while the south-east monsoon (Kusi) from April to September brings lower temperatures and stronger winds.

Vegetation

Six principal vegetation types are found in Jozani: forest, coral rag bushland and thickets, wooded grassland, shrubland with low, emergent trees, salt marsh and mangrove forest. Within the forest trees range from 5–40m in height. Trees include **Flat Crown** (*Albizia adianthifolia*), **White Milkwood** (*Sideroxylon inerme*), **Forest Olive** (**Ironwood**) (*Olea woodiana*) and **Broom Cluster Fig** (*Ficus sur*). Other notable plants to look out for are the **Wild Date Palm** (*Phoenix reclinata*) and the **Screw Palm**, or **Mkadi** (*Pandanus kirkii*), which grows to a height of about 10m and has distinctive stilt roots and large, orange, pineapple-like fruits. This species is mainly associated with salt marsh and forest edges. Bushes in the shrubland are diverse and rarely grow to more than a few metres but include the **Natal Karree** (*Rhus natalensis*) and the **Sea Guarrie** (*Euclea racemosa*). The mangrove forest in the park is the last remaining intact patch on the island, and several species grow here, including **White Mangrove** (*Avicennia marina*), which may grow to 10–14m and has smooth, light grey bark; **Black Mangrove** (*Bruguiera gymnorrhiza*) may reach 10m but is usually shorter, with rough, reddish-brown bark and characteristic spindle-shaped, green fruits. The **Red Mangrove** (*Rhizophora mucronata*) may reach heights to 25m but in most cases are less than 15m. Mangrove forests are flooded by daily tides and are important breeding grounds for a wide range of invertebrate and fish species.

Black Mangrove flowers

Black Mangrove fruit

Wildlife

Mammals

Some 54 species of terrestrial and aerial mammal are recorded from Unguja, with most known to occur in the park. The most obvious and frequently seen are the endemic **Zanzibar (Kirk's) Red Colobus** and **Blue Monkey**. Three dwarf antelope species are present, the endangered **Aders' Duiker**, **Blue Duiker** and **Suni**, but they are seldom seen, although their tracks may be visible along the forest trails. These species are under considerable hunting pressure, and poaching continues to be a problem in the park. **Leopard** used to occur on the island, but there have been no confirmed sightings for at least 25 years. Carnivores in Jozani include **Servaline Genet**, **Bushy-tailed Mongoose** and **Slender Mongoose**, the last being diurnal and most frequently seen. Two civets occur, the **African Civet** and the introduced **Javan Civet**, but they are nocturnal and are not

WILDLIFE FACTS

- Some 31 mammal species.
- 217 bird species recorded on Unguja, most found in the park, including several endemics.
- At least 157 fish species have been recorded from Chwaka Bay.
- 26 reptile and 21 amphibian species.
- At least 109 butterfly species occur.

Fischer's Turaco

Mangrove Kingfisher

Great Plated Lizard

!
- Unguja lies within a malaria zone.
- Do not feed any wild animals.

likely to be spotted. The two large sengis, or elephant shrews, **Four-toed Sengi** and **Black and Rufous Sengi**, are diurnal and commonly seen running across pathways, but a glimpse is usually all that the visitor gets. Although there are few records, sightings are possible of both the **Red-legged Sun Squirrel** and the **Red Bush Squirrel**.

Birds

The diversity of birds in the park is boosted by the diversity of habitats: the Jozani forest, thicket on coral rag, and mangroves. In the forest the list stands at 43 species, with specials being **Fischer's Turaco, Crested Guineafowl, Blue-cheeked Bee-eater, Little Greenbul, East Coast Batis, East Coast Akalat, Red-capped Robin-Chat, East Coast Boubou, Olive Sunbird, Mouse-coloured Sunbird, Zanzibar Red Bishop, Dark-backed Weaver** and **Golden Weaver**. Because forest-dwelling birds are often difficult to locate, it is well worthwhile taking on one of the local guides. In the mangroves and around Chwaka Bay look out for the **Mangrove Kingfisher**, numerous Palaearctic waders during summer, **Crab Plover** and **Western Reef Heron**.

Reptiles and amphibians

Although the diversity of reptiles and amphibians is remarkably high, most are elusive and cryptic. Two of the commonest lizards are the **Tropical House Gecko** and the **Speckle-lipped Skink**, the latter living among the leaf litter on the forest floor and in trees. In the coastal area you have a good chance of spotting the **Coral Rag Skink**. One of the largest lizards here is the **Great Plated Lizard**, which lives in holes in the ground and among coral rag. Although difficult to locate, the fairly large **Flap-necked Chameleon** occurs throughout the forest and thicket areas. The **Zanzibar (Dull) Day Gecko** is one of the few diurnal geckos and can be seen on tree trunks and branches. Most snake species on the island are harmless and include the **Brown House Snake, Cape Wolf Snake, Dwarf File Snake, Rufous Egg-eater** and the **Usambara Green Snake**. Venomous species include the **Boomslang** and **Forest Cobra**. Amphibians are abundant and diverse with several endemics, including the **Guttural Toad, Woodland Toad, Mrora Forest Toad** (known to occur only on Unguja and Mafia islands), **Jozani Kassina** (only discovered and described in 2006) and the **Southern Foam-nest Frog**.

KATAVI NATIONAL PARK

A group of Savanna Elephant crossing the Katuma River in Katavi

Lie of the land

Katavi National Park is located in the Mpanda district of western Tanzania, and at 4,471km² it is the country's third-largest park. The park lies at the heart of an ecosystem covering some 25,000km² that includes three game reserves, Rukwa, Lukwati and Luafi, as well as several forest reserves. Much of the park lies within the Rukwa Rift Valley and has an altitudinal range of 500–1,560m. Much of the park lies in flat to undulating seasonal floodplains but broken hill country is located in the north and east, with the Mlele Escarpment in the east. The western sector of the park forms the eastern boundary of the Karema Gap that separates the Tanzania-Malawi mountain zone from the Albertine Rift mountains to the north-west, an important zoogeographical boundary. The town of Mpanda, the district capital, lies 40km to the north of the park.

Brief history

A number of Stone Age and Iron Age sites are known from the area, including an iron kiln just to the north of Sitalike. Tribal groups, such as the Pimbwe, Fipa, Gongwe, Bende and Konongo, were already established in the area in the 19th century and probably earlier. Arab slave and ivory traders were in the area in the early decades of the 19th century and one of their principal routes between Lake Tanganyika and the coast passed through what is now the park. During the course of the early 20th century the human population was impacted by diseases, including sleeping sickness and rinderpest, destructive to man and cattle, warfare and severe drought. The Katavi ecosystem was first put under protection by

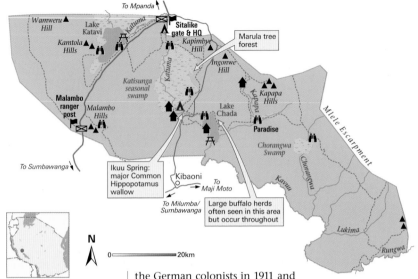

To Mpanda
Wamweru Hill
Lake Katavi
Kamtola Hills
Sitalike gate & HQ
Kapimbye Hill
Marula tree forest
Ingonwe Hill
Katisunga seasonal swamp
Katuma
Kapapa Hills
Malambo ranger post
Malambo Hills
Lake Chada
Paradise
Mlele Escarpment
To Sumbawanga
Ikuu Spring: major Common Hippopotamus wallow
Kibaoni
To Maji Moto
Chorangwa Swamp
Chorangwa
Kavuu
To Milumba/ Sumbawanga
Large buffalo herds often seen in this area but occur throughout
Lukima
Rungwa

N

0 ——————— 20km

- Visitor numbers are low.
- Great diversity of mammals, including all larger game species except Hook-lipped Rhinoceros.
- Large herds up to 1,000 strong of African Buffalo on the floodplains.
- Spectacular concentrations of Hippopotamus during the dry season; also Nile Crocodile.
- Scenic beauty, especially associated with the escarpments and hill country.
- Good birdwatching, especially during rainy season.

the German colonists in 1911 and called the Bismarck Hunting Reserve and in 1932 the British renamed it the Rukwa Game Reserve. By 1974 it had been raised to national park status and was expanded to its present size in 1996. The park takes its name from a Wabende spirit known as Katabi who is believed to reside in a pair of trees near Lake Katavi. In recent years the building of dams outside the park on the major feeder rivers has resulted in lower water flow and a reduction of water available to game species in Katavi during the dry season. This and poaching are reducing the numbers of some game species.

Geology and landscape

Most of the park lies in the Rukwa Rift Basin, part of the Central African Rift and a parallel arm to the Tanganyika Rift. The landscape can be broadly divided into the rift valley floor bordered by rift walls, and areas of rugged hills and plateaux. In the west lies the Llyamba lya Mfipa Escarpment and in the east the Mlele Escarpment. Much of the valley floor is flat and has extensive seasonally flooded plains, lakes that largely dry out between the rains, as well as a river network. The principal seasonal river is the Katuma, which forms much of the park's southern boundary and is the principal feeder of lakes Katavi and Chada, as well as the Katisunga floodplain. All rivers in Katavi drain towards Lake Rukwa except the Nkamba River, which flows into Lake Tanganyika. These rivers flow only during the rains, when much of the plain is transformed into a network of lakes, marshes and flowing waterways. The Rukwa Basin is made up of three geological age groups: Karoo sediments, Neogene deposits and rocks dating from the Cambrian. Most of the rock systems are made up of soft sandstones, silt stones and tuffaceous sediments.

Climate

Most rain here falls from October to April and there is an annual average of 930mm. Temperatures are moderately hot from August to December, cool in June and July, with the remaining months being mild to warm.

Vegetation

Up to 11 broad plant communities have been recognized for Katavi but two types dominate, dry miombo woodlands (hilltop miombo and mixed miombo) and grassland. Hilltop miombo is found at higher altitudes along hill ridges and upper escarpment and is dominated by the **Double-crown Julbernardia** (*Julbernardia globiflora*). Mixed miombo has greater tree diversity and includes several species of *Brachystegia* and **Bush Willow** (*Combretum* spp.), as well as **Double-crown** (*Isoberlinia angolensis*), **Zebra Wood** (*Dalbergia melanoxylon*), **Umbrella Thorn** (*Vachellia tortilis*), **Wild Teak** (*Pterocarpus angolensis*), **Sausage Tree** (*Kigelia africana*), **Ana Tree** (*Faidherbia albida*), **Doum Palm** (*Hyphaene compressa*) and **Borassus Palm** (*Borassus aethiopum*).

Similar tree mixes extend from the escarpment foothills along the river lines and around the scattered, seasonally flooded, grassy plains (known as dambos), but with a number of additional species. Thickets consisting of just a few tree species and climbing plants are scattered throughout the park, including around Kanyamkaa, Igongwe, Ikuu and Kapapa. Bushland with emergent trees can be found around Lake Chada and Lake Katavi; it is species rich, most bushes are multi-stemmed and rarely exceed 5m in height, sometimes with dense stands of **Sickle Bush** (*Dichrostachys cinerea*). Tall trees may be present, including **Baobab** (*Adansonia digitata*) and **White Gul Mohur** (*Delonix elata*), as well as extensive stands of **Marula** (*Sclerocarya birrea*). There are several areas with riverine forest, including along the Katuma, Kapapa and Rungwa rivers. The trees here tend to be tall, up to 25m, and many are evergreen, including **Sycamore Fig** (*Ficus sycomorus*), **Mountain Fig** (*Ficus glumosa*), **Giant-leaved Fig** (*Ficus lutea*), **Forest Newtonia** (*Newtonia buchananii*), **Red Mahogany** (*Khaya anthotheca*) and **Waterberry** (*Syzygium cordatum*).

FACILITIES AND ACTIVITIES

- Five privately run upmarket tented camps and lodges: Chada, Flycatchers Seasonal, Katavi Wildlife, Katuma Katavi and Palahala, most of which are closed during the rains.
- Park authorities have one guesthouse and six huts but these are not well maintained.
- Public and special campsites are situated near HQ.
- Road access is poor and may be difficult during rains; main access is Mpanda-Sumbawanga road; internal roads are limited.
- The park is best reached by air and has airstrips.
- No fuel or supplies available in the park.
- Local market in Mpanda.

Dry miombo woodland dominates the park.

WILDLIFE FACTS

- At least 74 mammal species.
- Latest game estimates include 20,000 Plains Zebra, 17,000 Topi, 15,000 Buffalo, 15,000 Impala, 4,000 Hippopotamus, 4,000 Giraffe and 750 Spotted Hyaena. These numbers may be lower due to recent poaching.
- More than 450 bird species in the park and adjacent areas.
- 226 species of tree have been identified.

Maasai Giraffe

Wildlife
Mammals

No detailed inventory of the smaller mammals has been compiled for Katavi. Of the 61 larger and medium-sized mammals recorded, the **Sitatunga**, **Klipspringer** and **Steenbok** have only been noted outside the boundary within the Rukwa ecosystem. It is likely that all three are present in Katavi. **Hippopotamus** are abundant, especially along the Kapapa and Ngolima rivers and at Ikuu. **African Buffalo** are common and can often be seen in great herds out on the floodplains but **Savanna Elephant** numbers have been greatly reduced by poaching throughout the Rukwa basin. Numbers of **Plains Zebra**, **Topi**, **Impala** and **Giraffe** are substantial and are easily observed on the floodplains. The numbers of **Roan**, **Lichtenstein's Hartebeest**, **Defassa Waterbuck**, **Bohor** and **Southern Reedbuck**, **Common Eland** and **Bushbuck** are also healthy but most favour woodlands to the open plains, except for the reedbuck. In total, 19 species of antelope are present but several are considered to be rare or have been sighted only outside the boundary. Carnivores are well represented, with no less than 26 species known to occur within and around the park. They range from all three big cats, **Lion**, **Leopard** and **Cheetah**, to **African Wild Dog**, **Side-striped** and **Black-backed jackals**, as well as eight species of mongoose. The most easily seen are those that are diurnal, **Dwarf**, **Banded**, **Egyptian** and **Slender mongooses**. Apart from the two nocturnal galago species, there are four diurnal primates, all readily seen: **Vervet Monkey**, **Blue Monkey**, and **Yellow** and **Olive baboons**. Most baboon records are from the fringes of the park in hilly country. The authors have records of **Cape Porcupine**, **Greater Cane-rat**, **Tree (Bush) Squirrel**, **Nile Grass Rat** and the **Four-toed Sengi**, which do not appear on the official list. In one study, seven species of small rodent were collected inside and in close proximity to the park. Potentially at least another 50 species of small mammal could be found in the park and surrounds.

Birds

More than 450 species of bird have been recorded in the Katavi-Rukwa ecosystem, at least 220 of which occur within the national park. Apart from resident and local migrant species, there is a major influx of Palaearctic migrants between November and April during the rains. Some of the specials include the resident **Dickinson's Kestrel**,

Racquet-tailed Roller, Stierling's Woodpecker, Tabora Cisticola, Kurrichane Thrush, White-headed Black-Chat, Miombo Rock Thrush, Tanzania Masked Weaver and the Broad-tailed Paradise Whydah. Several hundred **African Skimmers** are winter visitors. At least 17 species of heron, egret and bittern occur, substantial numbers of **Great White Pelican** seasonally and seven species of stork. There are resident waders, such as **Long-toed Plover**, and many rainy season visitors. Ducks and geese are well represented with both resident and migratory species. During the rains there are particularly large numbers present. Potentially 48 species of raptor could be present, of which a substantial number have already been confirmed. More prominent are the **African Fish Eagle, Martial Eagle** and **Tawny Eagle**, as well as **Palmnut Vulture**. Although many species of raptor are resident, there are a number of seasonal migrants. Both **Red-billed** and **Yellow-billed oxpeckers** occur and are best seen in proximity of the African Buffalo and other game species.

Palmnut Vulture are fairly frequently observed along the watercourses.

Reptiles and amphibians

The reptile fauna of the park and surrounds is considered to be particularly diverse. The **Nile Crocodile** is common and is especially seen in the dry season when groups mass in overhangs and cavities in the banks of the riverbed. There is at least one reptile endemic to the park, the **Katavi Burrowing Skink** (*Typhlacontias kataviensis*). One land tortoise, **Speke's Hinged**, and three freshwater terrapins occur, **Helmeted, Serrated Hinged** and **Pan Hinged**. At least 31 species of lizard call this area home, including the **White-throated Monitor** and **Nile Monitor**, as well as five species of gecko and eight skinks. There are 58 snake species, ranging in size from the **Southern African Rock Python** to the tiny **blind snakes** (*Rhinotyphlops* spp.), of which there are four species. Fairly commonly seen are **African Rock Python, Black Mamba, Boomslang** and **Puff Adder**. Some 28 species of amphibian have been recorded from within and close to the boundaries of the park.

Nile Crocodiles on the river bank

- **Katavi lies within the malaria area.**
- **Tsetse flies are abundant in some parts, so there is a slight risk of sleeping sickness.**
- **Be alert to potentially dangerous game: African Buffalo, Elephant, Lion and Nile Crocodile.**
- **In general, roads are in poor to very bad condition, especially during the rains.**
- **If you opt for self-drive, be prepared for breakdowns and long distances between reliable fuel supplies.**

KILIMANJARO NATIONAL PARK

Mount Kilimanjaro viewed from the city of Moshi

Lie of the land

The 1,688km² Kilimanjaro National Park protects the largest free-standing volcanic mass in the world, Mount Kilimanjaro. Rising 4,877m above the surrounding plains to a total height of 5,888m asl, Kilimanjaro is one of the largest dormant volcanoes in the world and the highest mountain in Africa. With its three principal peaks, Kibo, Mawenzi and Shira, it is often referred to as an Afromontane sky island. Kilimanjaro lies 300km south of the equator. The city of Moshi, often considered the gateway to the park, is situated 45km to the east of Marangu park headquarters.

Brief history

The Chaga people living on the slopes of Kilimanjaro are descended from Bantu groups that moved into the area around the 11th century. They are agricultural people and have heavily cultivated the fertile lower slopes and surrounding areas. The first European known to have reported on the existence of Kilimanjaro was the missionary Johannes Rebmann in 1848. The first attempted ascent was in 1861 by Baron Karl Klaus von der Decken, who turned back due to foul weather. He and Otto Kersten made another attempt in 1862 but only reached 4,300m. Others that attempted the climb were Count Samuel Teleki and Ludwig von Hohnel in 1887, as well as Hans Meyer in the same year, but all were defeated by the ice cap. The first successful ascent of Kibo took place in 1889, while the summit of Mawenzi was successfully climbed in 1912 by Edward Oehler and Fritz Klute. Today as many as 35,000 people attempt the ascent each year. The German colonists proclaimed Mount Kilimanjaro and its flanking forests as a game reserve. In 1921 the British gazetted it as a forest reserve, in 1973 part of the reserve was reclassified as a national park, and in 1987 the park was designated a World Heritage Site.

Geology and landscape

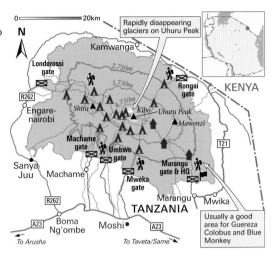

Kilimanjaro is a huge stratovolcano with three separate volcanic cones, Kibo, Mawenzi and Shira. Kibo boasts the highest point, known as Uhuru Peak. The base of the mountain measures about 80x48km. Mawenzi and Shira are classified as extinct, but Kibo is dormant and has the potential to erupt, with gas still being emitted from fumaroles within its crater. The last major eruption took place between 200,000 and 150,000 years before present. Kilimanjaro is the largest of an east-west belt of volcanoes strung across northern Tanzania.

Shira is the oldest peak and forms a relatively flat plateau, as only its western and southern rims survive. Mawenzi has a rugged peak, fragmented by erosion, a steep western wall and an eastern wall rising more than 1,000m, below which are two deep gorges, Great Barranco and Lesser Barranco. Kibo, the highest point, with two large concentric craters, is separated from Mawenzi by a 3,600ha plateau that is the largest area of high-altitude tundra in tropical Africa. Apart from its size, Kilimanjaro also stands out because of its white ice cap. However, more than 80% of the ice cap has been lost since 1912 and it is estimated that the remaining ice will be lost within 15–25 years.

Climate

There are two rain periods, late March to early June and late October to early January, with the driest times being February to mid-March and July to September. Levels of precipitation vary according to altitude and location, with the south and east slopes receiving about 2,500mm at around 3,000m asl but this drops to just 1,000mm on north-facing slopes. Rainfall decreases towards the summit and on the Saddle barely reaches 250mm, a true alpine desert. Above 3,000m temperatures often drop below freezing and at the summit may drop to -25°C at night. Days usually start with clear skies but as the air warms clouds form and precipitation in the form of rain, or sleet and hail from the upper forest and moorland upwards, may fall.

HIGHLIGHTS

- Spectacular and varied mountain scenery.
- Great diversity of plant and animal life.
- The opportunity to climb Africa's highest mountain.

The first aerial photograph of Kibo, taken in 1929

Kilimanjaro Senecio are common on the moorland zone of Mount Kilimanjaro.

Vegetation

There are five main vegetation zones on the mountain: savanna bushland on the southern and northern slopes and submontane agro-forest on the southern and south-east slopes; above these the montane forest belt; at higher altitude the subalpine moorland and alpine bogs; and alpine desert towards the peaks. Unlike Mounts Kenya or Meru, Kilimanjaro does not have a bamboo belt. At least 2,500 plant species have been identified from the mountain, of which 1,600 grow on the wetter southern slopes. Lower parts of the wet forest are characterized by **East African Camphor Wood (Mkulo)** (*Ocotea usambarensis*) and **Wild Poplar** (*Macaranga kilimandscharica*), with a dense understorey of woody herbs and shrubs. Above 2,400m **East African Yellowwood** (*Afrocarpus gracilior*) is common, festooned with bryophytes and lichens, mainly **Old Man's Beard** (*Usnea barbata*). Forests on the drier western and northern slopes differ in appearance and species composition up to about 2,400m when the yellowwood reappears, as well as **African Pencil Cedar** (*Juniperus procera*). Species here include **African Olive** (**Wild Olive**) (*Olea europaea*), **Cape Chestnut** (*Calodendrum capense*), **Croton** (*Croton megalocarpus*) and **Pillarwood** (*Cassipourea malosana*). Above the forest is a belt characterized by **Giant Heath** (*Erica arborea*). Between 2,800 and 4,600m one finds **Giant Groundsel** (*Senecio/Dendrosenecio* spp.), **Giant Lobelia** (*Lobelia deckenii*), **Kilimanjaro Protea** (*Protea kilimandscharica*) and several species of 'everlastings' (*Helichrysum* spp.). Here also are extensive areas of **tussock grassland**. At the highest levels lichens cling to the ice edge.

FACILITIES AND ACTIVITIES

- Six main trekking routes to the summit, with mountain huts and camp locations. If you intend to get to the summit you are obliged to hire a guide and porters; minimum five nights.
- Nature trails at lower elevations.
- Excellent birdwatching and great diversity of plants.
- Accommodation and campsites outside the park.

Wildlife
Mammals

Although a list of as many as 140 mammal species is available, this includes areas outside the park boundary. Primates include the **Olive Baboon** in the lower areas, with both **Blue Monkey** and **Guereza (Black and White Colobus)**, in the forest zone. The Guereza here has a distinctly bushy and all-white tail and is recognized as a distinct subspecies. Carnivores are well represented but most are seldom seen. Apart from occasional records of **African Wild Dog**, the only other canid record is of **Black-backed Jackal**, including a sighting from the Shira Plateau. **Striped Polecat, African Palm Civet** or **African Civet** are likely to occur. The **Common Large-spotted Genet** occurs in the forest but to what level is not known. **Slender Mongoose** are quite common, with several melanistic individuals observed, as well as **White-tailed Mongoose**. The **Spotted Hyaena** has been observed at 4,100m on Mount Kenya and is likely to range widely here but may not be resident. There are also records of **Striped Hyaena**. The **Serval** occurs up to the moorland to at least 3,850m and melanistic individuals are occasionally sighted. **Leopard** occur throughout all zones. **Lion** venture on to the moorland and Shira Plateau; it is not clear whether there is a resident population in the park. The **Savanna Elephant** population probably numbers less than 200 and they rarely venture above 2,900m. The **Southern Tree Hyrax** can occur at densities of up to 70 hyrax per hectare at about 2,600m on the north slope of the mountain. It lives in trees and on rocky slopes and is mainly nocturnal but may be active during the day. **Bushpig** occur but are uncommon.

Blue Monkey frequent the forest zone.

Leopard are secretive.

Apart from man, the only other mammal known to have reached the summit is the African Wild Dog.

WILDLIFE FACTS

- 140 mammal species, many outside, or only marginally in the park.
- The Kilimanjaro Mouse Shrew (*Myosorex zinki*) is endemic to the park.
- 179 bird species have been recorded, with several rarities.
- Up to 88 reptile species.
- 21 amphibian species recorded, but most occur outside the national park boundary.
- 130 tree species recorded on the mountain; 100 lianas; 130 ferns; 415 mosses; 181 liverworts; 120 lichens.
- 1,310 species of beetle have been identified; 537 butterfly and moth species; many endemic insect species.

!
- **To avoid altitude sickness, ascent over several days is recommended to acclimatize.**
- **Hypothermia and frostbite are also potential problems.**
- **Dangerous game species, such as Lion, Savanna Elephant and African Buffalo are present on the mountain.**

The highly restricted **Abbott's Duiker** seems to occur only above 2,000m but this may be due to poaching pressures at lower levels. This duiker also occurs at upper levels on a few other Tanzanian mountains. In contrast, the **Grey Duiker** is common and occurs up to 4,600m and is present on the Shira Plateau. The largest antelope here is the **Common Eland** and it is known to range widely and has been recorded quite regularly on the Shira Plateau. Given the sparse vegetation here, it is believed this and other species, such as **African Buffalo**, come to exploit mineral deposits. At least 15 species of rodent occur in the park, with the subterranean **Mount Kilimanjaro Mole Rat** occurring up to 4,300m and apparently common on the Shira Plateau. There are seven shrew species from three genera; the **Kilimanjaro Mouse Shrew** (*Myosorex zinki*) is the only mammal endemic to Mount Kilimanjaro.

Birds

Although forest birds are difficult to observe, there are many interesting species on Mount Kilimanjaro, such as the **Olive Ibis, Rufous-chested Sparrowhawk, Mountain Buzzard, African Crowned Eagle, Hartlaub's Turaco, Cinnamon-chested Bee-eater, Silvery-cheeked Hornbill, Narina** and **Bar-tailed trogons, Abbott's** and **Waller's starlings** and **Abyssinian Ground Thrush**. Beyond the forest at higher altitudes bird diversity is not great but **White-necked Raven** commonly seen and occasional sightings of **Bearded Vulture**. Of the 13 species of **sunbird** recorded on the mountain, high-altitude species include **Scarlet-tufted Malachite Sunbird** and **Tacazze Sunbird**. The **Moorland (Alpine) Chat** is common above 3,400m on moorland and in the alpine zone.

Reptiles and amphibians

Up to 88 reptile species have distributional ranges that may include Kilimanjaro. The **Side-spotted Dwarf Gecko** is known only from Kilimanjaro and the Taita Hills (Kenya), with the **Mount Kilimanjaro Two-horned Chameleon** known from here and several other mountains. There are 21 amphibian species recorded, many occurring only outside the park and just two common within the park, **De Witte's (Molo) River Frog** and the **Mount Meru Stream Frog**. The low diversity and lack of endemism here is surprising given that on mountains within the Eastern Arc these are particularly high but could be explained by the relatively young age of Kilimanjaro.

LAKE MANYARA NATIONAL PARK

Flocks of African Wood Stork and Great White Pelican gather at Maji Moto hot springs.

Lie of the land

Lake Manyara lies close to the town of Mto wa mbu ('Place of the Mosquito' or 'Mosquito Stream'), within Mbulu district, on the main route that links Arusha to the Serengeti. Near the headquarters of the Lake Manyara National Park is the confluence of three streams, Kirurumo, Simba and Mtowambu. Manyara lies on the floor of the Great Rift Valley and covers an area of 330km², of which about two-thirds consists of the lake. The shallow alkaline lake lies in the Natron-Manyara-Balangida branch of the East African Rift, with the Gregory Rift wall on its western flank. To the east lies the Kwakuchinja wildlife corridor and the Manyara Ranch Conservancy that allows for some game movement between the park and Tarangire National Park.

Brief history

Humans and human ancestors have lived in this area for millions of years, the Hadza (Hadzabe) hunter-gatherers have lived in the region for several thousand years, and Bantu tribes arrived in the area from the north some 1,500 years before present. Several tribes, such as the Iraqw, Datoga and Isanzu, were forced south into the area in the 19th century with the arrival of the pastoralist Maasai, a Nilotic people that have their origins in what is now South Sudan. The Maasai have dominated the area since their arrival. The area was proclaimed as a game reserve in 1957, given national park status in 1960, and declared a biosphere reserve in 1981. An ever-growing human population in the surrounding area has resulted in the destruction of habitats, pollution of the lake and poaching of game species. At least nine mammal species have been driven to extinction since the late 1950s. The park became known to the outside world when elephant researcher Iain Douglas-Hamilton undertook his groundbreaking research here.

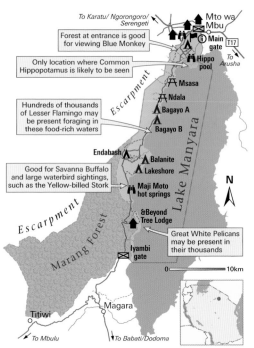

To Karatu/ Ngorongoro/ Serengeti

Mto wa Mbu

Forest at entrance is good for viewing Blue Monkey

Main gate

117

Only location where Common Hippopotamus is likely to be seen

Hippo pool

To Arusha

Msasa

Ndala

Hundreds of thousands of Lesser Flamingo may be present foraging in these food-rich waters

Escarpment

Bagayo A

Bagayo B

Endabash

Balanite

Lakeshore

Good for Savanna Buffalo and large waterbird sightings, such as the Yellow-billed Stork

Maji Moto hot springs

Lake Manyara

N

Escarpment

&Beyond Tree Lodge

Marang Forest

Great White Pelicans may be present in their thousands

Iyambi gate

0 ──────── 10km

Titiwi

Magara

To Mbulu

To Babati/Dodoma

Geology and landscape

Manyara lies in the north-western area of the Maasai-Steppe at an altitude of between 953m and 1,145m asl. The landscape is dominated in the west by the rugged wall of the Gregory Rift and to the east the shallow Lake Manyara. This is an alkaline lake but there are several hot springs at its edge, most notably at Maji Moto Ndogo and Maji Moto in the south of the park. There are several short streams that rise on the Gregory Rift but some flow only during the rains. The level of the lake can vary considerably but its bed is some 40km long and 13km wide. About 250,000 years before present the lake was part of the much more extensive Proto-Manyara.

Climate

There are two periods of rain (annual average of 579mm at Mto Wa Mbu) separated by dry seasons from June to September and to a lesser extent in January and February. Rainfall reaches its peak in April, with an average of 129mm. Summer temperatures have a mean range of 20–30°C and in winter 19–25°C.

Vegetation

The name of the park is derived from the Maasai word *emanyara*, the name they give to the **Pencil Tree** (*Euphorbia tirucalli*), which they use as a living stock-proof hedge. To the north the porous volcanic rock allows numerous small streams of fresh water to emerge and ground water forest dominates. Here are some of the largest trees in the park, including **Natal Mahogany** (*Trichilia emetica*), **Bark-cloth Tree** (*Antiaris toxicaria*), **Mitzeeri** (*Bridelia micrantha*) and **Sycamore Fig** (*Ficus sycomorus*). In other parts of the park there are also other distinctive tree species, such as **Baobab** (*Adansonia digitata*), **Sausage Tree** (*Kigelia africana*), the yellow-green-barked **Fever Tree** (*Vachellia xanthophloea*) and the tall, slender-trunked **Real Fan Palm** (*Hyphaene petersiana*). Another distinctive large, canopied tree is the **Umbrella Thorn** (*Vachellia tortilis*), which is frequently used

HIGHLIGHTS

- Ease of access and small size make it suitable for a day visit.
- Great diversity of habitats, mammals and birds.
- Lions that climb into trees to escape biting flies.
- Vast flocks of flamingos and pelicans gather during the wet season.

as a perch for the resident lions. The closest approach to the rugged escarpment is to the south of the Bagayo River, which is where you will see the massively trunked Baobabs but it is only in March that the numerous scrubby, thorned bushes called '**Wait-a-bit**' (*Senegalia brevispica*) blossom. Especially towards the south of the park, there are more open grassed areas with scatterings of small trees and bushes. In the vicinity of the hot springs there are some taller grasses and reeds. The Marang Forest lies in the south of the park but is largely inaccessible to visitors.

Wildlife
Mammals

There is a small resident **Savanna Elephant** population with decreasing numbers moving in from other areas due to human developments and activities around the boundaries. Elephants may be seen anywhere within the park but during the dry season are especially visible at permanent water sources and along the Ndala River. The only resident **Common Hippopotamus** are found in the Simba River in the north. Other large game includes herds of **Savanna Buffalo**, which wander the grassed areas of the park and are often seen at the springs at Maji Moto Ndogo, **Maasai Giraffe**, **Eastern White-bearded Wildebeest**, **Plains Zebra**, **Impala** and **Common Warthog**. There are **Klipspringer** on the slopes of the rift wall but they are difficult to spot. Among the most obvious mammals in the park are **Olive Baboons**, which occur throughout, as well as troops of **Vervet Monkey** and **Blue Monkey**. The last are most easily seen in the ground water forest close to the entrance gate. **Lions** are present in small numbers and are well known here for climbing into trees

Natal Mahogany fruits

FACILITIES AND ACTIVITIES

- One permanent luxury lodge (&Beyond Tree Lodge); public and special campsites; various options outside the park, from budget to top end.
- Network of game-viewing tracks starting and ending at the northern entrance.
- Viewing platform at Hippo Pools with boardwalk at Maji Moto hot springs.
- Good game viewing and birdwatching with amazing diversity given the small size of the park.

Savanna Buffalo occur throughout the park.

Savanna Elephant occur in small numbers.

Eastern White-bearded Wildebeest

WILDLIFE FACTS

- 60 mammal species known but no survey done of smaller species.
- 436 bird species; at times thousands of Lesser and Greater flamingos and pelicans.
- Diversity of reptiles and amphibians but poorly known.

to rest, often lying on the horizontal branches of the Umbrella Thorn. **Leopard** and **Spotted Hyaena** are present but seldom seen. A further 14 smaller carnivore species occur, of which only three are commonly seen, the social **Banded** and **Dwarf mongooses** and the solitary **Slender Mongoose**. Many of the smaller species present are nocturnal and are only likely to be seen during an organized night drive. Another small diurnal species that may be spotted is the **Rock Hyrax** on the rift wall.

Birds

Despite the park's small size it has 436 bird species on its list, in part thanks to the diversity of habitats. Depending on the level of the lake, hundreds of thousands of **Lesser Flamingo** may be present foraging in these food-rich waters. **Great White Pelicans** may also be present in their thousands (one estimate of 200,000 individuals) but do not breed here although large numbers of **Pink-backed Pelicans** do nest in the park. Great numbers of **Yellow-billed Stork** breed here and flocks can often be seen around the springs at Maji Moto Ndogo. The lake fringes are important feeding grounds for many bird species, including the migratory **Spotted Crake** and **Red-throated Pipit**. At least 13 heron species, seven of stork, 15 ducks and geese, as well as eight kingfisher species have been recorded. The area is also rich in raptors, including **African Crowned Eagle**, **Martial Eagle**, **Long-crested Eagle**, **African Fish Eagle**, **Palmnut Vulture**, **Augur Buzzard**, **African Marsh Harrier** and at least another 37 species are known. This is an important area for migrant waders, especially when lake levels are low. **Fischer's Lovebird** is at times common but not always present. Of the six hornbill species, the **Silvery-cheeked** is mainly found in the ground water forest. The **Rufous-tailed Weaver** occurs in the park but is more common on the eastern shore of the lake.

Reptiles and amphibians

No formal survey of the reptiles and amphibians of this park has been published but it is likely to be a rich herpetofauna.

- This is a malaria area.
- Camps are not fenced – be alert for potentially dangerous game species.
- Baboons can be a nuisance.
- Roads may be difficult to negotiate during the peak rains.

MAHALE MOUNTAINS NATIONAL PARK

Up to 900 Common Chimpanzees are believed to live in Mahale.

Lie of the land

Covering 1,613km², Mahale is located 128km south of Kigoma, the only official access point (by boat) to the park. It is situated in western Tanzania and forms a broad peninsula, with its western boundary formed by Lake Tanganyika. Unlike Gombe Stream National Park, Mahale incorporates a 1.6km-wide strip of the lake. Much of the park is rugged and hilly and dominated by the Mahale Mountain range, with its highest peak Mount Nkungwe rising to 2,462m asl.

Brief history

Mahale and the surrounding areas have been occupied for thousands of years with many waves of immigrant tribes from Congo, as well as from the Malagarasi River basin to the north, the Ufipa District further south and from northern Zambia. Each successive wave conquered and absorbed the tribes already in place. One of the most recent of these events saw the Baholoholo drive the Wamahare away from the lake shore into the Mahale Mountains, with the latter later fully absorbed. There are no villages within Mahale today and the Baholoholo, Waganza and Wagalawa live around the fringes of the park, speaking a common language, Tongwe, and are known collectively as the Watongwe. Large areas of the park were inhabited in the past and signs of cultivation (including a number of fruiting trees) and settlements can be observed in many locations. The people living outside the park rely principally on small-scale farming and netting the Lake Sardine (*dagga*) as well as producing palm oil (*mawese*).

One of the longest-running studies on Chimpanzees was initiated by researchers from the Kyoto University, Japan, in 1965, in Mahale. In 1980 all villagers were removed from the park and in 1985 Mahale was gazetted as a national park.

- Chimpanzee population with habituated animals, allowing for close viewing.
- Accompanied walking safaris of 2–7 days can be arranged.
- Great diversity of fauna and flora.
- Protected lake frontage allows good viewing of aquatic organisms.
- Scenic backdrop of the Mahale Mountains

Lagosa (Mugambo)
Igalula
Katumbi
Sitolo Bay
Kalilanio
Bilenge Bay
Pasagula Point
Miyako Point
▲ Mt Pasagulu
▲ Mt Mhensabantu
Kasiha
▲ Mt Humo
To Kigoma (by boat)
▲ Mt Kungwe
▲ Mt Sibindi
▲ Mt ▲ Mt Mfitwa
Kahoka ▲ Mt Sisaga
Habituated Common Chimpanzee in this area
Luagala Point
Mahale Mountains
Great diversity of cichlid fishes
Lake Tanganyika
Kasagulu
N
0 ————— 15km
Kibwesa
Kibwesa Point
Kalya

FACILITIES AND ACTIVITIES

- Guided Chimpanzee tracking.
- 2–7-day guided hiking trail.
- Snorkelling in Lake Tanganyika.
- Private luxury tented camps including Nomad Safaris and Nkungwe. Five self-contained tourist bandas.

Geology and landscape

Mahale is dominated by Lake Tanganyika to the west and the Mahale Mountain range from the lake eastwards. The rock is predominantly granite and metamorphic gneisses and schists. Most of the soils are thin, stony and porous.

Climate

There is a single wet season from mid-October to mid-May that deposits 1,500–2,500mm of rain, with altitudinal and localized variation. The dry season starts in mid-May and terminates in mid-October. Although there are seasonal, altitudinal and day-night temperature fluctuations, the maximum mean towards the end of the dry period is around 31°C.

Vegetation

About 75% of the park is covered by miombo woodland, with tree species of the genera *Brachystegia*, *Isoberlinia* and *Julbernardia* dominating, all with pinnate leaves and hard, woody pods when ripe. Where the mountains converge with the lake, to an altitude of about 1,300m asl, there is an area dominated by lowland forest. Trees here include a mix of **figs** (*Ficus* spp.), **false thorns** (*Albizia* spp.), **Red Mahogany** (*Khaya anthotheca*), **bitterwood** (*Xylopia* spp.), **Ochol** (*Pseudospondias microcarpa*) and **garcinias** (*Garcinia* spp.). The understorey is dominated by several species of evergreen creeper. Above and beyond the Kasoge forest is a mix of **bamboo** and montane forest, with **Wild Poplar** (*Macaranga kilimandscharica*), **Wild Elder (Muchorowe)** (*Nuxia congesta*), **yellowwoods** (*Podocarpus* spp.), *Bersama* spp., and **fever berries** (*Croton* spp.), among others.

Mahale Mountains National Park is accessed by boat only.

Wildlife
Mammals

The majority of visitors to Mahale come to see the habituated **Common (Robust) Chimpanzee** troops located in the north-west of the park. There are an estimated 700–900 Common Chimpanzees in the park, comprising about 15 communities, many of which have little or no contact with man. Along with the Gombe population, the Mahale chimps are among the most studied of any primates. Although the two populations have much in common, there are also minor behavioural differences. Some of the chimp groups here range through virtually all available habitats. The **Yellow Baboon** is common but the Olive Baboon of Gombe is absent. **Angolan Black and White Colobus** occur in the montane forest above 2,000m asl; other primates include **Vervet Monkey**, **Eastern Red Colobus**, **Red-tailed Monkey** and **Blue Monkey**, as well as **Brown Thick-tailed Galago**. One of the smaller galagos has been recorded but its identity still awaits confirmation. There are several species normally associated with Central and West Africa here, including **African Brush-tailed Porcupine** and **Giant Forest Squirrel**. Savanna-associated species occur mainly in the east and south of the park, such as **Savanna Elephant, Maasai Giraffe, Common Warthog, Savanna Buffalo, Sable Antelope, Roan Antelope, Lichtenstein's Hartebeest, Bushbuck (Imbabala), Common Duiker** and **Plains Zebra**. Predators are well represented but status and numbers are little known. **Lion** are wide ranging and on occasion include Chimpanzees in their diet, as no doubt do **Leopard**. **Spotted Hyaena** are resident but it is not clear whether **African**

Spotted Hyaena

WILDLIFE FACTS

- 82 mammal species recorded (may be up to 120).
- 700–900 Common Chimpanzees resident.
- 247 bird species.
- At least 28 reptile species and 22 amphibians; no intensive survey has been undertaken.
- More than 250 cichlid fish species in Lake Tanganyika.
- 1,174 plant species recorded; undoubtedly more occur.

Wild Dog are resident. Both the **Spotted-necked** and **Cape Clawless otters** occur along the lake shore and the latter probably also penetrates along some of the stream courses. Nine species of mongoose are known to occur.

Birds

Some 355 species of bird (247 within the park) have been recorded within and on the fringes of Mahale, including a number of rarities. Although birding is good throughout the year, from November to April northern migrants are present. A limiting factor here for birders is the fact that walking is only permitted with a guide, with emphasis on Chimpanzee watching. As within any forested habitat, birding is difficult and a knowledge of calls is a plus. The **African Fish Eagle** is commonly seen along the lake shore, as is the **Palmnut Vulture**, with **African Crowned Eagle** over forested areas. Other specials include the **Kungwe Apalis, Regal Sunbird, Bocage's Akalat, Yellow-streaked Greenbul, Shelley's Greenbul, Mountain Greenbul, Brown-chested Alethe, Bamboo Warbler, Yellow-throated Warbler** and **Yellow-bellied Wattle-eye. Stuhlman's Starling** in Tanzania is known to occur only in Mahale.

Reptiles and amphibians

Nile and **Slender-snouted crocodiles** are recorded from the lake, but only Nile has been confirmed off Mahale. The **Serrated Hinged Terrapin** occurs along the lake edge and it is likely other species occur. **Speckle-lipped** and **Striped skinks** are widespread and believed to be common. **Flap-necked** and **Smooth chameleons** are present. The **Nile Monitor** can be expected anywhere along the lake shore. Snakes are under-represented on current lists for the area but the **Southern African Rock Python** and **Brown House Snake** occur. Smaller species are often secretive and seldom seen. Arboreal snakes include **Blanding's Tree Snake, Boomslang, Gunther's Green Tree Snake** and both **vine snakes, Savanna** and **Forest**. An interesting aquatic snake in and around the lake is the fish-hunting **Banded Water Cobra**, with **Forest Cobra** on terra firma. There are 22 amphibians, including the **Kisolo Toad**.

Two chameleon species occur, here the Flap-necked Chameleon.

- **Malaria area; sleeping sickness (spread by tsetse flies) and bilharzia possible.**
- **Obey all rules when Chimpanzee tracking for your safety and the welfare of the chimps.**
- **An expensive location to visit, so it is wise to do your homework.**
- **Rainy season brings wet and slippery conditions.**

MIKUMI NATIONAL PARK

Johnston's Wildebeest in Mikumi is at the northernmost part of its range.

Lie of the land

Mikumi National Park is located close to the town of Morogoro, in Kilosa District, in east-central Tanzania and it is bisected by the A-7 highway that links the south of the country to Dar es Salaam. The park covers 3,230km² and is the northernmost, and most accessible, part of the Selous ecosystem. It has an altitudinal range of 500m to 1,250m asl and lies mainly on the floodplain of the Mkata River, which flows into the Wami River. To its north-east lie the Uluguru Mountains and to the south-west the Udzungwa Mountains, with the Uvindunda and Rubeho ranges to the west and the Ukaguru Mountains in the north-west. Much of the park is flat grassland, fringed with areas of dry woodland, with rocky hill country to the south of the tar road, known as the Vuma Hills, highest of which is Malundwe Mountain. The park's southern boundary adjoins the vast Selous Game Reserve.

Brief history

Unlike some other parts of Tanzania, very little is known about the prehistory of the Mikumi area. At about 10,000 years before present much of the country was sparsely populated by hunter-gatherer peoples, with the first Bantu people arriving from about 2,000 years before present in a series of waves from the north and north-west. The principal tribal groupings living on the fringes of the park today are the Wavindunda, Walugur and Wasagala. Early explorers that passed through the area of the present-day park, including H.M. Stanley in 1872, commented on the abundance of game on the Mkata plain. This was to change with the completion of the Iringa-Morogoro road in 1954, allowing hunters to reach the area, resulting in the slaughter of many head of game. The area was first proclaimed as a Game Controlled Area but upgraded to national park status in 1964. Extensions to the park were added to the north and south in 1975. The park is named for the local name of the Borassus Palm.

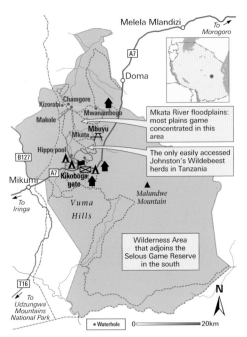

Mkata River floodplains: most plains game concentrated in this area

The only easily accessed Johnston's Wildebeest herds in Tanzania

Wilderness Area that adjoins the Selous Game Reserve in the south

● Waterhole 0 ▬▬▬ 20km

N

Geology and landscape

Much of the park that is accessible to the public consists of flat land on the Mkata River floodplain with long, very low ridges that are separated by shallow troughs filled with 'black cotton soil'. This soil, also known as Usterts Vertisol, is formed from very heavy clay and when dry can form cracks up to 2m deep but when wet becomes waterlogged, very sticky and difficult to impossible to negotiate. The low hardpan ridges are made up of near impervious soils that drain rapidly during rain. In the north of the park the 'cotton soils' remain swamp-like almost throughout the year but in the south form streams that flow into the Mkata River. There are low hills in the west and to the south (the Vuma Hills), with the Malundwe Mountains lying further south. The mountain ranges you may see to the north and south lie outside the park.

Climate

There is one rainy season, starting in November through into May with the highest falls March to May, when it can be expected to rain most days. The dry season is June to October and by mid-August most surface water has dried up and game must drink at the Hippo Pool, limited waterholes and the Mkata River. The wet season is hot and humid with average minimum temperatures of about 20°C and maximums of about 28°C, whereas the dry season averages marginally cooler with an average maximum of 26°C during the day and some 16°C at night.

HIGHLIGHTS

- Flat and largely open landscape makes for good game viewing.
- Great diversity of game species and large predators.
- Good locality for Common Eland sightings.
- Despite ease of access, relatively low visitor numbers.

Vegetation

The vegetation in Mikumi can be broadly divided into open grassland, wooded grassland, dry woodland, riverine and montane forest. The area of the Mkata River floodplain lies in the heart of the park and is dominated by open grassland with scatterings of **African Fan Palm** (*Borassus aethiopum*), **Real Fan Palm** (*Hyphaene petersiana*), **African Blackwood** (*Dalbergia melanoxylon*), **Tamarind** (*Tamarindus indica*) and the **Apple Leaf** (**Rain Tree**) (*Philenoptera violacea*). Apart from the palms, one of the most obvious trees here is the **Baobab** (*Adansonia* *digitata*). One of these massive Baobabs at the edge of the plain is hollow and was said to have been used as a hideout by poachers. Much of the south of the park is dominated by dry miombo or *Brachystegia* woodland with trees such as **Mnondo** (*Julbernardia globiflora*), **Mfuti** (*Brachystegia microphylla*) and **Mwanga** (*Pericopsis angolensis*). There are two other woodland types in the park, with **acacias** (*Vachellia/Senegalia* spp.), **Zebrawood** (*Dalbergia melanoxylon*) and **Granite Garcinia** (*Garcinia buchananii*) dominating in the north. To the south of this lies *Combretum* woodland with the **Russet Bushwillow** (*C. hereroense*) being abundant. Areas of mixed grassed woodland blend into these but grasses occur throughout. Along some of the streams and rivers there is thicket and forest with the more common trees here being *Sclerocarya caffra*, *Terminalia kilimandscharica* and *Haplocoelum inoploeum*.

Winged fruits of a bushwillow

Wildlife
Mammals

Mikumi has a great diversity of mammal species, ranging from **Savanna Elephant** to shrews but the official list gives just 60 species. Small-mammal surveys in recent years have added a further 21 species to this total. As with most areas of Tanzania, ivory poaching has been a serious problem here and elephant tend to be skittish. This is the only easily accessible park where you will see herds of **Johnston's (Nyasa) Wildebeest**. Of interest is that this species has a white band across the upper muzzle in the southern Selous Game Reserve and in Mozambique but in Mikumi either lacks this band or it is only faintly present. Herds are commonly seen on the Mkata Plains and the fringing more open woodland. This is one of the most important prey species for **Lion**. The park is one of the best for observing the **Common Eland** in Tanzania, with herds frequently seen on the open grassland. Other antelope present include **Impala**, **Lichtenstein's**

Savanna Elephant in Mikumi

FACILITIES AND ACTIVITIES

- Public and special campsites situated near HQ.
- Foxes Safari operate two lodges/tented camps, Vuma Hills and Stanley Kopje; other options on park fringes.
- Fairly extensive road network to north but difficult to negotiate during rains; limited and poor road network in south.
- No fuel or supplies in park; usually available in Mikumi and Morogoro.

Impala are common in Mikumi, especially in mixed grass and bush areas.

Common Warthog feeding on grass roots in fresh burn area

Hartebeest, Sable Antelope, Common Waterbuck, Bohor Reedbuck, Greater Kudu and **Bushbuck (Imbabala)**. Most of these are found in the woodland and fringes of the grass plains. **Savanna Buffalo** are common and may form into large herds. The **Common Warthog** occurs throughout the park and is frequently observed. **Maasai Giraffe** occur in the woodland but in relatively small numbers, although their great height makes them easy to see. Both the buffalo and warthog can often be seen near areas with water and mud. The **Plains Zebra** race here is **Crawshay's**, which has narrower stripes than those occurring further north in Tanzania. Small numbers of **Common Hippopotamus** are present and are most easily observed at the Hippo Pool just to the north of the main entrance gate. **Lion** are present but in small numbers, with **Leopard** occurring throughout but seldom seen. Other predators present include small numbers of **Spotted Hyaena** but the **African Wild Dog** is not believed to occur except as an occasional vagrant. Most of the smaller carnivores are nocturnal but the social **Dwarf** and **Banded mongooses** are sometimes seen, as is the solitary **Slender Mongoose**. The **Yellow Baboon** occurs throughout the park and is common, with troops sometimes numbering 100, or more, individuals. **Vervet Monkeys** are common in the woodlands but do not venture out on to the open grassed plains. **Angolan Black and White Colobus** only occur in the south in forest to the north of the Ruaha River. Watch for the diurnal **Yellow-spotted Hyrax** in the broken country of the Vuma Hills in the south.

Birds

Although the official list stands at 393 bird species, it is believed that at least another 50 species are resident or occur seasonally. Both the **Pale-billed** and **Grey hornbills** are common and **Southern Ground Hornbill** frequently observed. Some of the birding specials here include **Grey** and **Dickinson's kestrels,** the former is usually located along wooded watercourses but the latter mainly frequents the drier miombo woodland. A further 27 raptor species have been recorded but several occur only in the area as seasonal migrants. Of the five woodpecker species here, the **Speckle-throated Woodpecker** is quite common in those areas where there are mature trees on the fringes of the floodplain. Mikumi is considered to be the best locality to observe this bird in Tanzania. During the rains there are major influxes of herons, egrets and bitterns, with nine species recorded, as well as five species of stork, including the large **Saddle-bill Stork.** Other species to look out for are **Uluguru Violet-backed Sunbird, Dark-backed Weaver, Red-breasted Wryneck, Fischer's Greenbul, Black-throated Wattle-eye, Square-tailed Drongo, Cinnamon-breasted Tit** and **Golden-breasted Bunting.** The **Taita Fiscal** has a distinctive grey back patch and is common. The authors found the public campsite to the south of the main road to be particularly good birding territory.

Taita Fiscal

Reptiles and amphibians

No list of the reptiles and amphibians of Mikumi has been compiled but **Nile Crocodile** is present in limited numbers, with both the **White-throated Monitor** and the **Nile Monitor** occurring, the latter in proximity to streams and other waterbodies. The **Tropical House Gecko** can be seen around buildings and the **Striped Skink** on the trunks of trees. **Pythons** are also present but it is not clear whether it is the Southern or Central African rock python here. In the Malundwe Forest in the south, four species of reptile, two caecilians and six frogs have been recorded but certainly more will be found to occur.

WILDLIFE FACTS

- 81 mammal species recorded, certainly more mammals occur.
- About 10,000 Savanna Buffalo, 12,500 Johnston's Wildebeest, 3,000 Plains (Crawshay's) Zebra.
- 393 bird species listed but probably at least 450 species.
- Best locality to see Johnston's race of Common Wildebeest.

!
- **Mikumi is a malaria area.**
- **Tsetse flies are abundant in parts, so there is a slight risk of contracting sleeping sickness.**
- **Be alert for potentially dangerous game – Savanna Elephant, Savanna Buffalo, Lion – as picnic sites and camps are not fenced.**
- **Many internal tracks are difficult to negotiate during the rains.**

MKOMAZI NATIONAL PARK

Because of heavy poaching, game is quite skittish in Mkomazi, here Grant's Zebra.

Lie of the land

Mkomazi National Park lies within the Kilimanjaro and Tanga regions of north-eastern Tanzania and its northern boundary lies against that of Kenya's Tsavo West National Park. The park covers about 3,400km² and has spectacular scenery with views of the South Pare Mountains to the west and the Usambara Mountains to the south-east. Within sight to the north-west lies Mount Kilimanjaro, Africa's highest mountain. The western area of the park is mainly hill country with more open plains in the south. The Zange gate of Mkomazi is located some 112km from the town of Moshi.

Brief history

Mkomazi was a combination of the Umba and Mkomazi game reserves, gazetted as such in 1951. At this time the colonial government allowed members of the Parakuyo tribe to continue living within the reserve with several thousand head of cattle, goats and sheep but only in the eastern sector. But other pastoralists started moving into the reserve and by the mid-1980s about 80,000 head of cattle occurred throughout. This was unsustainable and by this time the Parakuyo had been joined by Maasai, Sambaa and Pare peoples with their livestock. By 1988 all people and their livestock had been evicted from the reserve and in 2008 the area was raised to national park status. Periodic livestock incursions occur to this day and poaching levels are said to be fairly high. From 1989 programmes to rehabilitate the park and reintroduce Hook-lipped Rhino and African Wild Dog were initiated and are ongoing today. The Mkomazi Rhino Sanctuary is a fenced area in the west of the park that is closed to the public. The name of the park is said to be derived from the Pare language, *mko* (small wooden spoon) and *mazi* (water). It is believed to be a reference to the dryness of the area.

Map

KENYA
TANZANIA

Spectacular hill scenery

Maore
Supa Bowl
Lechupa
Mlima Ng'ombe
Kamakota
Lolumesera
Lemuno

Umba gate

Vitewini
Mbula
Dindira
Norbanda

Mkomazi Rhino Sanctuary
Kisima
Kifukua
Nalvera

Good views of South Pare and Usambara mountains

Lelukunya

Njiro gate
Kisima Hill 1,356m

Kamba
Kivingo
Umba

Zange gate
Kisiwani
To Moshi

Gonja
Langoni

To Tonga

Same
B1

South Pare Mountains
Ndungu
Mkundi Mtae

Usambara Mountains

To Mombo
To Mombo

0 — 20km

• Waterhole

N

Geology and landscape

Mkomazi is flanked in the north-west by the South Pare Mountains that extend into the north of the park and the Usambara Mountains that approach its south-east boundary. The Usambaras and the Pare Mountains were formed at least 100 million years ago by faulting and uplifting and are made up of Precambrian metamorphic rocks. The altitudinal range is from 225m in the eastern lowlands towards the Umba River, the only natural source of permanent water, to about 1,530m in the hills of the north-west. Much of the north of the park is broken hill country interspersed with open sandy valleys, some of which become seasonal marshes during the rains, with the south being less rugged and with areas of well-bushed, open sand and gravel flats.

Climate

The park lies within the rain shadow of the West Usambara Mountains and as a result is relatively dry. There are two wet seasons, with 'long rains' falling from March to May and 'short rains' in November and December. Rain is often accompanied by thunderstorms. The dry season is between June and October but light showers can fall during this period. The mean annual average fall over much of the park is about 570mm but outside the park in the higher areas towards the South Pare Mountains the average may be as high as 1,900mm. Throughout the year temperatures are usually mild to hot, with night time minimums averaging 16° to 19°C, and daytime temperatures averaging 27° to 30°C. Temperature and humidity levels from November to May can be uncomfortable.

HIGHLIGHTS

- Stunning backdrop of South Pare and Usambara mountain scenery.
- Diverse landscapes.
- Very low visitor numbers.
- A number of arid area game and bird species.

Corkwood bushes have flaky bark.

- Public and special campsites, the latter without facilities.
- Babu's Tented Camp is the only lodge option in the park.
- Fairly extensive network of moderate to bad game-viewing tracks; mobility during the rains can be restricted.
- Game walks accompanied by an armed ranger can be arranged at Zange main gate.
- No fuel or supplies available in the park; special campsites do not have water.

Gerenuk are present in the thorn thickets in the south.

Vegetation

The vegetation can be broadly divided into four types, *Vachellia-Senegalia-Commpihora* bush country (known as Nyika Bush), which consists of low thorn trees and corkwood bushes and covers large areas of the park, areas of open wooded grassland, open grassland and dry montane forest in the north-west. There are thickets of **Sickle Bush** (*Dichrostachys cinerea*), with its distinctive mauve and yellow, bottlebrush-like flowers and clusters of tightly curled pods. The most obvious and distinctive tree is the **Baobab** (*Adansonia digitata*), especially on the better drained soils of the north. Although not comprehensively surveyed, 1,307 plant species are known to occur within Mkomazi, and lie within the Somali-Maasai vegetation zone.

Wildlife
Mammals

No detailed survey of the smaller mammal species occurring in the park has been undertaken but this would add considerably to the 78 mammal species recorded so far. During the rains up to 1,000 **Savanna Elephants**, including female groups with young, move into the park from adjoining Tsavo, Kenya, but the lack of surface water in the dry season forces most of them to move away. Although **Hook-lipped Rhinoceros** have been reintroduced they are held in an area that may not be accessed by the public. The park is best known for its arid area species, including **Gerenuk, Lesser Kudu, Fringe-eared Beisa Oryx** and **Common Eland**. Other species present include **Plains Zebra, Maasai Giraffe, Savanna Buffalo, Coke's Hartebeest, Impala** and **Grant's Gazelle**. Several species may be present only during the rains, or at least in reduced numbers. Large-predator numbers are low but include **Lion, Leopard, Cheetah** and **Spotted Hyaena**, with sightings of **Serval** being quite common. **African Wild Dog** has been reintroduced but these wide-ranging canids are seldom seen. **Black-backed Jackal, Bat-eared Fox**, solitary **Slender Mongoose**, as well as the social **Banded** and **Dwarf mongooses** also occur. The **Yellow Baboon** occurs throughout but is most obvious in the hill country in the north where it seeks out large trees to sleep in at night. Troops of **Vervet Monkey** may be seen foraging in trees or on the ground. Both the **Small-eared** and **Thick-tailed greater galagos** occur and are more likely to be heard than seen, with the much smaller **Northern Lesser Galago** present in the more dense stands of woodland. The diurnal **Unstriped**

Ground Squirrel is common and is frequently seen. Visitors should be aware that most game species here tend to be skittish and in most cases do not allow close approaches.

Birds

Although 402 bird species have been recorded in Mkomazi, it is believed that more than 450 species probably occur. What the reader must be aware of is that not all species will be present in a park at any one time, as it includes residents, local and seasonal migrants, as well as the occasional vagrant. This is the only area of Tanzania where you are likely to see **Three-streaked Tchagra**, **Shelley's Starling**, **Violet Wood-Hoopoe** and **Yellow-vented Eremomela**. A number of other specials occur and include **Rosy-patched Shrike**, **Golden-breasted Starling**, **Hunter's Sunbird**, **Tsavo Sunbird**, **Black-bellied Sunbird**, **Pink-breasted Lark** and **White-headed Mousebird**. **Lesser Kestrel** is a common summer visitor, with other raptor species including the **Long-crested Eagle**, **Wahlberg's Eagle**, **Martial Eagle**, **Red-necked Falcon**, **Eastern Chanting Goshawk** and **Pygmy Falcon**. Both the **Red-necked** and **Yellow-necked spurfowl** are common, as is **Crested Francolin**, with flocks of **Helmeted Guineafowl** frequently sighted but **Vulturine Guineafowl** less often encountered. This magnificent gamebird is close to the southernmost point of its range here. There is a good chance of spotting **Orange-bellied Parrot**, especially in the northern areas. The main entrance gate is always worth a half hour for birding.

Reptiles and amphibians

As with many East African parks, no comprehensive survey of the reptiles or amphibians has been undertaken in Mkomazi. Diversity is expected to be quite high, especially in the north. One of the most frequently seen lizards in rocky areas is the **Red-headed Rock Agama**, which is territorial and lives colonially. Two commonly seen skinks are largely tree-dwellers, the **Tree Skink** and **Striped Skink**.

Eastern Chanting Goshawk

Long-crested Eagle

WILDLIFE FACTS

- 78 mammal species recorded.
- 402 bird species occur as residents and seasonal migrants.
- Ideal place to see Gerenuk, Lesser Kudu and Fringe-eared Oryx.

- **Mkomazi is a malaria area.**
- **You may alight from your car but be alert for potentially dangerous game.**
- **Camps are not fenced and game moves freely through them, including Savanna Elephant and Lion.**
- **In general, roads are in moderate to poor condition and many cannot be traversed during the rains.**

RUAHA NATIONAL PARK

During the dry season Savanna Elephant dig for water in riverbeds.

Lie of the land

At 20,226km², Ruaha National Park is Tanzania's largest national park. To its north it is flanked by the Rungwa and Kizigo game reserves, which together form the major part of the Rungwa-Kizigo-Muhesi ecosystem that covers some 45,000km². The park lies in central Tanzania to the west of the Iringa Highlands and the main gate is located some 112km from the town of Iringa. Much of the park consists of a great, gently undulating plain that averages about 1,000m asl, but in the west the Ikungu Mountains rise to more than 1,800m, with the Datumbulwa range in the south. The Great Ruaha River flows through the south of the park and is a feeder to the Rufiji River.

Brief history

The name Ruaha is a corruption of the Wahehe tribe's name for a river. More correctly, the spelling should be *luvaha* and the actual local name for it is *Lyambangari*. So, here we have the Great River River! Arab trading and slaving caravans traversed the area from the coast in the early years of the 19th century but by the 1830s these routes moved to the north of the present-day park. The Ruaha area was the scene of several battles during the Maji-Maji Rebellion, when Chief Mkwawa led his warriors in the early 1890s against German colonial forces. The warriors fought pitched battles against the Germans and launched ambushes against the force under

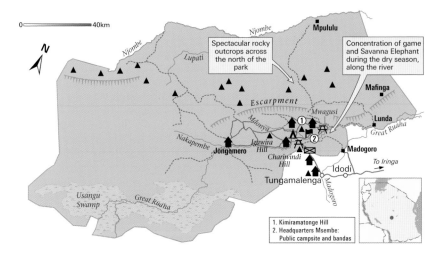

1. Kimiramatonge Hill
2. Headquarters Msembe:
   Public campsite and bandas

the legendary Von Lettow-Vorbeck. Mkwawa shot himself in 1898 rather than being captured. The Germans proclaimed the area as Saba River Game Reserve in 1910, which became part of the Rungwa Game Reserve in 1946. Ruaha was proclaimed as a national park in 1964 and its primary boundaries were finalized in 1973. In 2008 the park was expanded to include the area of the Usangu Game Reserve and its wetlands, a feeder source of the Great Ruaha River.

Geology and landscape

Ruaha has its lowest point at 723m asl in the Ruaha River valley in the north-east and its highest at 1,885m in the granitic peaks in the south-west. Much of the park consists of undulating plateaux with low, broken mountains in the south and west and rolling, open plains and hills. The Great Ruaha River rises in the Usangu wetland in the south of the park, running north-eastwards for 130km on the south-east boundary, exiting into the Lunda-Mkwabi Game Area. The Njombe River runs along part of the north-western boundary. Until relatively recently, only the Great Ruaha River was perennial while the others, such as the Mdonya, Mwagusi and Mzombe, flowed seasonally but in recent years the drawing off of water for rice cultivation in the south-west has caused this river to cease flowing during the dry season. This has serious implications for the long-term viability of areas of the park and its associated wildlife. Much of the visible geology here consists of ancient granites and gneiss, which is most clearly seen on such hills as Igawira and Chariwindi.

HIGHLIGHTS

- Unspoilt African wilderness with low tourist numbers.
- High game and bird diversity, including rarities.
- Of the big game, only Hook-lipped Rhinoceros absent.
- Some areas of great scenic beauty, especially in association with the great rock outcrops, such as Kimiramatonge Hill.

- Public and special campsites, the latter with no facilities.
- Basic tourist bandas run by the park.
- A number of upmarket lodges and tented camps in the park, including Jongomero, Kigelia, Kwihala, Mdonya River, Ruaha Flycatcher, Ikuka and Ruaha River.
- There are several lodges located short distances from the park.
- Some lodges offer armed escorts for walks.
- The road network is principally in the east-central area of the park. Roads and tracks vary from reasonable to poor condition. During the rains movement is limited.
- If you opt for self-drive bring in all fuel and supplies.

Borassus Palm

Climate

This is one of the driest areas of Tanzania, with the dry season extending from May to October and a single rainy season running from November to April. Rainfall is usually associated with thunderstorms in the afternoons. Average rainfall is 520mm per year in the east of the park, which is the area accessible to the visitor, but on the western high plateau it averages 800mm. However, timing and quantity of rain may vary from year to year and be lower or higher than the averages. The dry season is the coolest period with July sometimes dropping to 8°C at night but daytime temperatures may reach 30°C. The hottest months are November and December with average lows of 17°C (but up to 25°C) and highs averaging 28°C (but can reach 40°C).

Vegetation

The park is of particular importance because it is in the region where elements of southern and eastern African flora and fauna meet, and to date more than 1,600 species of plant have been recorded here. Ruaha can be broadly divided into four vegetation types but this is a great simplification. In the far east is an area dominated by **thorn tree** species (*Vachellia/Senegalia*), then westwards a broad belt of miombo woodland with a preponderance of *Brachystegia* trees. Much of the west of the park lies in a zone that is dominated by **corkwood** or **paperbark** (*Commiphora*) trees and bushes, with a small area in the south-west with dense stands of evergreen submontane forest. This forest area is outside the tourist circuit. There are areas of open, largely treeless grassland, swamp areas, especially the recently incorporated Usangu Swamp in the south-west, with floodplains along the river courses. In many areas of the park you will encounter the **Baobab** (*Adansonia digitata*), a species mainly pollinated by fruit-eating bats. Especially along the river courses there are stands of the tall **Ana Tree** (*Faidherbia albida*) with grey-green foliage, dull grey bark and distinctive orange-brown, sickle-shaped to curled seedpods. The distinctive **Sausage Tree** (*Kigelia africana*), with grey, sausage-like fruits, may be seen throughout but most commonly along the rivers. Other common trees include the **Tamarind** (*Tamarindus indica*) and several wild fig species, including giant **Sycamore Fig** (*Ficus sycomorus*). The **Candelabra Tree** (*Euphorbia candelabrum*) is scattered throughout the park and is a 'cactus-like' succulent that may reach a height of 10–15m.

Above: Maasai Giraffe
Left: Greater Kudu bull

Wildlife
Mammals

The best time for mammal viewing is June to October in the dry season, when game has access only to limited water sources and foliage cover is greatly reduced. Ruaha has a large **Savanna Elephant** population but ivory poaching has resulted in a substantial reduction in recent years. However, elephant are frequently observed and during the dry season they dig into the dry riverbeds to access water. There are believed to be about 20,000 of the gentle grey giants within the greater Ruaha-Rungwa ecosystem, making it the largest single population in East Africa. There is a substantial **Common Hippopotamus** population, principally in pools along the Great Ruaha River such as at Msembe. **Savanna Buffalo** can be expected anywhere in the park. There are good numbers of **Plains Zebra**, **Maasai Giraffe** and **Common Warthog**, especially in areas of wooded grassland. Antelope are well represented and include both the **Greater** and **Lesser kudu**, the latter at the most southern limit of its range. Both **Sable** and **Roan antelope** occur, as does the **Defassa Waterbuck**. Another antelope at its southern range limit here is the **Bohor Reedbuck**, usually found in association with the river courses and seasonal swamps. **Grant's Gazelle** occurs no further south than Ruaha. The **Impala** is common in wooded grassland and is an important prey species for several predators. In the thicket country and in bush along rivers watch for the **Bushbuck (Imbabala)**, which is a solitary species but occurs at fairly high densities. Among the smaller antelope are **Common (Grey) Duiker**, **Steenbok**, **Klipspringer** (in the rocky

WILDLIFE FACTS

- At least 200 mammal species in the Ruaha-Rungwa ecosystem, many in the park.
- All large predators present, including substantial numbers of Lion and African Wild Dog.
- Large Savanna Elephant population despite poaching pressure.
- 40,000 Savanna Buffalo, 30,000 Plains Zebra, 8,000 Maasai Giraffe.
- 578 bird species, including two near endemics.
- No detailed reptile and amphibian list but potentially more than 100 species.
- More than 1,600 plant species identified.

Lionesses on a river bank

Banded Mongoose

Yellow Baboons

hills) and **Ugogo Dik-dik** (formerly Kirk's Dik-dik). With such a rich prey base the carnivore diversity is great and includes good populations of **Lion, Leopard** and **Cheetah,** with one of the continent's most important populations of **African Wild Dog.** The African Wild Dogs are easiest to see when they have pups at a fixed den between June and August. **Spotted Hyaena** is relatively common but **Striped Hyaena** is rare and seldom seen. **Black-backed Jackal, Bat-eared Fox, Aardwolf, Honey Badger** and eight species of mongoose occur. The most commonly seen are the solitary **Slender Mongoose** and the social **Banded** and **Dwarf mongooses,** as they are diurnal. In rocky areas watch for the tailless **Yellow-spotted Rock Hyrax,** which lies in the sun on ledges and boulders in the early morning. The most frequently seen primates are the troops of **Yellow Baboon** and **Vervet Monkey,** usually in proximity to the river courses and rock outcrops. Within the Ruaha-Rungwa ecosystem about 200 mammal species occur, with many of these in the national park. There are at least 23 bat and 22 rodent species in western Ruaha alone; many areas have not been surveyed.

Birds

With the current list standing at 578 species, this is one of the best birding destinations in Tanzania. Two recently described species are the **Ruaha (Tanzanian) Red-billed Hornbill** and the **Ruaha Chat.** There are important populations of the Tanzanian endemics **Ashy Starling** and **Yellow-collared Lovebird.** Apart from resident and local migrant species, there is a major influx of Palaearctic migrants between November and April, including large numbers of **White Stork**. **African Skimmers** breed on sandbanks in the Ruaha River, and there are important seasonal populations of **Black-winged Pratincole** and **White-headed Lapwing**. No less than 15 heron species have been recorded, from the diminutive **Dwarf Bittern** to the giant **Goliath Heron**. Storks are also well represented with eight species, resident and migratory. Of the nine waterfowl, the noisy **Egyptian Goose** is the most frequently sighted, most obvious during the rains. Raptor diversity is great with 53 species on record, several of which are palaearctic migrants and present only during the summer months. **Verreaux's Eagle** is associated with the rocky hills but the **Bateleur** and **Martial Eagle** are more wide ranging. On the other side of the size scale is the diminutive **Pygmy Falcon**, which breeds in the nests of buffalo weavers. There are 12 species of dove and pigeon, including **Blue-spotted** and **Emerald-spotted wood doves**, often most evident by their distinctive calls. Apart from the Ruaha Red-billed Hornbill, there are six other hornbill species including **Von der Decken's Hornbill**. The **White-naped Raven** is mainly associated with the rocky hills but the **Pied Crow** can be expected anywhere. The shrikes are very well represented with 15 species. Some, such as the **Grey-headed Bushshrike**, are best known by their calls but the long-tailed **Magpie Shrike** often sits exposed and is easily seen.

Von der Decken's Hornbill male

Red-throated Bee-eater

Reptiles and amphibians

Species most commonly seen include **Nile** and **White-throated monitor lizards**, the largest in East Africa. **Nile Crocodiles** are common, especially in the larger pools along the Great Ruaha River. In rocky areas look out for the **Red-headed Agama** (*Agama lionotus*, previously *A. agama*). **Tropical House Gecko** is commonly seen at night catching insects around lights. The largest snake here is the **Southern African Rock Python** but it is also possible that the very similar **Central African Rock Python** occurs. At least another 28 species of snake could occur but only **Puff Adder**, **Black Mamba**, **Red-lipped Herald** and **Spotted Bush Snake** can be confirmed.

African Bullfrog

> **!**
> - **Ruaha is a malaria area.**
> - **Tsetse flies are present in more wooded areas, especially along river courses, so there is a slight risk of sleeping sickness.**
> - **Camps, lodges unfenced, so be alert for potentially dangerous game.**
> - **Roads and tracks are of variable condition and can be difficult to negotiate, especially during rains.**

SERENGETI NATIONAL PARK

White-bearded Wildebeest and Grant's Zebra moving northwards to the Mara River

Lie of the land

To the Maasai this area is *siringet* – 'the place where the land runs on forever' – modified by the British colonists to Serengeti. This is arguably Africa's most famous game sanctuary and home to the continent's greatest antelope herds. The Serengeti covers 14,763km² and is bounded by the Maswa Game Reserve (2,200km²) to the south, Grumeti and Ikorongo game reserves in the west, Loliondo Game Controlled Area to the east and the Maasai Mara National Reserve in Kenya (1,672km²) to the north. To the south-east it adjoins the Ngorongoro Conservation Area, which extends over 8,280km². Together they are usually referred to by scientists as the greater Serengeti ecosystem, extending to more than 30,000km². The park lies to the east of Lake Victoria with the Western Corridor extending to within a few kilometres of it. Much of the park is dominated by vast flat to undulating open plains, with a scattering of isolated low hills and granitic outcrops located mainly in the west and north-east. The tourist centre of Arusha lies 325km from the park headquarters at Seronera.

Brief history

Given the evidence from the adjoining Ngorongoro, ancestral pre-humans were walking the area 3.6 million years before present and peoples from the three Stone Ages called the area home. The first German to reach Serengeti in 1892 was Dr Oscar Baumann, explorer and naturalist, and it took him 23 days to cross the area that is now the park. The first detailed account of the northern sector of the Serengeti came from the pen of the American hunter

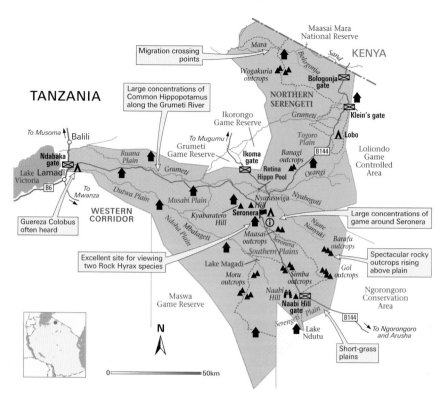

Map labels:

Maasai Mara National Reserve
KENYA
Mara
Bologonja
Wogakuria outcrops
Bologonja gate
Migration crossing points
NORTHERN SERENGETI
Klein's gate
TANZANIA
Large concentrations of Common Hippopotamus along the Grumeti River
Ikorongo Game Reserve
Grumeti
Togoro Plain
Lobo
Loliondo Game Controlled Area
To Musoma
Balili
To Mugumu
Grumeti Game Reserve
Ikoma gate
Banagi outcrops
B144
Ndabaka gate
Ruana Plain
Grumeti
Retina Hippo Pool
Orangi
Lake Lamadi
Victoria
B6
To Mwanza
Dutwa Plain
Musabi Plain
Nyaraswiga Hill
Nyabogoti
WESTERN CORRIDOR
Kyabaratero Hill
Seronera
Large concentrations of game around Seronera
Guereza Colobus often heard
Ndoha Plain
Mbalageti
Maasai outcrops
Seronera
Ngare Nanyuki
Barafu outcrops
Southern Plains
Excellent site for viewing two Rock Hyrax species
Lake Magadi
Moru outcrops
Simba outcrops
Gol outcrops
Spectacular rocky outcrops rising above plain
Ngorongoro Conservation Area
Maswa Game Reserve
Naabi Hill
Naabi Hill gate
Serengeti Plain
B144
To Ngorongoro and Arusha
N
0   50km
Lake Ndutu
Short-grass plains

Stewart Edward White in 1913, who wrote, 'Never have I seen anything like that game. It covered every hill, standing in the openings, strolling in and out among groves, feeding on the bottom lands, singly, or in little groups. It did not matter in which direction I looked, there it was; as abundant one place as another'. Little is recorded of the area during the German colonial period and it was only during the 1920s that it was slowly opened by professional hunters. In 1929 the British colonial authority declared the central core of Serengeti to be a Closed Reserve and its boundaries were gazetted as a national park in 1951. The Maasai moved into the Serengeti area about 200 years before present. They were moved out of the Serengeti by the British to an area of 7,800km² now known as the Ngorongoro Conservation Area, which forms the eastern boundary to the Serengeti. The Maasai population in the conservation area has grown from 10,000 in 1954, when they were moved, to more than 50,000 today. It was during the 1950s that the work of Bernard Grzimek helped to establish the importance of this park in the eyes of the world.

HIGHLIGHTS

- Great diversity and numbers of plains game.
- The great migration covering around 1,000km in an annual cycle.
- One of the best locations to observe Lion, Leopard, Cheetah and Spotted Hyaena.
- Best place in Tanzania to see large numbers of Grant's and Thomson's gazelles.
- Great bird diversity.

Open, lightly wooded grassland near the Lobo Hills

Geology and landscape

The Serengeti is a vast upland area ranging from 1,162m asl at Lake Victoria to 2,177m asl towards the north-east and rising to the Ngorongoro Highlands. Much of the area consists of flat to rolling plains, interspersed with isolated granitic outcrops, such as Moru, Simba, Gol and Barafu in the south and Lobo and Wogakuria in the north. The plains were formed 3–4 million years before present when ash blew from volcanoes erupting in the vicinity of the Ngorongoro Highlands. Fresh ash is contributed to the plains from time to time from the still-active Ol Doinyo Lengai. It is the resulting nutrient-rich soil that sustains the grass that provides grazing for so many antelope and zebra. The rock outcrops, or kopjes, are technically known as inselbergs and are composed of ancient granites of volcanic origin. The underlying base rocks date to the Precambrian and are made up of granites, gneisses and schist. Hill ranges occur throughout but mainly on the fringes of the park, some of the most obvious being on the south of the Western Corridor and to the east of Lobo. There are a number of seasonal and perennial rivers, the most important of which are the Mara in the north and the Grumeti in the Western Corridor, both of which play a role in the great migration.

Migrating wildebeest at Bologonja

Lobo Hills, home to Klipspringer

Climate

Generally it has a semi-arid climate with two rainy seasons, the 'short rains' in November and December and the 'long rains' running from March through to early May. The dry months run from June to October. The lowest annual rainfall of 514–688mm falls on the south-eastern plains, with 850–976mm in the central woodlands and Western Corridor and up to 1,100mm in the north. Dry-season temperatures average 25°C at midday to as low as 8°C at night. During the hot months average temperatures are about 35°C at midday and 14°C at night. During the main rains high temperatures and humidity can become uncomfortable.

Vegetation

The principal vegetation feature of the Serengeti is its vast grass resources. In the south-east, short annual grasses dominate the great treeless plain. Areas to the west and north are dominated by longer grassland and extensive areas of woodland and bush. There are many species of **acacia** (*Vachellia* and *Senegalia*) growing in the west and north. The most intriguing is the **Whistling Thorn** (*Vachellia drepanolobium*), which seldom reaches more than five metres in height as it is favoured browse of several game species. A greater variety of tree and bush species grow along the watercourses, and along the Grumeti River there is well-developed riverine forest. A few of the commoner trees include the **Sausage Tree** (*Kigelia africana*), **Fever Tree** (*Vachellia xanthophloea*), **Umbrella Thorn** (*Vachellia tortilis*) and the **Wild Date Palm** (*Phoenix reclinata*). The so-called **Desert Date** (**Soapberry**)(*Balanites aegyptiaca*) is a common tree on the fringes of the grassed plains and its fruits are readily eaten by a range of species. Scattered throughout the park are the giant cactus-like **Common Tree Euphorbia** (**Candelabra Tree**) (*Euphorbia candelabrum*), often standing alone, sometimes in groups. There are many small flowering annuals that are at their best on the short-grass plains during the rains but in the Western Corridor the dry months tend to be more productive. On the rock outcrops various **aloe** species are a feature when they flower.

FACILITIES AND ACTIVITIES

- Serengeti is one of the most heavily lodged parks in East Africa, with structured, tented and mobile camp facilities, mostly upmarket.
- Public and special campsites with basic to no facilities.
- Extensive road and track network, often in poor condition, particularly during the rains; approach road from Ngorongoro can be one of the most corrugated in the country.
- Most lodges offer night drives, some offer guided walks with armed guard.
- Fuel may be available at Seronera but best to carry your own backup.

The Whistling Thorn has characteristic swellings at the thorn bases, which are inhabited by ants.

At Lobo Hills aloes occur mainly on rocky outcrops.

Kongoni (Coke's Hartebeest) bull

WILDLIFE FACTS

- About 3,500 Lion in the Serengeti-Ngorongoro ecosystem; 1.2–1.5 million Western White-bearded Wildebeest and more than 200,000 Plains Zebra; 400,000 Thomson's Gazelles.
- 40,000–200,000 game animals poached each year in the ecosystem.
- At least 100 mammal species but detailed surveys of bats, shrews, small rodents lacking.
- >500 bird species (residents, migrants and vagrants) in Serengeti ecosystem.
- At least 48 reptile and 36 amphibian species.

Wildlife
Mammals

At least 17 antelope species occur, the most obvious being the **Western White-bearded Wildebeest (Common Wildebeest)**. It is the migration of this and other game species that draws many visitors. Because of the annual migration during the dry season they are absent from the eastern short grasslands (see migration block p16). Although numbers fluctuate, there are usually 1.2–1.5 million wildebeest, of which about 250,000 die during each full migration cycle. **Grant's Gazelle** and the smaller **Thomson's Gazelle** are common and widespread, as are **Topi**, **Kongoni (Coke's Hartebeest)**, with smaller antelope such as **Oribi**, **Klipspringer** (on rock outcrops) and **Ugogo Dik-dik** (dry thicket). In the more wooded areas you may see **Common Eland, Impala, Roan Antelope, Defassa Waterbuck** and along the rivers **Bushbuck (Imbabala)**. There are also large numbers of **Plains Zebra**, the local race being **Grant's**, with up to 250,000 animals. Many zebra also participate in the migration. Both **Savanna Buffalo** and **Savanna Elephant** occur and are mainly located in the west and north of the park, with an estimated 8,000 **Maasai Giraffe**, which is one of the largest giraffe populations in Africa. **Common Hippopotamus** are common along the Mara and Grumeti rivers. Of course one of the biggest drawcards of Serengeti is the abundance and diversity of predators. With about 3,500

Topi bull

Lion, this is Africa's single largest surviving population. There are also substantial numbers of **Cheetah** and **Leopard**, with chances of sightings being particularly high in this park. **Spotted Hyaena** are common and form large clans but the **Striped Hyaena** is seldom seen. Smaller carnivores that may be observed include the **African Wolf** (previously Golden Jackal), **Black-backed** and **Side-striped jackals**, **Bat-eared Fox**, **Serval** and the **Banded Mongoose**. **African Wild Dog** disappeared from the park in the early 1990s and, although occasionally sighted in peripheral areas, are unlikely to be seen by visitors. In the wooded and hill country, particularly in association with the river courses, **Olive Baboon** are common whereas **Guereza (Black and White Colobus)** are only found along the Grumeti River, with troops of **Vervet Monkey**, **Red-tailed Monkey** and **Blue Monkey** at several locations but mainly tied to river courses. Three **hyrax** species occur, two rock-dwellers, **Rock** and **Yellow-spotted**, as well as the nocturnal **Southern Tree Hyrax**, the latter best known by its harsh call. Both rock-dwelling hyrax species are common around the restaurant and park headquarters at Seronera.

Yellow-spotted Rock Hyrax in a tree

Kori Bustard

Birds

Most references give a bird list of 458 bird species recorded from the park but if the greater Serengeti area is taken into account this rises to more than 500 species. This park holds the largest population of **Ostrich** in Tanzania, here the **Maasai** subspecies. Roughly a third of the entire **Rüppell's Vulture** population uses the Serengeti ecosystem, with a further 58 species of raptor known both as residents and seasonal migrants, as well as a few rare vagrants. Of the eagles, only the **Tawny Eagle** is commonly seen, but in the hills and rock outcrops **Verreaux's Eagle** may be sighted hunting its hyrax prey. Of the six bustard species known here, only the **Kori Bustard** and **White-bellied Bustard** are often seen, with the former frequently

Male Maasai Ostrich

D'Arnoud's Barbet

Male Mwanza Flat-
headed Agama

on recently burned areas. The grassland areas are favoured by the nine lark species, three sandgrouse, of which the **Yellow-throated Sandgrouse** is the most abundant, as well as eight pipit and longclaw species. Here also are three courser species, **Temminck's**, **Double-banded** and the **Three-banded**. Species to watch for include **Grey-breasted Spurfowl, Brown-chested Lapwing, Grey-crested Helmet Shrike, Karamoja Apalis** (area of Moru Kopjes), **Fischer's Lovebird,** which is locally common, **Red-throated Tit, Usambiro Barbet** and **Rufous-tailed Weaver.** The campsites and lodges are good birding locations as birds here are used to people moving around.

Reptiles and amphibians

Nile Crocodiles are common in the Mara and Grumeti rivers. They are most visible during the migration crossings when they prey on the antelope and zebra that cross. The large **Nile** and **White-throated monitors** occur, the former in association with permanent water. One of the most visible of the smaller lizards is the **Tropical House Gecko,** which is common at lodges, emerging at night to feed on insects attracted by lights. Of the many skink species, the most frequently encountered is the diurnal **Striped Skink,** seen on buildings and in trees. One of the most obvious lizards is the **Mwanza Flat-headed Agama,** especially the large vividly coloured males that sit on boulders and rocks in hill country and occur on the rock walls around Seronera. Two species of chameleon occur but only the large **Flap-necked Chameleon** is likely to be seen. Of the tortoises, you are likely to see the **Leopard Tortoise** only but **Helmeted Terrapins** are commonly spotted on the banks of the Mara and Grumeti rivers. Snakes are seldom spotted but **Southern African Rock Python** occur, as do **Black-necked Spitting Cobra, Black Mamba** and **Puff Adder.** No comprehensive reptile or amphibian list has been compiled for the park. Although 36 amphibian species are known, most are unlikely to be encountered. One of the few exceptions is the **Guttural Toad,** which forages for insects under the lights around the lodges, particularly during the rains.

- Serengeti is a malaria area.
- No camps or lodges are fenced; always be aware of your surroundings and the presence of potentially dangerous animals.
- Roads and tracks are generally in poor condition and mobility during the rains can be restricted, especially in areas with black 'cotton soil'.
- During peak season (dry) the park can get very congested in parts with safari vehicles.

The swamp areas in Tarangire are crucial to the Savanna Elephant during the dry season.

Lie of the land

Tarangire National Park forms the core of the Tarangire-Manyara ecosystem that lies mainly on the Maasai Steppe in north-eastern Tanzania, with Lokisale Game Controlled Area and Simanijiro GCA to the east and Mkugunero GCA to the south. The park covers 2,850km^2 and serves as a retreat for game herds during the dry season. It derives its name from the Tarangire River, which provides the only permanent water during the dry season. During the rains many species disperse on to the plains to the east and north outside the boundary of the park. The dominant features of the park are the Tarangire River, the seasonal swampy floodplains, plains and broken granitic ridges. Much of the park lies between 1,100m and 1,300m asl. Tarangire lies some 112km to the south of Arusha and 70km from Lake Manyara National Park.

Brief history

The greater Tarangire ecosystem has been occupied by humans for many centuries, both farming and pastoral Bantu groups, but between the 16th and 19th centuries they were displaced by Maa-speaking peoples. By 1880 the Maasai had occupied all of what is now the Tarangire ecosystem and more were moved to the area during the establishment of Serengeti National Park. Shortly after independence, the Tanzanian government promoted large-scale agricultural development, which pushed the Maasai into marginal areas and disrupted migration patterns of game from the Tarangire National Park during the rains, when species such as wildebeest and zebra move to the calving and foaling grounds to the east (Simanjiro Plain) and north (Lake Manyara and Lake Natron). Efforts are under way to try to restore the traditional migration routes but numbers of some game species are still in decline. Tarangire was proclaimed a game reserve in 1957 and gazetted as a national park in 1970.

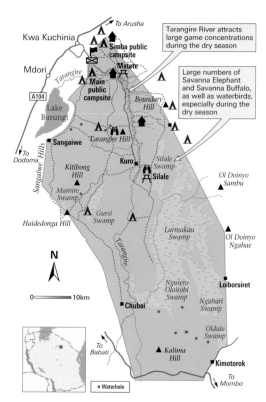

To Arusha

Kwa Kuchinia

Simba public campsite

Tarangire River attracts large game concentrations during the dry season

Mdori

Matete

Main public campsite

A104

Lake Burungi

Boundary Hill

Large numbers of Savanna Elephant and Savanna Buffalo, as well as waterbirds, especially during the dry season

Sangaiwe

Tarangire Hill

To Dodoma

Kitibong Hill

Kuro

Silale Swamp

Silale

Ol Doinyo Sambu

Mamire Swamp

Gursi Swamp

Haidedonga Hill

Larmakau Swamp

Ol Doinyo Ngahae

N

0 ——— 10km

Ngusero Oloirobi Swamp

Loiborsiret

Chubai

Ngahari Swamp

Oldule Swamp

To Babati

Kalima Hill

Kimotorok

To Mombo

Waterhole

Geology and landscape

The park lies in the eastern branch of the East African Rift Valley. About 250,000 years before present it was partly inundated by a lake known as Proto-Manyara. The dominant landscape feature in the park is the Tarangire River and its associated marshes, with scattered granitic ridges and flat plains. Most of the park lies on the western side of the Maasai Steppe, with much of the park's rocks consisting of granites and gneiss. The soil here has very low concentrations of phosphorus, a mineral that is essential for lactating ungulates. As soon as the rains arrive, many of the ungulates migrate east and north out of the park, where the soils are phosphorus rich. The dominant soil in the park on the plains and swamps is black cotton soil, hard in the dry season but glutinous in the wet. Soils to the north and east of the park are of largely volcanic origin.

Climate

Rainfall is bi-modal, as in much of the north of Tanzania, with the 'short rains' occurring between November and December and the 'long rains' March to May. Annual average rainfall is about 650mm but varies greatly from year to year. June to October are the driest months. The annual mean temperature is maximum 27°C and minimum 16°C, with an extreme high of 40°C in January and extreme minimum of 4°C in July.

Vegetation

Two wooded savanna types are dominant in the park, **acacia** tree grassland mainly along the riverine zone in cotton soil, with the flat-topped **Umbrella Thorn** (*Vachellia tortilis*) the most important and obvious species. The other type is deciduous woodland savanna on the well-drained, red loamy soils of the ridges and upper hill slopes, with **bushwillow** (*Combretum* spp.), **corkbark/paperbark** (*Commiphora* spp.) and **African Ebony** (*Dalbergia melanoxylon*) dominant. The

HIGHLIGHTS

- Greatest concentration of game during the dry season (best July to mid-November), including Savanna Elephant, Savanna Buffalo, Eastern White-bearded Wildebeest and Plains Zebra.
- Landscape dotted with Baobab trees.
- Substantial Lion population.
- Good birding.

The Baobab occurs in the drier areas of the park.

Solanum in flower

most obvious tree in the park is the **Baobab** (*Adansonia digitata*). There are also some areas of extensive grassland with scattered trees. The seasonal grassy swamps are treeless and provide important grazing areas during the dry season. In areas with taller trees the **Fever Tree** (*Vachellia xanthophloea*) is often dominant, with the **Paperbark Thorn** (*Vachellia sieberiana*) also common. Along seasonal watercourses – less so along the Tarangire River because of elephant damage – there are **Sausage Trees** (*Kigelia africana*), **Tamarind** (*Tamarindus indica*) and the **Candelabra Tree** (*Euphorbia candelabrum*). Along the river, stands of **Soapberry (Desert Date)** (*Balanites aegyptiaca*) trees are dominant in places, and can be identified by the straight green spines that form spirals around the branches. Stands of tall **Doum Palm** (*Hyphaene compressa*) produce fruits from only about the 30th year. The extensive swamp areas, known locally as *mbuga*, are grass and sedge dominated and usually dry up between the rains. It is the grasses throughout that are most important to the large ungulate herds.

Wildlife
Mammals

As with many East African parks, there is no comprehensive checklist of all the mammals occurring here but four shrews, seven bat species and 15 species of rodent have been identified as being present. Tarangire is one of the best places in Africa to see large herds of **Savanna Elephant**, with hundreds gathering along the Tarangire River from August to November, and large breeding herds from February to May. It is the only park in the

FACILITIES AND ACTIVITIES

- Public and special campsites, the latter have no facilities.
- Number of lodges and tented camps in Tarangire and in surrounding area; note some are advertised as located inside the park but in fact are outside.
- Network of game-viewing tracks, mainly in north; many become difficult to negotiate in the rains.
- No fuel or supplies available in the park.

Above: Bohor Reedbuck ram grazing in Tarangire

Right: Grant's Zebra mare and foal

Immature Common Waterbuck ram

Black-backed Jackal in threat posture

north that has large numbers of elephant present throughout the year. The largest swamp in the east attracts many of these gentle grey giants. Unlike the elephants in many other East African parks, these are calm and largely non-aggressive. It is estimated that about 2,500 Savanna Elephant occupy the Tarangire ecosystem. **Common Hippopotamus** are rare but may be seen, or at least heard, in the Silale Swamp. During the dry season large numbers of **Savanna Buffalo** are present, especially in the vicinity of the seasonal swamps. Large herds of **Eastern White-bearded Wildebeest** and **Plains Zebra** are present during the dry season, but at the onset of the rains they migrate to the east and north outside the park. Human developments outside the park have caused reductions in the populations of both species. **Maasai Giraffe** may be seen anywhere within the park. Previously, sightings of **Gerenuk** and **Lesser Kudu** were relatively common but for unknown reasons populations have declined. Other antelope present, either throughout the year or seasonally, include **Fringe-eared Oryx** (uncommon), **Common Waterbuck**, **Bohor Reedbuck**, **Kongoni**, **Grant's Gazelle**, **Thomson's Gazelle** (rare in north) and **Impala** (particularly common). Of the smaller antelope, the **Ugogo Dik-dik** (previously Kirk's) is common everywhere except the swamps, **Steenbok** is common but **Klipspringer** is restricted to a few rocky outcrops. Carnivores are well represented, with a substantial **Lion** population and healthy **Leopard** numbers. **Cheetah** are uncommon and sightings of **African Wild Dog** are rare and no packs are known to be resident in the park. Although both **Spotted** and **Striped**

hyaena occur, numbers are low. Of the six mongoose species, just the **Slender**, **Banded** and **Dwarf** are regularly seen. Of the two hyrax species present, the **Yellow-spotted Rock Hyrax** is diurnal and is found in rocky outcrops throughout, but the nocturnal **Southern Tree Hyrax** is most likely to be heard giving vent to its scream-rattling call but they may be seen sun-basking in large trees along the river and its side streams. Two squirrels are very common, the **Ochre Bush Squirrel** occurs throughout and commonly in and around the lodges, with the **Unstriped Ground Squirrel** common in the north. On the primate front, only the **Olive Baboon** (particularly common in the north) and **Vervet Monkey** are common throughout, both not infrequently a pest around lodges and camps.

Birds

The shallow soda waters of Lake Burungi, just outside the north-western park boundary, attracts large numbers of **flamingos** during the rains. The current bird list stands at 446 species, with good birding throughout. More than 50 species of raptor have been recorded, with a number being seasonal migrants, including large numbers of **Lesser Kestrel** around

Vervet Monkey female

April but they do not remain in the area. There are 13 eagle species, with regular sightings of **Bateleur**, **Black-breasted Snake-Eagle**, **Long-crested Eagle** and **Tawny Eagle**. **Augur Buzzards** are relatively common and **Black-shouldered Kite** is frequently sighted. There are five species of bustard, **Kori**, **White-bellied**, **Buff-crested**, **Black-bellied** and **Hartlaub's**, easiest to observe during the dry season when grass is at its shortest and less dense. For good viewing of water birds, it is well worth sitting along part of the main swamp when it has not completely dried out. Elephant and buffalo trample the edges, creating more or less open pools that are attractive to a wide range of birds, including 14 heron species, of which **Goliath Heron**, **Black Heron** and **Striated Heron** are quite commonly observed. Here also are **Glossy** and **Sacred ibises**, 15 duck and goose species, large numbers of **African Jacana** and a wide diversity of resident and migratory waders. Ever present in the woodlands are **Bare-faced** and **White-bellied turacos** (go-away-birds) with their distinctive calls. If you are familiar with the different owl calls you could identify up to eight species present here, including **Barn Owl**, **African Scops**, **Spotted Eagle-Owl** and **African Wood Owl**. Most species can be heard from the lodges and campsites. You would have to have good knowledge of the nightjars to differentiate

WILDLIFE FACTS

- 94 mammal species listed but in-depth surveys lacking.
- Migratory population of Eastern White-bearded Wildebeest and Plains Zebra present in dry season.
- Greatest Savanna Elephant concentration of any northern Tanzanian park.
- 446 bird species recorded, including rarities.
- No reptile checklist has been compiled.

White-headed Buffalo Weaver

White-browed Sparrow-Weaver colony

between the nine species, remembering not all are there throughout the year. During breeding the **Pennant-winged Nightjar** is the most dramatic of all with its long outer-wing plumes. The swifts are a difficult group to identify to species level but with 11 species recorded a serious challenge to the keen birder. Around the Doum Palms watch for the extremely slender-winged **African Palm Swift**. Both **Yellow-collared** and **Fischer's lovebirds** occur, with the latter at the most eastern fringe of its range. **Meyer's** and **Red-bellied parrots** also occur in the park. For LBJ fans this is a good area for the **Little Tawny Pipit**, which occurs in substantial numbers. Other smaller species to look for here include **Northern Pied Babbler**, **Northern White-crowned Shrike**, **Slate-coloured Boubou**, **Pink-breasted Lark** and **Rufous-tailed Weaver**.

Reptiles and amphibians

The Tarangire ecosystem is rich in herpetofauna, with three species of land tortoise, two terrapins, at least 28 lizard species (including eight geckos), as well as 25 different snakes. But of this impressive list, only a few are likely to be seen by the average visitor. The large **Leopard Tortoise** may be seen feeding along the roads, and both large **monitor lizards**, **White-throated** and **Nile**, are quite commonly sighted, the latter mainly along the river and in swampy areas. The most frequently seen lizard in rocky areas is the **Mwanza Flat-headed Agama**, particularly the pink-and-blue male, as he usually sits on top of rocks and boulders. Around lodge buildings at night you are likely to see **Tropical House Geckos** foraging for insects around lights. The only other gecko you are likely to see, the **Cape Dwarf Gecko**, which measures up to 8cm, is diurnal and commonly seen around the lodges on posts and trees, often hunting small insects in the shade. The chances of seeing a snake, at least for long enough to identify it, are small. Both the **Southern African Rock Python** and **Central African Rock Python** are believed to be present but are difficult to separate in the field. Several large venomous species occur, including **Puff Adder**, **Black Mamba** and **Black-necked Spitting Cobra**.

- Tarangire is a malaria area.
- Tsetse flies occur in denser woodland, so there is a slight risk of sleeping sickness.
- Camps and lodges are unfenced; be alert for potentially dangerous game.
- Olive Baboons can be a problem in some camps and lodges. Never feed them!
- Many roads and tracks are difficult to negotiate during the rains from early April to May.

UDZUNGWA MOUNTAINS NATIONAL PARK

The Udzungwa Red Colobus is relatively easy to locate near park headquarters.

Lie of the land

The Udzungwa Mountains lie within what are called the Eastern Arc Mountains, a string of isolated mountains that run down eastern to south-western Tanzania. The park extends over 1,990km², covering about one-fifth of the Udzungwas, with several forest reserves forming buffers with surrounding farmland. The range extends from a low of about 400m asl to 2,576m on Mount Luhombero, with Mwanihana Peak rising to 2,111m. The park entrance lies 350km south of Dar es Salaam and 65km from Mikumi. Some 80% of the park lies in Kilolo District and the remainder in Kilombero District. The park borders Mikumi National Park in the north-east, the Great Ruaha River in the north and the Ruipa in the south-west. The park is so rich in biodiversity that it has been called the 'Galapagos of Africa'.

Brief history

Udzungwa Mountains National Park was first gazetted in 1992. The park was a result of a consolidation of five existing forest reserves established in the 1950s, Mwanihana, West Kilombero Scarp, Nyanganje, Matundu and Iwonde. The name Udzungwa is derived from the Kihehe word *Wadzungwa*, which means the 'people who live on the sides of the mountain'. There are a number of caves in the mountains that have cultural significance.

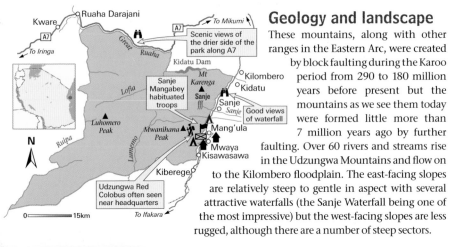

Kware
Ruaha Darajani
A7
To Iringa
Great Ruaha
Lofia
Luhomero Peak
Lumemo
Rulpa
N
0 ——— 15km
A7
To Mikumi
Scenic views of the drier side of the park along A7
Kidatu Dam
Mt Karenga
Sanje Mangabey habituated troops
Sanje
Kilombero
Kidatu
Sanje
Sanje
Good views of waterfall
Mwanihana Peak
Mang'ula
Mwaya
Kisawasawa
Kiberege
To Ifakara
Udzungwa Red Colobus often seen near headquarters

Geology and landscape

These mountains, along with other ranges in the Eastern Arc, were created by block faulting during the Karoo period from 290 to 180 million years before present but the mountains as we see them today were formed little more than 7 million years ago by further faulting. Over 60 rivers and streams rise in the Udzungwa Mountains and flow on to the Kilombero floodplain. The east-facing slopes are relatively steep to gentle in aspect with several attractive waterfalls (the Sanje Waterfall being one of the most impressive) but the west-facing slopes are less rugged, although there are a number of steep sectors.

Climate

Most of the rain here falls between November and May, with an average of 2,000mm falling in the east but only 600mm in the north-west. The hottest period is October to March and coolest May to July. Throughout the year temperatures average highs of 25° to 35°C with average lows from 17° to 23°C. Higher altitudes are cooler.

Vegetation

Natural forest in the Udzungwas covers some 2,103km^2; this is the largest area of open forest in the Eastern Arc. It is believed that the forests are some 30 million years old and were once connected to the forests of the Congo Basin. More than 2,500 plant species have been recorded from the park, at least 50 of which occur only here, including 10 tree species. The vegetation is a mosaic of forest, miombo woodland, dry bush and upland grassland. There are species differences at altitudinal level, as well as on the east- or west-facing slopes. The drier western slopes have numerous **Baobabs** (*Adansonia digitata*) and the similar but much smaller **Impala Lily** (*Adenium multiflorum*).

Wildlife
Mammals

Populations of **Savanna Elephant** and **Savanna Buffalo** are present mainly in the northern forests and the dry woodland on the western slopes, with the former extending into the moist forested eastern slopes. Both species move out of the park to the

Impala Lily in bloom

HIGHLIGHTS

- Unique access to forest related to that found in the Congo Basin.
- Many species found nowhere else, including Udzungwa Red Colobus, Sanje Mangabey and Udzungwa Forest Partridge.
- Can only be accessed by walking trails, giving unique insight.
- Interesting mountain scenery.

south and west but these movement corridors are increasingly under human disturbance. There is a small **Common Hippopotamus** population in the Matundu Forest on the Ruipa River. Although **Leopard** occur throughout, **Lion** and **Spotted Hyaena** are mainly found in the drier western wood and grassland but do on occasion enter the forests. At least 26 carnivore species are known to occur, including such rarities as **Jackson's Mongoose** and **Servaline Genet**. To date, 120 species of mammal are known to occur here, including five species that occur nowhere else. There are at least 13 species of primate in the Udzungwas, including the two endemics, **Udzungwa Red Colobus** and the **Sanje Mangabey**, the latter only discovered by scientists in 1979. There are also more widespread species such as the **Angolan Black and White Colobus, Sykes's Monkey**, as well as the **Vervet Monkey** and **Yellow Baboon**, with the last two mainly in the drier woodlands and forest edges. An Eastern Arc endemic, the **Mountain Galago**, is more frequently heard than seen. The **Kipunji** is found only in the north-western Ndundulu Forest (Vikongwa) sector and is one of Africa's most recently described and most endangered species. Another endemic here is the **Grey-headed Giant Sengi**, a diurnal denizen of the forest floor. This massif and its forests is also the last major stronghold of the large and endangered **Abbott's Duiker**, but **Harvey's Red Duiker** and **Blue Duiker** are common and widespread. Other antelope include **Suni, Bushbuck (Imbabala)** and in the drier west, small populations of **Sable Antelope, Common Eland** and **Common Waterbuck. Bushpig** are widespread in the forests and **Common Warthog** occur in the dry woodland and grassland. Although seldom seen, the **Eastern Tree Hyrax** can be identified by its large dung middens below denning trees and its rattling calls at night. They are only found here in closed canopy forest.

The Sanje Mangabey is one of Africa's rarest primates.

FACILITIES AND ACTIVITIES

- Hiking trails of various durations (hours to days); most trails are fairly difficult, especially when wet, and require guides.
- Viewing of habituated troops of Udzungwa Red Colobus and Sanje Mangabey.
- Several bird endemics and restricted-area species.
- Public campsite near park headquarters.
- Hondo Hondo Forest Tented Camp lies on boundary of park; camping and accommodation.

Birds

Considered one of the best birding destinations in Tanzania, with a number of endemics to near endemics. **Udzungwa Forest Partridge**, first scientifically discovered in 1991 and more closely allied to Asia than to Africa, is known only from the Udzungwas and the Rubeho Mountains (north of Kibakwe), at an altitudinal range of 1,300–2,400m in montane and submontane forest. However, like many other forest birds here, it is not easy to track down. Among other species highlights are **Usambara Eagle-Owl** (more likely to be heard), **Swynnerton's Robin, Dappled Mountain Robin** and **Iringa Akalat**. Along

Lower forest trail in Udzungwa

the forest edges and interior are **White-winged Apalis, Banded Sunbird, Rufous-winged Sunbird, Usambara Weaver**, with **Green-throated Greenbul** only in higher-altitude forests. As far as is known, a number of species appear to be restricted to certain altitudinal ranges, with **Fülleborn's Boubou** recorded at 1,200–1,800m, **Chapin's Apalis** 1,500m, **Spot Throat** 1,400–1,700m and **Kenrich's Starling** in forest at about 1,500m. The **Red-capped Tailorbird** is known only from forest on the slopes of Mount Luhombero. The most obvious large raptor here is the **African Crowned Eagle** and is usually easy to observe as it soars above the forest canopy. An obvious and colourful species is **Livingstone's Turaco** because of its call and also the broad red patches visible on the wings in flight. There is good birding around park headquarters and at the Hondo Hondo private camp, ideal for those not seeking strenuous hikes.

Reptiles and amphibians

The Udzungwas are rich in reptile (>65) and amphibian (71) species, with a number being endemic to these mountains. On the south-eastern slopes of the Udzungwa Scarp Forest Reserve alone (just 200km^2 of these mountains) 33 reptile and 36 amphibian species have been recorded, many of which are endemic. Among the endemics, or Eastern Arc endemics, are the **Red-snouted Wolf Snake, Usambara Eyelash Viper, Udzungwa Viper, Spiny-flanked Chameleon, Udzungwa Chameleon, Moyer's Pygmy Chameleon, Bearded Pygmy Chameleon, Uluguru One-horned Chameleon, Werner's Three-horned Chameleon, Udzungwa Mountains Limbless Skink, Udzungwa Five-toed Skink** and the **Ukinga Girdled Lizard**. The amphibian fauna is equally rich and diverse, with a number of endemics. There are common and widespread species in the Eastern Arc Mountains, such as the **Amani Screeching Frog, Poroto Screeching Frog, Shovel-footed Squeaker, Dwarf Squeaker** and the **Bagomoyo Forest Tree Frog**, but a few occur only in the Udzungwas. These include the **Udzungwa Toad, Poynton's Forest Toad, Dabaga Leaf-folding Frog, Kihanga Reed Frog, Tiny Reed Frog** and **Keith's Striped Frog**.

WILDLIFE FACTS

- 120 mammal species.
- 13 species of primate, including the endemic Udzungwa Red Colobus and Sanje Mangabey.
- 160 bird species in the Mwanihana Forest sector alone and at least 400 species across the massif.
- 539 species of butterfly in the range.
- >65 reptile species and at least 71 amphibian species; more can be expected.

- **The Udzungwas lie in a malaria area.**
- **No unaccompanied walking is allowed on trails.**
- **Many trails are steep, often not clearly defined, and become very slippery during rain.**
- **Although potentially dangerous game occur in the park, such as Savanna Elephant, Savanna Buffalo and Lion, you are unlikely to encounter them, but be alert.**

SELOUS GAME RESERVE

Selous has substantial populations of Maasai Giraffe and Nyasa (Johnston's) Wildebeest.

Lie of the land

The legendary Selous Game Reserve covers 54,600km², lying within the greater Selous ecosystem of about 90,000km², and is located in south-east Tanzania. Adjoining the reserve to the north are the Mikumi and Udzungwa Mountains national parks, in the west the Mahenge and Kilombero game controlled areas and in the south the Selous-Niassa Wildlife Corridor linking to the park of that name in northern Mozambique. It is a blend of open plains, woodland, rivers, floodplains, lakes, swamps and hill ranges, the latter including the massifs of Nandanga, Mbarika, Mberera and Ngalwa. There is an altitudinal range of 80–1,300m asl (Mbarika Mountains). This vast area lies partly within the following regions: Coast, Morogoro, Lindi, Mtwara and Ruvuma. The Matambwe entrance gate is a 350km drive south from Dar es Salaam.

Brief history

The earliest human records for the area date to about 2,000 years before present, with the discovery of steel-smelting kilns, operated by the ancestors of the local Haya tribe. These people produced medium carbon steel long before it was developed in Europe. Arab slavers and ivory traders passed through here from the interior to the coastal trading town of Kilwa. Kisaki village, close to the northern boundary of the Selous, was a transit station for slaves, with at times more than 1,000 of the unfortunates waiting for the next stage in their journey. The reserve takes its name from the great hunter, Frederick Courtenay Selous, whose grave is located on the bank of the Beho Beho River in the north. By 1905 the German colonizers

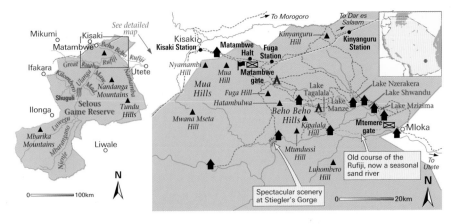

See detailed map

- Vast tracts of wilderness.
- Very low tourist numbers.
- Great diversity of animals and plants.
- Long, accompanied, walking safaris.
- Boat safaris offer unique game viewing.

Large areas of Selous are covered by woodland.

started to demarcate wildlife reserves. In 1910 Kaiser Wilhelm gave his a wife a vast expanse of land in what was then Tanganyika and it became known to locals as *shamba la bibi* ('field of the woman'). In 1912 a large area between the Mgeta and Rufiji rivers was added to the steadily growing park. The British enlarged the reserve further and between 1933 and 1955 it was under the management of game ranger Constantine J.P. Ionides, who was first tasked with killing man-eating Lion that were plaguing the local people. The ashes of Ionides are buried at the foot of Nandanga Mountain in the heart of the reserve. The reserve was declared a World Heritage Site in 1982. Much of the park has been divided into 46 large hunting blocks, which are closed to tourists. Recent poaching history has seen a massive reduction in elephant from more than 100,000 in 1976 to about 15,000 today. However, the population remains one of the largest in Tanzania and East Africa.

Geology and landscape

The Selous is often referred to as the place of sand rivers, at least in the dry season, although in the rains all streams pour their waters into the Rufiji River, which in turn cuts its way to the Indian Ocean. Larger rivers, such as the Rufiji and Great Ruaha, flow throughout the year, but in recent years flow levels have fallen. The Rufiji watershed is drained by a veritable lacework of rivers and streams, the Beho Beho, Ulanga, Luhombero, Madaba, Mawera, Lung'onyo, Namamba, Luwegu, Mbarangano and the Njenje, to name but a few. During the rainy season many of the rivers spill over their banks, turning vast tracts of the reserve into seasonal swamps. There are several small lakes that hold water throughout the year, and there are crystal-clear springs that continuously bubble from the earth. Much of the Selous consists of flat to gently undulating terrain but in the south, lying along a fault line, are precipitous red cliffs flanking the Luwegu River. Within the ecosystems in the south-west are the Ukumu Hills, in the north the Uluguru Mountains and in the north-west the Udzungwa Mountains. Just below the confluence of the Great Ruaha and Rufiji rivers lies the deeply cut Stiegler's Gorge. At the centre of the park the Kilombero River joins the Rufiji just above the Shuguli Falls. The Selous lies on one of the oldest geological formations on Earth, the Tanzania Craton, formed some

Despite heavy poaching, the Selous Elephant population is one of the region's largest.

3 billion years before present, with, among others, sedimentary rocks of the various Karoo sandstones. Soils are generally poor and thin.

Climate

Averaging 750mm in the east to 1,300mm in the west, the rains generally start in November, peak in March and are over by May. The coolest months, between June and the end of October, are the most pleasant. January and February are very hot and uncomfortable.

Vegetation

In the tourist area in the north the vegetation is predominantly *Vachellia-Senegalia-Terminalia* woodland. More than 60% of this magnificent wilderness is bedecked with miombo woodland and is dominated by trees of the genus *Brachystegia* (sometimes referred to as **Miombo**) and various **bushwillows** (*Combretum*), the latter characterized by most species having four-winged fruits. Most trees are deciduous or semi-deciduous within the miombo belt. One of the common trees is **Spiny Terminalia** (**Mwanga**) (*Terminalia spinosa*), which can reach 15m but is often shorter. Along the major rivers there are stretches of riparian forest with one of the most obvious plants being the **Borassus Palm** (*Borassus aethiopum*). Other prominent trees include **Star Chestnut** (*Sterculia appendiculata*) and stands of **Marula** (*Sclerocarya birrea*) with its eagerly sought-after plum-like fruits. There are also majestic, massively trunked **Baobabs** (*Adansonia digitata*), usually located in drier areas. Within the woodland there are open grassed areas throughout.

FACILITIES AND ACTIVITIES

- Several upmarket lodges and camps in the north of reserve, in proximity to the Rufiji and associated lakes; most close March to May/June.
- Walking safaris of varying length.
- Boating safaris.
- Very good and diverse game viewing but wildlife viewing circuit quite small, with game often skittish due to trophy hunting to the south.
- Not a first choice self-drive park but a good safari pick.

Selous has Africa's largest African Wild Dog population.

Wildlife
Mammals

The smaller mammals of the reserve have not been studied much, but at least 124 species of mammal are known, or expected, to occur. The reserve was previously known for its vast herds of **Savanna Elephant** (some 110,000 in 1976), but by 2015 just 15,000 remained as a result of largely unchecked ivory poaching. Despite the poaching, this still remains one of the largest populations of these gentle grey giants in East Africa. Likewise, **Hook-lipped Rhinoceros** used to occur in the thousands but now only a few small scattered populations survive and are rarely seen. Selous has the largest surviving **Savanna Buffalo** population of about 150,000 and a substantial **Common Hippopotamus** population of perhaps 20,000. A substantial population of **Giraffe** is present and there is some discussion as to whether this is the **Maasai Giraffe**, or an as yet undescribed form. There are also large populations of **Common Eland, Nyasa (Johnston's) Wildebeest, Lichtenstein's Hartebeest, Common Waterbuck, Sable Antelope** (which is the largest single protected population), **Greater Kudu** and **Bohor Reedbuck**. Other antelope present include **Bushbuck (Imbabala), Suni, Klipspringer, Sharpe's Grysbok, Common Duiker** and **Blue Duiker**. It is not clear whether it is the **Natal Red Duiker** or **Harvey's Red Duiker** that occurs, or possibly both. The Selous is also, as one would expect, a hotspot for predators, with a large number of **Lion; Leopard**, though elusive, occur throughout. **Cheetah** are rare and seldom seen. Selous is probably the last great stronghold of **African Wild Dog**, which has been decimated across the rest of its range. Because of their relatively high density these dogs are fairly frequently seen. Small carnivore diversity is great, but as most species are nocturnal they are seldom seen, with the exception of the two communal mongooses, **Dwarf** and **Banded**, as well as the solitary **Slender Mongoose**. Two species of squirrel, **Striped Bush Squirrel** and **Smith's Bush Squirrel**, are common in the woodland here and are easy to observe.

WILDLIFE FACTS

- At least 124 mammal species.
- Savanna Elephant numbers down to only some 15,000 (2015); remnant Hook-lipped Rhinoceros population; +20,000 Common Hippopotamus; 150,000 Savanna Buffalo; 7,000 Sable Antelope; 20,000 Lichtenstein's Hartebeest; 80,000 Johnston's Wildebeest. There may have been recent declines in some of these populations.
- 3,000 Lion; perhaps 1,000 African Wild Dog.
- Official bird list has 430 species.
- 2,149 plant species so far recorded.

Birds

The Selous bird list (which also includes adjacent areas on the outer boundary) stands at 430 species but it is expected to be higher, as several areas have not been fully explored. Birds associated with the rivers, especially the Rufiji River, are particularly diverse, with up to 17 species of heron, egret and bittern. This is also one of the best locations to watch the **African Skimmer** and the less commonly seen **Pel's Fishing Owl**. Other birds of interest include **African Crowned Eagle** in riparian forest, **African Fish Eagle**, **Dickinson's Kestrel**, **White-headed Lapwing**, **Blue-spotted Wood Dove**, **Brown-necked Parrot**, **Green Turaco**, **Barred Long-tailed Cuckoo**, **White-eared Barbet**, **African Broadbill**, **Eastern Bearded Scrub-Robin**, **Spectacled Weaver** and **Yellow-fronted Serin**. Other specials include the **Kilombero Weaver**, which is known only from the area where the Kilombero River forms the north-west boundary of the Selous. The **African Pitta** is known to breed on the south bank of the Rufiji and Kilombero rivers. The park is an important over-wintering area of the **Madagascar Squacco Heron**.

African Fish Eagle occur wherever there is permanent water, but mainly along the Rufiji River.

Reptiles and amphibians

No comprehensive reptile and amphibian list has been compiled for this reserve, although much preliminary work was undertaken by Ionides, the first game ranger at Selous. The **Nile Crocodile** is abundant, especially along the Rufiji River, as are the **Nile** and **White-throated monitors**. The waters of the Selous are home to at least four species of freshwater turtle or terrapin, including the **Zambezi Flap-shelled Turtle**. The only chameleon the visitor is likely to encounter is the widespread **Flap-necked Chameleon**, which can reach a length of 43cm, but is usually not longer than 25cm. The largest snake here is the **Southern African Rock Python**, but at least another 32 snake species should occur in the area.

Nile Monitor are common along the Rufiji.

- Selous falls within the malaria area.
- Many tsetse flies in parts, not so much in the north; low risk of sleeping sickness.
- Safari camps are not fenced; be alert for potentially dangerous game.
- Much of Selous is set aside for trophy hunting (92%) and only a limited area in the north can be accessed by visitors.
- For those with limited time and finances Selous is not a prime destination.
- Most lodges close during the rainy season.

NGORONGORO CONSERVATION AREA

Empakaai Crater in the Ngorongoro Conservation Area

Lie of the land

The Ngorongoro Conservation Area lies within the crater highlands of north-western Tanzania and forms part of what is known as the Serengeti-Ngorongoro-Maasai Mara ecosystem. Its eastern boundary is formed by the western wall of the Great Rift Valley, while its western boundary adjoins the world-famous Serengeti National Park. To the east lies Mount Kilimanjaro, Africa's highest mountain, and Mount Meru, with Lake Victoria to the west. The conservation area covers 8,292km² and is a mix of mountains, volcanoes and calderas, open and wooded plains. The focal points for most visitors are the Ngorongoro Crater and the Oldupai Gorge. From Arusha to the entrance gate is about 154km.

Brief history

This is one of the few areas in East Africa where there is a comprehensive record of the ancestral beginnings of modern man on the continent. Some 3.5 million years before present our ancient ancestors walked across a rain-dampened volcanic ash deposit at a place we know today as Laetoli. A fresh eruption covered these tracks with ash, thus preserving them until their discovery in 1978. Approximately halfway between the Ngorongoro Crater and Serengeti lies one of the world's most important sources of fossil animal and hominid remains. Oldupai (incorrectly given as Olduvai) Gorge is named for the Maasai word for the succulent Wild Sisal that grows in abundance in the area. In the gorge successive lava flows, ash deposits and mud layers preserved an incredible array of fossils. Crustal movements, faulting and volcanic action resulted in Oldupai being deeply incised. The periodic flow of water in the gorge exposed series of evolutionary events from ancient lava to the most recent

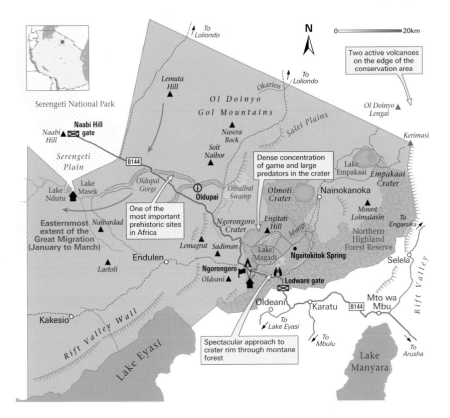

Two active volcanoes
on the edge of the
conservation area

One of the
most important
prehistoric sites
in Africa

Dense concentration
of game and large
predators in the crater

Easternmost
extent of the
Great Migration
(January to March)

Spectacular approach to
crater rim through montane
forest

Naisiusiu bed that was laid down in the past few thousand years. This was the domain of the Leakey family, who through their excavations were able to trace the development of humans in Africa and their ancestral forms over several million years. Here were found remains of *Australopithecus robustus*, *Homo habilis* (Handy Man), with the first modern humans appearing some 17,000 years before present. About 10,000 years before present modern humans known as the Stone Bowl people occupied the area, but they disappeared about 1,000 years ago. Another group, still present in the Ngorongoro highlands, that appeared about 2,000 years ago, are the Mbulu people. The Datoga, a warrior pastoral people, arrived as recently as 300 years before present, but were driven out by the Maasai, who currently occupy the area. Although said to live in harmony with the game herds and natural environment, this is not strictly true, as when their numbers increase, so do those of their cattle.

Oldupai Gorge, north-west of the crater, is one of Africa's premier prehistoric sites.

- Ngorongoro Crater, with very high game and predator densities.
- Great mammal and bird diversity.
- Access to Oldupai Gorge and insights into human ancestral prehistory.
- Vast herds of White-bearded Wildebeest and other game during the rains on the short-grass plains.

Geology and landscape

The landscapes of Ngorongoro are a combination of both ancient and modern geological processes. The Ol Doinyo Gol Mountains and the gneiss and granite outcrops scattered across the Serengeti Plain originated several hundred million years before present. Some 20 million years before present the eastern side of Africa started to crack and rift, causing the land between the rifts to subside. The Earth's crust gradually thinned and softened, allowing molten materials to thrust to the surface to form lava beds, and later volcanoes. Within the Ngorongoro area the oldest volcanoes – Lemagrut, Sadiman, Oldeani, Ngorongoro, Olmoti, Sirua, Lolmalasin and Empakaai – were formed along the Eyasi Rift. In the north the rift separates the Ol Doinyo Gol range from the Salei Plains, but much of this early rift is obscured by lava. It is believed that Ngorongoro volcano rivalled Kilimanjaro in size. The lava that filled the volcano formed a solid cap, which subsequently collapsed to form the caldera we see today. It covers just 304km², is about 14.5km across, and the depth from rim to floor ranges from 610m to 760m. The smaller volcanoes of Olmoti and Empakaai suffered the same fate. Two volcanoes of more recent origin in the north-east, Kerimasi and Ol Doinyo Lengai (the Maasai 'Mountain of God'), are active and periodically erupt. The vast quantities of ash spewed out by the volcanoes past and present, produce incredibly fertile soils that are able to sustain the great herds on the grass plains. The landscape is dominated by mountains in the east and north and by flat and undulating plains in the west. Altitudinal range is 1,009–3,645m asl.

The floor of the Ngorongoro Crater is a microcosm of the adjacent Serengeti.

A view of the Ngorongoro Crater from the southern rim

Climate

Because of its altitude the area has a mild, temperate climate with two periods of rain: 'short rains' October and November and 'long rains' March to May. Most rain falls in the afternoon. Day temperatures during the dry season (June to October) are mild (average 19°C), but nights can be cold and at times even frost occurs. During the rainy season, day temperatures average in the low 20°s and at night some 6°C. Depending on location, annual rainfall averages 500–1,700mm, with more falling in the high-altitude areas than on the lower-lying grass plains.

Vegetation

In its broadest sense, the vegetation of Ngorongoro can be divided into montane forest and tussock grassland, as well as montane heath, dry woodland that varies from open to dense thicket, and short grassland on the plains. The montane forests have great diversity, with important trees being **White Stinkwood** (*Celtis africana*), **Wild Elder** (**Muchorowe**) (*Nuxia congesta*), **Pillarwood** (*Cassipourea malosana*), **East African Yellowwood** (*Afrocarpus gracilior*), **Peacock Flower** (*Albizia gummifera*), **Sweet Olive** (*Olea chrysophylla*), **Strangler Fig** (*Ficus thonningii*), **Wild Mango** (*Cordyla africana*) and **East African Rosewood** (*Hagenia abyssinica*). In these forests you will notice many trees have long, tangled grey tufts of lichen hanging from their branches, which is known as **Old Man's Beard** (*Usnea* sp.). On Oldeani Mountain in the south is an extensive stand of **African Alpine Bamboo** (*Yushania alpina*). In the Crater itself grassland dominates, but there are stands of **Fever Tree** (*Vachellia xanthophloea*) and **Quinine Tree** (*Rauvolfia caffra*). On the descent into the Crater you will see tall, succulent cactus-like trees, **Candelabra Tree** (*Euphorbia candelabrum*) and *Euphorbia bussei*. The open plains to the west sustain few trees but the distinctive **Umbrella Thorn** (*Vachellia tortilis*) has roots able to penetrate the shallow calcrete layer.

FACILITIES AND ACTIVITIES

- Wide choice of mostly upmarket lodges and tented camps; very basic public campsite, private camps with no facilities.
- Network of 'roads' and tracks but generally in poor condition, including the main route from Lodware Gate into Serengeti. Most tracks are difficult during rains.
- If you enter the Crater you have to hire a guide if you opt for self-drive.
- Small museum at Oldupai Gorge.
- Cultural tours to Maasai villages.
- Guided bush walks and hiking.
- Most visitors visit only the Crater and move straight to Serengeti, but much of the rest of this area is well worth exploring.
- Carry enough fuel, food and water if you opt for self-drive.

Zebra and wildebeest in the Crater do not migrate.

Caracal with hyrax prey

Wildlife
Mammals

The mammal fauna of this conservation area is diverse, and the appeal for many visitors is the density of predators and prey in the Crater. Most of these species can also be seen elsewhere in the conservation area, the only exception being the remnant **Hook-lipped Rhinoceros** population on the Crater floor. **Savanna Elephant** bulls are also found here but cow and calf herds remain beyond its rim, the descent too difficult for small calves. The **Maasai Giraffe** are commonly seen along wooded river courses, or crossing the plains between feeding grounds. **Savanna Buffalo** are mainly found in the highlands but are commonly seen in the Crater, especially groups of bulls. **Common Hippopotamus** occur in small numbers in the Mandusi and Gorigor swamps on the Crater floor. Unlike the **Western White-bearded Wildebeest** and **Plains Zebra** on the open plains (best here January to April), the populations in the Crater do not participate in the migration. Apart from the vast herds of wildebeest and zebra seasonally present, out on the plains are large numbers of **Thomson's Gazelle, Grant's Gazelle, Topi** and **Kongoni (Coke's Hartebeest)**, with **Impala** found mainly along the wooded watercourses and woodland. It is here also that you have your best chances of seeing the diminutive **Ugogo Dik-dik** (previously known as Kirk's Dik-dik). Only the ram carries the short, back-angled horns. **Common Eland** also occur but they are not frequently seen as they are constantly on the move. **Lion** are relatively common both in and outside the Crater, as are clans of **Spotted Hyaena**. Both **Leopard** and **Cheetah** occur but are not as easy to observe as their Lion cousin. Among the smaller carnivores are the recently described **African Wolf** (previously called Golden Jackal), **Black-backed** and **Side-striped** jackals, **Bat-eared Fox, Serval, Caracal**, the social **Banded** and **Dwarf** mongooses, as well as the solitary **Slender Mongoose**. In the hills and rocky areas are the colonial **Rock** and **Yellow-spotted Rock** hyraxes, always alert for predators, including Verreaux's Eagle. In the forests there is the nocturnal **Southern Tree Hyrax**, which is seldom seen but its screaming cry gives its presence away. The most obvious primate is the troop-living **Olive Baboon**, which can be expected anywhere but rarely ventures far onto the open grass plains. **Vervet**

Lion occur throughout the conservation area.

Monkeys are common in the wooded areas but avoid the forested uplands, where the distinctive **Black and White Colobus (Guereza)** occurs. This magnificent monkey is most easily seen in the early morning and late afternoon when it sits in fairly prominent positions. If you are staying on the forested rim you are likely to hear their far-carrying deep throaty croaking call, a warning to neighbouring troops to keep their distance. Another forest dweller is the less flamboyant **Blue Monkey**, with **Northern Lesser Galago** and **Thick-tailed Greater Galago** occurring mainly in the drier woodlands. The latter two are nocturnal and seldom seen, but they have distinctive calls. No detailed inventory has been made of the smaller mammals of the conservation area.

Olive Baboon male grooming female

Birds

The birdlife in Ngorongoro is diverse with at least 560 species on record but some ornithologists believe this could rise to 600 species, however some species are seen only as seasonal migrants and are not always present. On the open grassland and in lightly wooded areas **Maasai Ostrich** are common, as are other large species such as **Kori Bustard**. Both **Helmeted** and **Crested guineafowl** occur, also **Hildebrandt's Spurfowl** and the most secure population of **Grey-breasted Spurfowl** in Tanzania. One of the most colourful sights is when **Lesser** (usually most abundant) and **Greater flamingos** are present at Lake Magadi in the Crater, with sometimes huge numbers in Empakaai Crater

Male Grey-crowned Crane dancing around a female prospect

Although they gather in vast numbers in the Crater, flamingos do not breed here.

White-crowned Shrike nest with large chicks

to the north-east. Their presence is seasonal and is influenced by water levels and abundance of the microorganisms that constitute their food. At highest altitudes both **Alpine Chat** and **Scarlet-tufted Malachite Sunbird** occur, with a resident population of **Jackson's Widowbird** on the high grassland and on the Crater floor. The Crater highlands is the only location in Tanzania where you are likely to see the **Cape Rook (Black Crow)**. All seven East African vulture species occur, with a substantial population of **Rüppell's Vulture** (a large breeding colony in Olkarien Gorge, east of Gol Mountains), and at least 50 raptor species are recorded throughout, among the most obvious in the highlands being **Augur Buzzard**, **Crested Eagle** and the **African Crowned Eagle**. **Lesser Kestrels** are common during the periods of migration, with **Pallid Harriers** seen over-wintering on the short-grass plains. Other species to look for include **Livingstone's** and **Hartlaub's turacos** in forested areas. There is a good population of **Fischer's Lovebird** and a local race of the **Brown-backed Woodpecker**. One can usually enjoy good birding in the grounds of the various lodges.

Reptiles and amphibians

No comprehensive list of the area's reptiles and amphibians has been compiled. One of the most easily observed in rocky areas is the **Mwanza Flat-headed Agama**, especially the large pink-and-blue male. Around the lodges look for the **Tropical House Gecko** around lights at night, but other geckos are seldom seen, although there are five species. Skinks are fairly commonly seen in woodland and include **Striped Skink**, usually on trees or buildings, and the smaller **Variable Skink**, most commonly found in rocky areas. Although it is likely that more species of chameleon occur, only the large **Flap-necked Chameleon** is known to be present. The large **Leopard Tortoise** is sometimes seen feeding along track verges. The **Southern African Rock Python** is present at lower altitudes, especially in moist habitats. Generally snakes are difficult to observe and are seldom seen.

WILDLIFE FACTS

- 85 mammal species, of which 20 antelope species; 28 carnivore species; no inventory of bats, shrews or small rodents.
- Super abundance of Western White-bearded Wildebeest, Plains Zebra and Thomson's Gazelle on short grass plains during rainy season.
- About 560 bird species.

- Ngorongoro is a malaria area.
- Be alert for potentially dangerous game, such as Lion, Savanna Buffalo and Savanna Elephant; lodges are not fenced, and as you are allowed to alight from your vehicle (not in the Crater), do so with caution.
- Roads and tracks are generally in poor condition.
- If you intend exploring some of the more isolated areas you will need to be well supplied and equipped; usually a guide is required.

KITULO NATIONAL PARK

Kipengere range viewed from the Kitulo Plateau

The Kitulo Plateau is an area of montane grassland and forest in the southern highlands of Tanzania. It lies within Njombe and Mbeya administrative regions, covers 442km² and rises to an altitude of 2,600m. The highest-lying peak in the area is Mount Mtorwi, at 2,961m (the maximum altitudinal point in southern Tanzania). The plateau was formed some 2.5 million years before present with great quantities of ash from the erupting Mount Rungwe to its west. Base rocks are granites, gneisses and schists. It lies between the Kipengere and Poroto mountains and close to the Mount Rungwe forest, home to one of Africa's most recently described primates, the Kipunji. The park runs into the Livingstone Mountains and lies parallel to the shoreline of Lake Nyasa. Kitulo is known to the locals as *Bustani ya Mungu* ('Garden of God') and to botanists as the 'Serengeti of Flowers'. Peak flowering is November to April, clearest months September to November, wet December to April, cold and foggy June to August. The park's headquarters are in Matamba, 100km away from the town of Mbeya. A 4x4 is essential, as access roads and internal tracks are in poor condition. There are hiking trails and campsites, but no accommodation. Kitulo was gazetted as a national park in 2005 to protect the unique flora, especially the numerous ground orchids. Some 350 flowering plants have been identified, including 45 species of ground orchid, many of which are endemic. No big game is present but there are small populations of, among others, **Southern Reedbuck**, **Common Duiker** and **Klipspringer**, at least 12 carnivore species and 7 primates, including the endangered **Kipunji** in Livingstone Forest. In the forest 106 bird species have been recorded and the plateau is the only location in Tanzania where **Denham's Bustard** is resident. Other species of special interest include **Blue Swallow**, **Mountain Marsh Widow**, **Njombe Cisticola**, **Kipengere Seed-eater** and **Short-tailed Pipit**.

MOUNT RUNGWE NATURE RESERVE

Foothills of Mount Rungwe over the Kiwira River in Tanzania's Southern Highlands

The reserve is located in the Tanzanian Southern Highlands, just to the west of Kitulo National Park and north of Lake Nyasa. It lies to the south-east of the district town of Mbeya and extends over just 150km², centred on Mount Rungwe. The area serves as an important water catchment for cultivation and has a very dense human population (some 200–400 per km²). Mount Rungwe adjoins the Livingstone Forest. It is the 'meeting place' of three great montane regions of endemism, southern, eastern and central African. In 2009 it was raised from catchment forest reserve to nature reserve to try to reduce poaching pressure. Altitudinal range is from 1,500m to 2,981m, the peak of Mount Rungwe, a dormant volcano that was active up to some 2.5 million years before present. The rains fall from November to May but some rain can be expected during the June to October dry season. Mean annual average rainfall is 2,133mm but in the south-east up to 3,000mm has been recorded. Apart from the montane forest, there are areas with **bamboo** thicket, montane grassland and areas of mixed bush and heath at the highest points. There are rough, steep trails and wild camping is allowed. The very determined person comes here to see the endangered monkey, **Kipunji**, which numbers no more than 1,000, lives in troops of 25–39 individuals, and is genetically most closely aligned with the baboons. The reserve is also home to the endangered **Abbott's Duiker**, as well as **Leopard, Side-striped Jackal** and **Southern Tree Hyrax**, and at least 100 additional mammal species, as well as 230 bird species, 34 recorded reptiles, 45 amphibians and 550 recorded plant species. There are a number of endemic species, as well as several that are restricted to this and other parts of the Eastern Arc Mountains.

RUBONDO ISLAND NATIONAL PARK & SAANANE NATIONAL PARK

Sitatunga on Rubondo Island

Rubondo Island is situated in the south-west corner of Lake Victoria and is located about 150km due west of the town of Mwanza. It was proclaimed as a game reserve in 1965 and raised to national park level in 1977. The main island is 28km long and 3–10km wide, with 11 much smaller islands incorporated in the national park. The highest point on the main island is the 350m-high Masa Hills. The archipelago is of volcanic origin. Much of the main island is covered by mixed evergreen and semi-deciduous forest with a dense understorey. A number of species have been released on the island, including **Common Chimpanzees** that were introduced between 1966 and 1969 and are now believed to number about 40 individuals. They are not habituated and are seldom seen. Another introduced primate is the **Guereza** but **Vervet Monkeys** occur naturally. Small numbers of **Savanna Elephant, Maasai Giraffe** and **Suni** were also released. **Common Hippopotamus, Sitatunga** and **Bushbuck (Imbabala)** are resident. Birdlife is rich, and there are large numbers of **Nile Crocodile**. Access is by park boat or light aircraft. There are various park-operated accommodation options. In the view of the authors this is not a prime wildlife destination but the relatively large forest block is of interest as most of those on the mainland have been destroyed.

Saanane National Park, gazetted as such in 2013, consists of three small islands (2.18km²) and lies in Lake Victoria just off the town of Mwanza. A number of species have been introduced, including **Impala, Vervet Monkey** and **De Brazza's Monkey**. It was originally set up as a zoo by the authorities and is said to be developed as an education centre. There is little here that cannot be seen elsewhere in the Lake Victoria basin.

SAADANI NATIONAL PARK

Palm woodland in Saadani National Park

Saadani, officially gazetted as a national park in 2005, comprises the original Saadani Game Reserve, Mkwaja Cattle Ranch and Zaraninge and Kwamsisi forests (only partly in the park). It lies some 110km to the north of Dar es Salaam and is the only park in Tanzania that in part borders the Indian Ocean. It has an ongoing history of controversy, including the release of game species that probably never occurred here, poaching and lack of consultation with local people. It covers about 1,100km² and lies within the districts of Pangani, Handeni and Bagamoyo. Several rivers cut through the park to the ocean, including the Wami, Mvave and the Msangazi. Apart from the two larger forests, there are several smaller forest pockets, riverine forest, savanna and grassland mosaics and mangrove thicket. In some areas with high water tables there are many **Borassus Palms**, but outside the forested areas various **acacia** species dominate. Because of relatively low visitor numbers game is not accustomed to vehicles and humans and is not always easy to observe, but among others there are **Savanna Elephant, Common Hippopotamus, Maasai Giraffe, Savanna Buffalo, Common Waterbuck, Lichtenstein's Hartebeest, Bushbuck (Imbabala), White-bearded Wildebeest, Common Eland, Sable Antelope (Roosevelt race), Bohor Reedbuck, Suni** and **Harvey's Red Duiker**. Although in relatively small numbers, predators are well represented with **Lion, Leopard, Serval, Spotted Hyaena, Side-striped Jackal** and **Banded Mongoose**, among others. **Yellow Baboon** and **Vervet Monkey** are common, with **Angolan Black and White Colobus** in the largest forest block. **Humpback Whales** occur seasonally but **Bottlenosed Dolphins** and **Humpback Dolphins** may be seen at any time. It is a good birding destination with many rarities, especially in the forests. **Nile Crocodile** and **Nile Monitor** are common, and there are 17 forest-dependent reptiles and 10 amphibian species. The coast here is an important nesting ground for the **Green Turtle**. There are upmarket lodges (mostly on the fringes), public and special campsites.

AMANI NATURE RESERVE

A stream running through the forest in Amani Nature Reserve

Covering just under 84km², Amani lies in the East Usambara Mountains in the Tanga Region of north-east Tanzania and was proclaimed as a reserve in 1997 to protect an area of submontane evergreen forest with at least 264 tree species. It is part of the Eastern Arc ranges and is rich in endemic or near-endemic species. There are 60 known mammal species in the reserve, including at least 16 species of bat. Although there are no large game species present, the seriously endangered **Abbott's Duiker** may occur, as well as **Harvey's Red Duiker**, **Blue Duiker**, **Bushbuck (Imbabala)**, **Bushpig** and **Angolan Black and White Colobus**. **Peter's Giant Sengi** is common and the **Eastern Tree Hyrax** occurs. Of interest to most visitors to Amani is the birdlife, especially the endemics and near-endemics. The elusive **Long-billed Forest-Warbler** is known only from here and Mount Namuli in Mozambique; others include **Usambara Weaver**, **Usambara Hyliota**, **Usambara Eagle-Owl** and the **Amani Sunbird**. Among others here are **Red-capped Forest-Warbler (African Tailorbird)**, **Sokoke Scops Owl**, **Swynnerton's Robin**, **Red-headed Bluebill**, **Pied Mannikin** and **Usambara Akalat**. The reserve and East Usambaras are rich in reptiles and amphibians, with at least 49 species of the former and 34 of the latter, of which eight are endemic. To date, seven chameleon and 26 snake species have been recorded. For those interested in the invertebrates, at least 30 of the 41 millipede species occur only in the East Usambaras and 55 species of gastropod occur only here. There are a number of accommodation and camping options in the East Usambaras, but movement in the reserve is only on foot.

KENYA

The world-renowned wildebeest migration is a key attraction of the Maasai Mara.

Kenya extends over 582,646km² and is bisected by the equator. It is bordered by the Indian Ocean to the south-east, Somalia to the east, Ethiopia and South Sudan to the north, Uganda to the west and Tanzania to the south and south-west. The dominant landform is the Great Rift Valley, which cuts through the centre of the country from north to south and shows numerous signs of the region's volcanic past. Extinct volcanoes, such as Africa's second-highest peak, Mount Kenya (5,199m), and Mount Elgon (4,321m), tower above the plateaux. Along the valley floor a chain of lakes runs from the Ethiopian to the Tanzanian borders and beyond. Some of these lakes dry up occasionally, many are alkaline and provide a primordial brew that favours algal growth to feed millions of flamingos. The largest lake in the chain, Turkana in the north, covers 6,400km². In the south-west lies Africa's largest lake, Victoria, which is shared with Tanzania and Uganda. Much of Kenya lies on a high plateau, with a coastal plain that is only a few kilometres wide in the south, broadening towards Somalia. The longest river is the Tana (1,000km), which rises in the Aberdare Mountains in the central highlands, and the Galana (390km) in the south-east, which in part cuts through Tsavo East.

The Kenyan coastal belt is warm to hot and humid throughout the year. The zone that lies between the coast and the inland plateau and the north of the country is dry and frequently hot. Although the central plateau has a temperate and mild climate, the floor of the Great Rift Valley is drier, with generally higher temperatures. The hottest months are December to March. The principal rainfall months are from March into June, with a less significant wet period in October and November.

Man's pre-human ancestors, the upright-walking *Australopithecus*, were living in the land we know today as Kenya at least 3 million years before present. Recent finds in

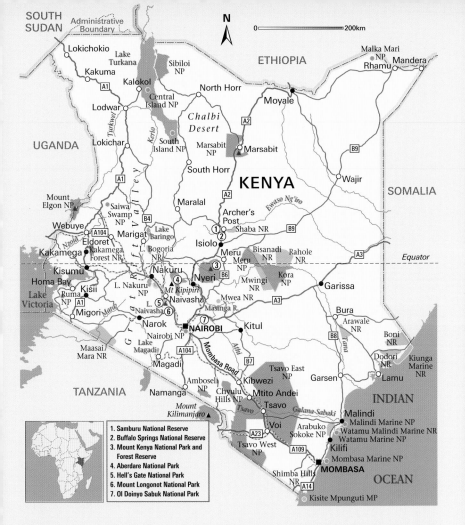

1. Samburu National Reserve
2. Buffalo Springs National Reserve
3. Mount Kenya National Park and Forest Reserve
4. Aberdare National Park
5. Hell's Gate National Park
6. Mount Longonot National Park
7. Ol Doinyo Sabuk National Park

neighbouring Ethiopia indicate this age may be even greater. At sites such as West Turkana, Koobi Fora, Lothagam and Lake Baringo our distant ancestors once hunted. Scattered across Kenya are many later sites associated with the three stone ages. Roving bands of *Homo erectus* hunter-gatherers started calling this region home at least 500,000 years before present. Certainly up to 3,000 years before present, and probably even more recently, much of East Africa was occupied by small nomadic bands wandering the landscape. Bantu-speaking peoples started occupying the region about 2,000 years ago after crossing the Congo Basin from West Africa in a succession of waves. Much later arrivals were the Nilotic-speaking tribes such as the Luo, Maasai and Samburu. The Kenyan coast and its associated islands became important for a succession of outside traders, with the first being the Persians in about 800AD. But it was the Omani Arabs who were to be the principal force here for hundreds of years.

The British colonial authorities initially set aside tracts of land in 1896, with the purpose of protecting wildlife for controlled hunting. In 1945 the first national park was proclaimed, Nairobi Royal Park, to be followed by Aberdare Royal Park and Mount Kenya Royal Park. The Kenya Wildlife Service today manages 19 terrestrial national parks, 14 national reserves (except Maasai Mara NR), 4 marine parks/reserves and the Kakamega Forest Reserve and used to manage Tana River Primate Reserve, which was, sadly, de-proclaimed. Kenya's total wildlife estate covers 44,359km², or 7.6%, of the country's surface area. Four small national parks lie away from the main circuits, **Ol Doinyo Sabuk** (near Nairobi and mainly visited for its scenery), **Ruma** (close to the shore of Lake Victoria, which protects a small number of Roan Antelope and is rarely visited) and **Saiwa Swamp**, which is Kenya's smallest park (known for small populations of Sitatunga and De Brazza's Monkey), as well as **Mwea National Reserve**, and we have not covered these. The following have little, or no, infrastructure and are difficult or inadvisable to visit: **Arawale National Reserve**; **Boni National Reserve**; **Dodori National Reserve** (close to Boni National Reserve and Somali border and known for its population of Coastal Topi and its birdlife); **Malka Mari National Park** (in north-east Kenya, shares its northern border with Gerale National Park, Ethiopia, is some 200km from the Somali border and is best known for its plant life; game apparently heavily poached). There are four marine national parks/reserves, namely **Kisite-Mpunguti**, **Malindi**, **Mombasa** and **Watamu**. The authors are well aware of the numerous privately owned reserves, conservancies and sanctuaries in Kenya, including **Laikipia**, **Ol Pejeta**, **Sweet Waters**, **Ngutuni**, **Taita Hills**, **Lewa Downs** and **Solio**, but we have chosen to leave them out of this natural history guide. It is not that we do not like these properties – we praise the good work that they have done and continue to do for conservation – but somewhere we had to draw a line on what to cover. Biodiversity is high in Kenya, with at least 410 mammal species, 1,106 birds, 39 geckos, 24 chameleons, about 120 snakes, and approximately 100 amphibians.

Conservation areas are vital to protect endangered species like Hook-lipped Rhinoceros.

Leopard in Aberdare National Park

Lie of the land

The Aberdare National Park lies within the Aberdare mountain range (known to locals as *Nyandarua*), extending over 160km and running roughly north to south. The boundary line of the park lies on the 2,800m contour and includes several peaks that exceed 3,500m asl, with the highest being Satima, or Oldoinyo Lesatima, at 4,001m. This conservation area covers 766km² and lies just 80km from the continent's second-highest peak, Mount Kenya, of which there are magnificent views from several locations. It is located in Nyandarua County in west-central Kenya, just to the south of the equator and about 100km north of Nairobi. It is a critical watershed, with several rivers rising here. The national park is almost completely ringed at lower altitudes by the Aberdares Forest Reserve, with the much smaller Kipipiri Forest Reserve in the west and the Kikuyu Escarpment Forest along the southern boundary.

Brief history

The Aberdares was named in 1884 after Lord Aberdare, then President of the Royal Geographical Society, but was previously known as the Sattima Range. The park was proclaimed in 1950 as the Aberdare Royal Park. The Aberdare Mountains, and especially their forests, were part of the scene of one of the bloodiest episodes in recent Kenyan history, the Mau Mau uprising in the 1950s. These forests formed the 'headquarters' of one

- Easiest access to subalpine area in Kenya and unique vegetation.
- Outstanding scenic beauty and views across to Mount Kenya.
- Best location to see Bongo and Giant Forest Hog but numbers low of former.
- Highest waterfall in Kenya, Karuru at 273m, in three steps.
- Two of the best-known upmarket lodges in Kenya – The Ark and Treetops.

FACILITIES AND ACTIVITIES

- Upmarket lodges: The Ark and Treetops; Kenya Wildlife Services basic accommodation; four public campsites, special campsites.
- Eight entrance gates.
- Network of roads/tracks; can be difficult going when very wet.
- Hiking with KWS guard but usually not required on higher moorland.
- Game viewing and birdwatching.

of the rebellion leaders, Dedan Kimathi, who ran his wave of terror from here into the surrounding countryside. He was captured and executed in 1957. The Aberdares are believed by the Kikuyu to be one of the homes used by Ngai (god) and called Nyandarua, meaning a 'drying hide' because of its superficial resemblance to a pegged out cattle hide. This is one of the few parks in East Africa that have been fenced in order to better protect the Hook-lipped Rhinoceros population and prevent elephants destroying crops on farmland ringing the park and forest reserve.

Geology and landscape

The Aberdares make up a section of the easternmost wall of the Great Rift Valley, formed by tectonic movement of the Earth's crust. Much of the rock structure is made up of basalts, trachytes and phonolites and the slopes are rather steep to the west but more gently sloping to the east. The range is about 160km in length and has four major peaks, Satima at 4,001m asl, Kinangop at 3,906m, Maratini at 3,698m and Chubuswa

A view of Mount Kenya from the Aberdares

at 3,364m. Altitude ranges from 2,000m to 4,000m asl. Deep ravines slice through the eastern and western slopes and most have streams and impressive waterfalls. Kenya's highest waterfall, Karuru, is located here, as well as Gura and Chania falls. Kenya's longest river, the Tana, rises in the Aberdares, as does the Ewaso Ng'iro, with important flows into Lake Naivasha. It is a critical source of water for the city of Nairobi. Much of the national park lies above the treeline with forest located mainly in the Salient area.

Climate

Mist and rain can be expected pretty much throughout the year. An average 1,000mm falls on the north-western slopes but rising to as much as 3,000mm in the south-east. Generally the heaviest rains fall from October to May. Depending on the season nights can be cool to cold. Temperatures are fairly even throughout the year, with the lowest at the highest altitudes. One can experience thick mist, blue sky, rain and a hail storm all within a space of just two hours.

The Aberdares has some of the most impressive waterfalls in Kenya.

Vegetation

Much of the park lies above the treeline, where there is a rich alpine and subalpine flora referred to largely as moorland, mostly above 3,000m. The most typical and obvious species to be seen here are the **giant lobelias** (*Lobelia deckenii* subsp. *sattimae, L. bambuseti*), which have some of the most impressive flower heads, or inflorescences, in the plant world. Three species of **giant groundsel** (*Dendrosenecio keniensis, D. battiscombei* and *D. keniodendron*) occur, conspicuous with their terminal leaf rosettes atop stout woody trunks. There are several species of **heath** (*Erica* spp.), including the **Giant Heath** (*E. arborea*), which forms dense thickets, and **everlasting** (*Helichrysum* spp.), as well as extensive areas of tussock grasses. At about the 3,000m contour there are extensive stands of the **African Alpine Bamboo** (*Oldeania alpina*). Montane rainforest on the western and north-western slopes is dominated by **African Pencil Cedar**

Giant Lobelias have prominent flower heads.

East African Rosewood thickets form the highest tree belt.

(*Juniperus procera*), **Common Yellowwood** (*Podocarpus falcatus*) and **Wild Elder** (**Muchorowe**) (*Nuxia congesta*). In the south-eastern forests **East African Camphor Wood** (*Ocotea usambarensis*) trees dominate, with mixed **East African Yellowwood** (*Afrocarpus gracilior*) forest in the east. In sheltered gullies on the edge of the moorland are small, almost pure stands of **East African Rosewood** (*Hagenia abyssinica*) woodland with their distinctive thick, peeling bark and dense pinkish-red flower clusters up to 60cm long.

Wildlife
Mammals

Although 73 mammal species are listed, this number can expected to be higher with further studies of smaller species. Although numbers are reduced, **Savanna Elephant** still occur and there is a population of **Hook-lipped Rhinoceros** but they are not commonly seen. **Savanna Buffalo** are common and seen throughout, as they utilize all habitats. **Mountain (Eastern) Bongo** (*Tragelaphus eurycerus isaaci*) are known to survive only in small numbers in the forests of the Aberdares, Mount Kenya, Mount Eburu and the Mau Forest complex.

Bushbuck occur throughout the Aberdares.

In the Aberdares there are perhaps just 50 individuals, constituting about half of the total in the country. The Bongo and **Giant Forest Hog**, the latter now fairly common, were decimated when **Lion** were reintroduced into the park. Since at least most, if not all, of the Lion were removed the hogs, especially, have rebounded. Apart from the Giant Forest Hog, both **Bushpig** and **Common Warthog** occur but only the latter is regularly seen. There are populations of **Common Eland**, and **Bushbuck** (**Imbabala**) are common below the subalpine zone. **Common Duiker** occur throughout but **Black-fronted Duiker** and **Harvey's Red Duiker** are rarely seen. **Bohor Reedbuck, Chanler's Mountain Reedbuck** and **Common Waterbuck** are present but in relatively small numbers. **Leopard** is an important predator but is secretive and seldom seen. The smaller **Serval** is not infrequently seen, especially in the tussock grassland and forest fringes, with melanistic (dark) specimens sometimes observed. The **African Golden Cat** has been reported but we feel that this needs photographic proof. **Spotted Hyaena** occur, even in the forest, and are fairly common but sightings are infrequent. There are occasional sightings of **African Wild Dog** but you would be very lucky to get a view. A number of small carnivore species are present, with the best sightings of **White-tailed Mongoose** and **Common Large-spotted Genet** at the two lodges. **Olive Baboons** are present, as are **Guereza, Sykes's Monkey** and **Vervet Monkey**. The nocturnal **Thick-tailed Greater Galago** occurs but the presence of other galago species has not been confirmed. There are two endemic species, the **Aberdare Mole-shrew** (*Surdisorex norae*), which occurs at altitudes of 2,700–3,350m, and the **Aberdare Mole-rat** (*Tachyoryctes audax*), which is rarely seen but its surface earth mounds are abundant.

Giant Forest Hog is fairly commonly seen in the Aberdares.

Olive Ibis

Birds

At least 290 bird species have been recorded from the Aberdares, of which at least 31 are forest specialists and 20 are considered to be rare species. The highly localized **African Green (Olive) Ibis** is difficult to locate but frequents swampy glades within forest. Other forest dwellers to look for include **African Crowned Eagle, Bar-tailed Trogon, Narina Trogon, Cinnamon-chested Bee-eater, African Green Pigeon, Hartlaub's Turaco, Silvery-cheeked Hornbill** and **White-headed Wood-Hoopoe**. There are three spurfowl to look out for, the **Moorland Spurfowl** (which occupies the

Jackson's Spurfowl

WILDLIFE FACTS

- 73 mammal species, including two endemics.
- Best location in Kenya for Giant Forest Hog.
- 290 bird species, with several specials.

area above the forest line), the **Scaly Spurfowl** (restricted to the forest) and **Jackson's Spurfowl** (a species that is near endemic to the Aberdares and is found in forest and within the bamboo belt). Both lodges put out bird feed and this attracts a wide array of forest species, which is especially the case at Treetops. Another near endemic is **Sharpe's Longclaw**, which can be located on the moorlands, as can **Alpine Chat, Scarlet-tufted Malachite Sunbird** (at least 12 species of sunbird occur in the park), **Aberdare Cisticola** and **Hunter's Cisticola**.

Reptiles and amphibians

No full list of the reptiles and amphibians of the Aberdares has been published but the park is home to many interesting species, including the **Kenya Montane Viper**, known only from the montane moorlands above the 2,700m contour on Mount Kenya and in the Aberdares. Another high-altitude dweller is **Von Höhnel's Chameleon**, known in Kikuyu as **Kimbu**, which occurs above 1,500m in bushes, tall grass and thicket, rarely in large trees, and can occur at high densities. The large (to 38cm) **Kikuyu Three-horned Chameleon** is widespread but in the Aberdares is found only on the forested eastern slopes. The beautifully marked **Aberdare Chameleon** is apparently restricted to a small area at about 3,500m in heath thickets on the slopes of Mount Kinangop in the park. Other lizards of interest include the **Alpine Meadow Lizard** found in the moorland and known only from here and Mount Kenya. A similar species, **Jackson's Forest Lizard**, occurs only on the forest floor. On the amphibian front, the greatest diversity is associated with the forest areas but in the moorland one will find the **Kisolo Toad** (at 3,000m in the Aberdares) and the localized **De Witte's River Frog**. Several reed frog species occur, with one of the largest being the aptly named **Mountain Reed Frog**, which can be found at up to 3,200m and appears to be quite common in the belt where the East African Rosewood trees grow. Other habitat-restricted species include the **Giant Puddle Frog**, which is not large but it is the largest member of the group, with females measuring up to 5cm.

Van Höhnel's Chameleon occurs above 1,500m here.

The Mountain Reed Frog is particularly common in the East African Rosewood belt.

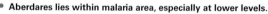

!
- Aberdares lies within malaria area, especially at lower levels.
- Weather can change dramatically and rapidly, so be prepared.
- Camping sites are not fenced, so be alert for potentially dangerous game, such as Savanna Elephant and Savanna Buffalo.
- Rain is frequent and some tracks may become difficult to negotiate.

AMBOSELI NATIONAL PARK

The backdrop of Mount Kilimanjaro is one of the major drawcards of Amboseli.

Lie of the land

Amboseli National Park lies close to the Tanzanian border and in close proximity to Africa's highest mountain, Kilimanjaro. It lies within Loitoktok District, Rift Valley Province, and covers just 392km² within an ecosystem of up to 8,000km² that spans the Kenya/Tanzania border. Several clearwater springs within and close to the park are fed by ice-melt water and rain from Kilimanjaro that filters underground through great layers of volcanic rock. The park lies 240km to the south-east of Nairobi via Namanga. Bordering the park is the Kitirua Game Conservancy to the west and the Elerai Conservancy to the south-east.

Brief history

The Maasai arrived in the area in the 18th century, but evidence shows that the area was occupied by other pastoralists as early as 3,800 years before present and by hunter-gatherers before then. Thus, as with most areas in Africa, humans had a major impact on the environment long before the arrival of Europeans. This area forms part of the tribal range of the Ilkisongo Maasai peoples, who have had a profound impact on the recent history of Amboseli. The first European known to have traversed the area was Joseph Thompson in 1883 and at that time the warlike Maasai referred to the area as *Empusel* meaning 'salty, dusty place' or 'open plain'. In 1906 the British colonial authority set aside the area for the Maasai and it was known simply as the Southern Reserve, an area that was used for resettlement of Maasai from the Great Rift Valley, where their place was taken by white settlers. In 1948 it was designated as a national game reserve. Conflict was inevitable

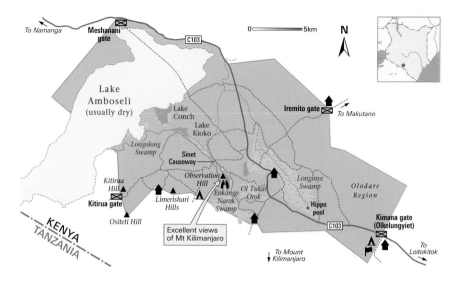

with this proclamation, especially when cattle herders were restricted from bringing their cattle into certain areas within the reserve. At independence, management of Amboseli was taken over by the Kajiado County Council, but numerous conflicts of interest ensued. In 1974 Amboseli was raised to national park status by presidential decree but in 2005 control was once again handed to a local council. Growing human populations and their activities around the boundaries of the park are placing increasing pressures on the ecosystem, with numerous settlements, agriculture and increasing numbers of livestock. This is the second most popular park in Kenya, only behind the Maasai Mara National Reserve.

Geology and landscape

Amboseli lies within a lake basin that was formed during the Pleistocene when lava flows from an erupting Kilimanjaro blocked the course of the Pangani River, Lake Amboseli. Today the lake is mostly dry but it is prone to seasonal flooding. Although the basin floor is flat, there are a number of small extinct volcanic vents such as Lemomo, Kitirua, Ositeti and Nomatior within the greater ecosystem. To the north the park is bounded by the old lake shoreline and to the south it rises gradually to the north-facing flanks of Mount Kilimanjaro. Two fairly large ice-melt swamps, Longinye and Enkongo Narok, lie within the park, as do a number of small freshwater springs and smaller swamps. These are all fed by melting snow and rainfall that fall on

HIGHLIGHTS

- Game viewing with the backdrop of Mount Kilimanjaro.
- Excellent Savanna Elephant viewing.
- The ice-melt springs attract game and a good diversity of birds.
- Cultural visits to local Maasai village.

White-bearded Wildebeest against the spectacular backdrop of Mount Kilimanjaro

Kilimanjaro and then percolate through the porous rocks and soils to keep a subterranean aquifer topped up, which in turn feeds water to the surface. It is these swamps and springs that form the lifeblood of the park. The rocks and soils are of volcanic origin and form clouds of dust in the dry season and glutinous mud during the rains.

Climate

Amboseli is a semi-arid area that receives 200–400mm of rain each year and is prone to extensive droughts. In 1993 unusually heavy rains forced the park to close for several months. Most rainfall is concentrated within two peaks, March to April and November to December. Temperatures are generally moderate but days can be hot and nights mild to cool. Strong winds are relatively frequent.

Vegetation

The vegetation is classified as semi-arid savanna. In its broadest sense the vegetation can be divided into five types, open grassed plains, rocky scrub thornveld, stands of **Fever Tree** (*Vachellia xanthophloea*), open woodland, and wetlands in the form of swamps, marshes and springs. In the open woodland areas the **Umbrella Thorn** (*Vachellia tortilis*) is common but stands are no longer as abundant as in the past due to elephant activity. There are thickets of **Toothbrush Tree** (*Salvadora persica*), more a bush than a tree, and *Suaeda monoica* on the open alkaline plain.

FACILITIES AND ACTIVITIES

- Several lodges in and just outside the park, a number of tented camps and a public campsite.
- Road network very dusty in dry season, often difficult to negotiate after heavy rain.
- Bush walks with armed guard from some lodges outside the park.

Elephant here have been the subject of the longest continuous study of elephant in Africa.

Wildlife
Mammals

Amboseli is best known for its stable **Savanna Elephant** population, which is the subject of the longest study (ongoing since 1972) ever undertaken on Africa's largest land mammal. There are up to 1,500 Savanna Elephant within the ecosystem, many of which concentrate here during the dry season to access the springs and swamps for water and food. They commonly wade into the swamps to feed, as do **Savanna Buffalo**. It is one of the few Elephant range areas in East Africa that have not been heavily impacted by ivory poaching. Amboseli was once home to a population of **Hook-lipped Rhinoceros**, but these were targeted and wiped out by poachers. There are reasonable numbers of **Plains Zebra** and **White-bearded Wildebeest**, but there is some movement out of the park and numbers fluctuate. There are also **Common Waterbuck, Bohor Reedbuck, Grant's** and **Thomson's gazelles, Impala, Coke's Hartebeest (Kongoni)** and **Maasai Giraffe**. There is also a small population of **Common Hippopotamus** in the swamps and reasonable numbers of **Common Warthog**. The **Spotted Hyaena** is the most commonly observed large carnivore, with sightings of **Lion, Leopard** and **Cheetah** much less frequent. The **African Wolf** (previously Golden Jackal) is sometimes sighted but the **Black-backed Jackal** is more commonly seen. **Bat-eared Fox** also occur, as do **Serval**

Spotted Hyaenas cooling off on a hot day in Amboseli

Plains Zebra drinking water at a snow-melt spring

and **Caracal**, but sightings are not common. The **Common Large-spotted Genet** is sometimes seen at night around the camps and lodges, as are the **African Civet** and **White-tailed Mongoose**. The most commonly seen small carnivores are the diurnal and troop-living **Banded Mongoose** and **Dwarf Mongoose**. Primates are not well represented but include **Yellow Baboon** and **Vervet Monkey**. Although the current mammal list stands at 92 species it is likely higher, as small rodents, bats and shrews have not been fully surveyed.

Birds

The current bird list of more than 400 species, of which some 47 are raptors, is believed to cover the Amboseli ecosystem and not just the park, which includes forest on the slopes Oldoinyo Orok. The best birding is to be found around the swamps and thorn thickets in the vicinity of the lodges and camps. The largest of all is the **Maasai Ostrich**, which is fairly common throughout. Of the 14 heron, egret and bittern species, several are resident, including **Goliath Heron**, and the **Madagascar Squacco Heron** is a non-breeding migrant. Another large wading resident is the **Saddle-billed Stork**, with **Marabou** regularly sighted. The marsh areas are particularly productive with resident **Long-toed Lapwing, Blacksmith Lapwing, Black Crake** and **African Jacana**, among others. Many other species visit the swamps seasonally, including non-breeding

WILDLIFE FACTS

- More than 400 bird species, including at least 47 different raptors.
- 92 mammal species but likely not a full inventory.
- One of the best locations in Kenya to observe relaxed Savanna Elephants.

Long-toed Lapwing

Clear views of Mount Kilimanjaro are limited due to frequent cloud cover.

Toads commonly forage under the lodge lights at night.

Palaearctic waders. On the plains and in the open woodlands no less than six bustard species occur, ranging from the large **Kori Bustard** to the smaller **White-bellied Bustard** and the relatively common **Buff-crested Bustard**. The three species of **sandgrouse, Chestnut-bellied, Black-faced** and **Yellow-throated**, are best observed when they come to the swamps and spill-overs to drink, especially during the dry season, when numbers are highest. In the thickets around the lodges 13 weavers are recorded, including the **Taveta Golden Weaver**, which is one of the most localized weavers in Kenya but is common here. Also around here are the **Superb Starling, Grey-headed Silver-bill** and eight waxbill species. This is also a hotspot for shrikes and their relatives, with no less than 18 species (several of them seasonal migrants), mostly found in the thickets and woodland.

Reptiles and amphibians

A comprehensive list is not available for Amboseli but both the **Leopard Tortoise** and **Speke's Hinged Tortoise** occur and **Helmeted Terrapin** are present in the swamps. Potentially at least five gecko species could be present, with **Scheffler's Dwarf Gecko** confirmed. Several skink species occur, including **Short-necked Skink, Tree Skink, Striped Skink** and **Variable Skink**. The large (to 55cm) **Great Plated Lizard** is present in the area but it is secretive and difficult to observe. Only two chameleon species are known to occur, the widespread **Flap-necked Chameleon** and the **Slender Chameleon**. One of the most obvious lizards is the **Red-headed Rock Agama** (the male having a red head and contrasting blue body), which occurs in rocky areas among thorn thicket. Snakes are usually retiring and seldom seen but, among others, the **Southern African Rock Python** is present, which cannot be mistaken for any other. When visiting the park the only snake the authors saw was the **Black-necked Spitting Cobra**.

The amphibian list is probably not great but several toads – including **Garman's Toad** and **Guttural Toad** – may be seen at the lodges, where they hunt insects that are attracted by the lights. During the rainy seasons you are likely to hear frog choruses, especially around the swamps.

- Amboseli is a malaria area.
- Be alert for potentially dangerous game – lodges and camps are not fenced.
- Roads are very dusty in the dry season and very muddy during rains.
- This is the second-busiest park in Kenya, so expect many safari and lodge vehicles.

LAKE NAKURU NATIONAL PARK

This small park is home to an incredible diversity of birds and mammals.

Lie of the land

Lake Nakuru National Park has Nakuru town at its fringe, which lies 156km from Nairobi. The park covers 188km² (of which about one-third is taken up by the lake when full) and lies at an altitude of 1,754m asl. Nakuru lies between the Aberdares in the east and the Mau escarpment in the west, and is dominated by the soda lake and an escarpment known as Baboon Cliffs to the east of the road.

Brief history

Excavations at Hyrax Hill near Nakuru have shown that seasonal and permanent human settlements were present at least 3,000 years before present during the Neolithic, with more recent indications of Iron-Age burial pits and various stone structures. It is likely that the lakeshore area was occupied at least 30,000 years before present by a people known as the Eburran, with the most recent settlers being the Maasai. The park was proclaimed in 1968 with the main intention of protecting the large numbers of flamingos. In 1974 the park was expanded to include more of the surrounding savanna. It has become a significant location for the protection of Hook-lipped and Square-lipped rhinoceroses and for this reason it has been completely fenced. Its name is derived from the Maa language, *en akuro*, which translates as 'swirling dust', a reference to the clouds of fine dust that are raised around the lake's edge when the wind blows. Issues of pollution into the lake from the growing town of Nakuru and offtake of water in the catchment are growing problems. The only fish species here is the introduced alkaline-tolerant cichlid (*Oreochromis alcalicus*), which was introduced in an attempt to control mosquito numbers. They now serve as a food source for numerous piscivorous birds.

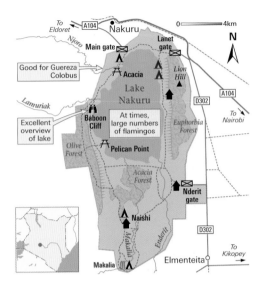

Geology and landscape

Lake Nakuru catchment basin is a closed drainage system, without outlets, covering some 1,800km². The lake is fed by the Makalia, Njoro and Enderit rivers. The lake itself is small, shallow, and has alkaline-saline water that once covered a much larger area, estimated at 700km², and incorporated the lakes Elmenteita and Naivasha. At that stage, some 10,000 years before present, it was a freshwater lake. Nakuru is subject to considerable variation in extent and depth (maximum 3m) and at times has totally dried out. The park lies in the eastern arm of the Rift Valley and has steep broken cliffs rising in the east. The rocks here are largely of volcanic origin (including lava flows and pyroclastics) from the Tertiary-Quaternary era.

Climate

The area is classified as dry sub-humid to semi-arid with a warm and temperate climate. March is the hottest month and July the coldest but there is only 2°C difference between the averages. Rain falls mainly during the winter months (April to August) with an annual average of 895mm, with lowest falls December to February.

HIGHLIGHTS

- Greater and Lesser flamingos, sometimes in vast numbers.
- Great mammal and bird diversity.
- High densities of Defassa Waterbuck and Common Warthog.
- One of the best locations for Chanler's Mountain Reedbuck and Guereza Colobus in Kenya.
- Easy access.

The view of Lake Nakuru from Baboon Cliffs is impressive.

Vegetation

Areas around the lake fringes consist mainly of short grassland dominated by **Bunchgrass** (*Sporobolus spicatus*), with other grasses taking its place further from the lake. On slightly higher ground there are extensive areas of large **Fever Trees**, with **East African Olive** (**Black Ironwood**) (*Olea hochstetteri*) and in bushland there are thickets of **Camphor Bush** (known locally as **Leleshwa**) (*Tarchonanthus camphoratus*) and the woody shrub **Sticky Psiadia** (*Psiadia punctulata*) with its abundance of small yellow flowers. On the rocky hills of the east the succulent **Candelabra Tree** (*Euphorbia candelabrum*) is common and forms woodland in places. In the north of the park there are a number of **acacia** tree species (*Vachellia* and *Senegalia*).

Wildlife
Mammals

This is an important park for the conservation of both **Hook-lipped Rhinoceros** and **Square-lipped Rhinoceros** (introduced from South Africa), as well as **Northern Giraffe** (form **Rothschild's**). There are high populations of **Defassa Waterbuck** and **Common Warthog**, with significant numbers of **Chanler's Mountain Reedbuck, Bohor Reedbuck, Impala,**

FACILITIES AND ACTIVITIES

- Nine campsites, two privately owned lodges.
- Limited road network.
- Game viewing and birdwatching.
- Picnic and viewing sites.

Square-lipped Rhinoceros introduced from South Africa

Lake Nakuru has one of the highest densities of Defassa Waterbuck in Kenya.

WILDLIFE FACTS

- A bird list of about 450 species, including seasonal migrants.
- 57 mammal species (incomplete).
- 575 plant species.
- No reptile or amphibian list.
- One of the densest Defassa Waterbuck populations in Kenya.

Bohor Reedbuck ram and ewe

Guereza are localized but quite common.

Thomson's Gazelle, Grant's Gazelle, Common Eland, Bushbuck (Imbabala), Naivasha Dik-dik and Savanna Buffalo, Common Hippopotamus (not easily observed), Plains Zebra, Olive Baboon, Vervet Monkey and Guereza (Black and White Colobus). The latter are usually associated with the Fever Tree forest. On the predator front there are small populations of Lion, Leopard and Cheetah, as well as Spotted Hyaena, but one has to wonder how sustainable these large predators are in such a small park. Striped Hyaena is also present but is rarely seen. Smaller predators include Black-backed Jackal, Bat-eared Fox and the social Banded Mongoose. Both Rock Hyrax and Yellow-spotted Rock Hyrax are present in the eastern rocky areas and are easily observed.

Birds

Great White Pelicans at Lake Nakuru

Most people visit Lake Nakuru to experience one of Africa's greatest spectacles, the immense concentration of Greater and Lesser flamingos. Within the soda lake 'necklace' system of East Africa these great pink-and-white flocks are highly mobile, and may number up to 2 million, with Lesser Flamingos outnumbering Greater. The flamingos use the lake for feeding but do not breed here. Unfortunately, pollution and other issues have reduced the spectacle, as they have largely dispersed to other soda lakes such as Lake Bogoria. Substantial numbers of Great White Pelican and Wood Stork are often present along the fringes of the lake, especially in the south. Apart from resident wading species,

Lake Nakuru is one of the easiest areas to reach for mass flamingo viewing.

large numbers of Palaearctic waders arrive during the northern winter but viewing is difficult as it is not possible to approach the lake edge in most areas. The area is rich in raptors with 42 species, including **Verreaux's Eagle, Long-crested Eagle, African Fish Eagle, Augur Buzzard** and **African Marsh Harrier** being commonly sighted. On the smaller side, a few specials include **Kenya Rufous Sparrow, Speke's Weaver, Schallow's Wheatear, Northern Puffback, Long-tailed Widowbird** and **Brown-backed Scrub-Robin.**

Reptiles and amphibians

Little has been recorded on the herpetofauna of this park but **Southern African Rock Python** occurs, as does the **Puff Adder.** The country endemic **Kenya Horned Viper**, known by the Maasai as **Nturububwa en-kiti**, is recorded from here. The **Yellow-throated Plated Lizard** is not commonly seen but has distinctive yellow stripes. The **Elmenteita Rock Agama** (Kenya's largest agama at up to 45cm) occurs in the rocky areas in the east. If you stay in one of the lodges watch for the **Tropical House Gecko** hunting insects around lights at night.

- Lake Nakuru is a malaria area.
- Be alert for potentially dangerous game at camps and viewpoints.
- Nakuru town is a notorious con artist zone.

Augur Buzzard

MERU NATIONAL PARK COMPLEX

Grevy's Zebra are endangered outside the few parks where they occur.

Lie of the land

Meru National Park covers just 870km² and is flanked to the south by Mwingi National Reserve and Kora National Park (1,788km²), and to the east by Bisanadi National Reserve. Rahole National Reserve borders on Kora in the east and lies within Eastern Province. This complex of conservation areas extends over 5,278km² but only Meru is seriously managed and is the second-largest such area in Kenya after the Tsavo complex. It lies 85km to the east of the town of Meru and 350km north-east of Nairobi. The park lies astride the equator and is bisected by 13 spring-fed rivers and streams, centred on the Tana River. It lies within the Somali-Maasai Regional Centre of Endemism.

Brief history

Meru was made famous during the course of the 1960s by the reintroduction of lions here by Joy and George Adamson, best known of which was the lioness Elsa. A memorial commemorates Joy's conservation work. George was killed by poachers in the adjoining Kora National Park in 1989. Poaching levels were extremely high, mainly during the 1980s and 1990s, to the point where there seemed little hope for the park's revival, and the government gave serious consideration to de-gazetting the park and turning part of the area over to rice farming. At the beginning of the 1980s some 3,500 Savanna Elephant lived within the Meru ecosystem but by 1989 there were just 210 individuals remaining. Since there has been an effort to improve management and reduce poaching levels.

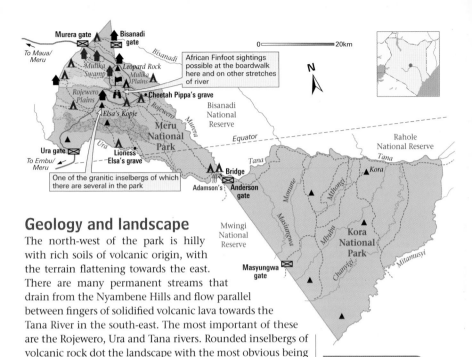

African Finfoot sightings possible at the boardwalk here and on other stretches of river

0 ————————— 20km

One of the granitic inselbergs of which there are several in the park

Geology and landscape

The north-west of the park is hilly with rich soils of volcanic origin, with the terrain flattening towards the east. There are many permanent streams that drain from the Nyambene Hills and flow parallel between fingers of solidified volcanic lava towards the Tana River in the south-east. The most important of these are the Rojewero, Ura and Tana rivers. Rounded inselbergs of volcanic rock dot the landscape with the most obvious being Mughwango Hill and Leopard Rock.

Climate

A semi-arid area with irregular rainfall within the April to June and November to December wet seasons, with the heaviest falls in April and May. The highest rainfall is in the west of the park with an annual average of about 700mm, while the east averages some 325mm. There can be considerable variation year on year and the area is drought prone.

Vegetation

The higher-lying ridge country is dominated by grassland well wooded with **bushwillow** (*Combretum*) species, especially **Red Bushwillow** (*Combretum apiculatum*), and blends into **acacia** wooded grassland eastwards. Species such as **Umbrella Thorn** (*Vachellia tortilis*) and **Gum Acacia** (*Senegalia senegal*) usually dominate. The tall and abundant **Doum Palms** (*Hyphaene coriacea*) are commonly associated with the river courses, as well as **Raffia Palm** (*Raphia farinifera*), **Wild Date Palm** (*Phoenix reclinata*), **Sycamore Fig** (*Ficus sycomorus*) distinguished by its large size, spread and light-coloured bark, **Newtonia** (**Mukui**) (*Newtonia hildebrandtii*), **River Acacia** (**Mgunga**) (*Vachellia*

HIGHLIGHTS

- Not frequented by the mass tourism industry.
- High game and bird diversity.
- Semi-arid area specials including Grevy's Zebra, Lesser Kudu and Gerenuk.

Hippo viewing platform at Meru

A diversity of creepers grow here.

A school of Common Hippopotamus in a pool on the Tana River

Bright's Gazelle ram

elatior) and **Broadpod Robust Thorn** (*Vachellia robusta*). The **Tana River Poplar** (*Populus ilicifolia*) can reach 30m in height, is commonly associated with the river of the same name and is the most southerly growing member of the genus in the world. In the more arid east and south-east there is a mix of fairly uniform *Vachellia-Senegalia-Commiphora* bush country that in places forms dense thickets. The **Baobab** (*Adansonia digitata*) is fairly common, particularly in the northern reaches of the park. **Rhodes Grass** (*Chloris gayana*) occurs pretty much throughout and is critical for grazing species. In the extreme north the southern fringe of the Ngaia Forest extends into the park.

Wildlife
Mammals

Both **Hook-lipped** and **Square-lipped rhinoceros** (South African origin) are under heavy guard in a fenced 84km² area within the park. Naturally occurring Hook-lipped Rhino were wiped out by poachers. **Savanna Elephant** numbers are increasing and there is a healthy population of **Common Hippopotamus**, especially in the pools along the Tana and Rojewero rivers. There are populations of **Reticulated Giraffe, Grevy's Zebra, Plains Zebra (Grant's), Lesser Kudu, Coke's Hartebeest (Kongoni), Common Waterbuck, Impala, Bohor Reedbuck, Beisa Oryx, Gerenuk** and **Bright's Gazelle** (previously a subspecies of Grant's Gazelle). **Savanna Buffalo** are also present, as are **Common Eland** and **Kirk's Dik-dik**. Of the five primate species known to

Square-lipped Rhinoceros in Meru

occur in the park, only troops of **Olive Baboon** and **Vervet Monkey** are commonly seen. **Lion**, **Leopard** and **Cheetah** occur, as do **Spotted Hyaena** and **African Wild Dog**. On one visit the authors stopped at the tree under which Joy Adamson had her camp when raising a cheetah cub, Pippa, and as we sat there two Cheetah strolled past within 20m, a special experience. Small carnivores are well represented but many are nocturnal and seldom seen, however **Serval** are fairly common and not infrequently seen hunting small rodents in well-grassed areas. Troops of **Banded** and **Dwarf mongooses** are the most frequently seen, as they are diurnal and social. Being nocturnal, the large **African Civet** is rarely seen but its large dung middens are a sure sign of its presence. Among the rock outcrops both the **Rock Hyrax** and **Yellow-spotted Rock Hyrax** are common, the latter being more grey, with a light dorsal spot and white eyebrow stripes. They often lie together when sunning, but when feeding the latter often forages in the bushes and trees, whereas the Rock Hyrax feeds mainly on the ground. Another diurnal mammal commonly seen here is the **Unstriped Ground Squirrel**. No detailed survey of the smaller species has been undertaken in Meru but the mammal list should easily exceed 100 species if bats are taken into account.

Cheetah are quite frequently seen in the more open areas.

Birds

More than 300 bird species occur in Meru, with at least another 120 species in the entire complex. Some 59 of the 94 Somali-Maasai biome species in Kenya have been recorded in the park. Some specials include **African Finfoot**, **Pel's Fishing Owl**, **Saddle-billed Stork**, **Martial Eagle** and **Grant's Wood-Hoopoe** (previously given as a subspecies of the Violet Wood-Hoopoe). Apart from the Martial Eagle, a further 37 species of raptor have been recorded, most as residents, some as seasonal migrants, of which six are vultures. The small **Red-necked Falcon** is closely associated with the areas of Doum Palms, particularly in the north-east. Wherever there are clusters of social weaver nests one should watch for the diminutive **Pygmy Falcon**. **Yellow-necked Spurfowl** and **Crested Francolin** are common, as is the **Helmeted Guineafowl**, and although less abundant both the **Vulturine** and **Kenya Crested guineafowl** occur. Of the seven owl species, most are widespread but **Pel's Fishing Owl** is largely restricted to the taller trees along the banks of the Tana and Rojewero rivers. This area is a **nightjar** hotspot with six species, but as they

- Several KWS self-catering options, one private lodge (Elsa's Kopje) and 10 campsites, public and special.
- There are several lodges just outside the park boundary.
- Network of game-viewing tracks.
- Game viewing and birdwatching.
- Hiking with an armed ranger might be feasible.

Crested Francolin

Serrated Hinged Terrapin

WILDLIFE FACTS

- 300 bird species in Meru; 427 species in the complex.
- About 720 plant species, with a number of endemics.
- Probably >100 mammal species but not fully surveyed; 22 carnivore species known, 16 antelope and five primates.

are nocturnal a knowledge of their calls is required. Of the five swift species the most easily identified is the extremely slender-winged **African Palm Swift**, especially around stands of Doum Palms. With 20 shrike species, this is a true shrike hotspot but several species skulk and seldom show themselves, including the tchagras and bushshrikes. However, some species, such as the **Long-tailed Fiscal**, **Fiscal** and **Rosy-patched shrikes** commonly sit in prominent positions affording good views. Of the eight starling species the **Golden-breasted Starling** and the aptly named **Superb Starling** stand out from the 'flock'. The limited-range **Smaller Black-bellied Sunbird** favours areas with flowering parasitic plants growing in acacia trees, usually in association with the rivers. Most of the 15 **weaver** species are associated with riverine vegetation, but **Buffalo** and **Social weavers** are mainly in woodland. The restricted-range **Golden Palm Weaver** occurs.

Reptiles and amphibians

Once again, as with many Kenyan parks, very little is known about the herpetofauna of the Meru ecosystem. **Nile Crocodiles** are common in some of the river systems, as is the large **Nile Monitor**, with **White-throated Monitor** in drier areas. Another large lizard here is the **Great Plated Lizard**, which can reach a length of 55cm and may be encountered in most habitats, especially on rock outcrops. Here also the **Red-headed Agama** is fairly common, with the territorial brightly coloured males standing on the top of boulders watching for rival males. Pythons are present, most likely the **Central African Rock Python**, as this is recorded from much of the length of the Tana River. Although the Black Mamba is not known from Meru the **Green Mamba** does occur. Other venomous species include **Black-necked Spitting Cobra**, **Red Spitting Cobra**, **Puff Adder**, **Rhombic Night Adder** and **Boomslang**. **Serrated Hinged Terrapins** are common wherever there is permanent water and may be seen at times on the backs of partially submerged hippos.

A preliminary survey of amphibians in Meru identified just 13 species in seven genera but it is likely that with further sampling this tally will be much higher.

- **Meru lies within a malaria area.**
- **Roads can be difficult to negotiate after heavy rain.**
- **Dense vegetation can make game viewing difficult.**
- **Tsetse flies present.**

MOUNT KENYA NATIONAL PARK

The view towards Lenana, which rises to 4,985m asl on Mount Kenya

Lie of the land

Mount Kenya is the second-highest mountain in Africa, rising to 5,199m asl, surpassed by Mount Kilimanjaro in Tanzania. Only the area above the forest line, from the 3,150m contour, is national park and extends over 715km². The mountain dominates the skyline of the central highlands and lies just on the equator, about 200km north of Nairobi. There are six entry points to the park.

Brief history

Mount Kenya, known locally as Kirinyaga, is considered to be holy by the Kikuyu and Meru peoples that live in the surrounding areas. Although early man almost certainly lived on the lower slopes of the mountain, the only certain evidence relates to the Early and Recent Iron Ages, known for the Kwale and Gatung'ang'a wares and relating to Bantu-speaking settlers. Tribes in the vicinity of Mount Kenya today derive from a group known as the Thagicu, who migrated from the north between the 12th and 14th centuries, with a splinter group settling on the mountain's south-western slopes. Archaeological evidence indicates that these people hunted game, kept sheep and goats, and forged iron tools and weapons. Dr Johann Ludwig Krapf, a missionary, was the first European to sight the mountain in 1849. The first successful ascent of the highest peak, Batian, was by Sir Halford J. Mackinder, Josef Brocherel and Cesar Ollier in September of 1899. Mount Kenya National Park was gazetted in 1949 and in 1997 was proclaimed as a UNESCO World Heritage Site. The forest reserves on the lower slopes are heavily exploited and there are logging, poaching and other illegal activities in the park itself.

- Incredible scenery.
- Relatively low visitor numbers.
- Great diversity of plants, especially in the subalpine zone.
- One of best locations to see Mountain Bongo (at Mount Kenya Safari Club).

- Vehicle tracks go no further than the trail heads. Guides and porters are recommended if you go to the peaks.
- There are a number of public campsites and mountain huts, with a number of lodge options near the park boundary.
- Game viewing limited but good birdwatching.

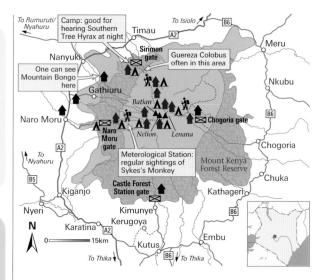

Geology and landscape

Mount Kenya, Africa's second-highest mountain, is a complex of three distinct peaks: Batian at 5,199m, Nelion at 5,188m and Lenana rising to 4,985m. Unlike Kilimanjaro, this is an extinct stratovolcano that was formed between 3.1 and 2.6 million years before present. It is estimated that its original height might have been a massive 7,000m. However, erosion, to a large extent the work of glaciers, has exacted a severe toll, a whole 2,000m eroded away. All volcanic activity in the central vent probably ceased more than 2 million years ago but some activity continued until 100,000 years before present in the

Rugged gorge and valley on the Chogoria route, Mount Kenya

vicinity of the volcano. As with Kilimanjaro, Mount Kenya's glaciers are in rapid retreat. Eight of the original glaciers described by Professor J.W. Gregory have since melted, and it is unlikely that the remainder will survive far into the 21st century. The mountain is deeply dissected by glacial valleys and there are 20 small glacial tarns, or lakes, with large deposits of glacial moraine above 3,950m. The rocks on Mount Kenya are mainly basalts, porphyrites, phonolites, kenytes and trachytes.

Remnant of Lewis Glacier

The mountain is an important source of water for the country both from snowmelt and rainfall runoff.

Climate

Mount Kenya has an equatorial mountain climate that has been described as having winter each night and summer every day. This is, of course, a rather dramatic simplification. Mid-March to June receives the heaviest rain, with lower falls from October to December. The months between the rainy seasons receive lesser falls but are not completely dry. A typical day starts with a crystal clear sky. As the ground begins to warm up, heated air starts to rise up the mountain and by mid-morning the cloud layer is at about 3,000m. By midday the entire mountain is shrouded in dense cloud. In the afternoon, rain, sleet, hail or snow (depending on the altitude) is common, but as the rising air begins to cool in the evening the cloud descends, leaving only the stars and planets to commune with the peaks. At the highest altitudes frost usually occurs every night. Highest average rainfall of about 2,500mm occurs in the south-east at around 3,000m (at 4,500m only 700mm falls).

Tussock grasses dominate above the tree line.

Vegetation

The vegetation of Mount Kenya can be divided into six broad zones, from the lower slopes forest zone, bamboo zone (lacking in the north), cloud forest, heathland, Afro-alpine and the nival zone on the peaks. The lower mixed forest belt has mainly evergreen trees on the wetter slopes and more semi-deciduous species where less rain falls. There are extensive stands of **African Pencil Cedar** (*Juniperus procera*) and **East African Yellowwood** (*Afrocarpus gracilior*), and the northern slopes have some magnificent stands of the latter. Here also are **East African Camphor** (**Muwong**) (*Ocotea usambarensis*), which can reach heights of 35–45m, and **African Olive** (**Wild Olive**) (*Olea europaea*). In the wetter areas of the south-west and

Trunk of an African Pencil Cedar

Giant Groundsel, or Senecio

Giant Groundsel are common in the subalpine zone and have evolved to survive the frequent freezing temperatures.

north-east **Pillarwood** (*Cassipourea malosana*) is dominant. As one rises to the cloud (mist) forest one also starts to encounter the **African Alpine Bamboo** (*Oldeania alpina*) belt, which is intermingled with the higher forest, including **Yellowwood** (*Podocarpus milanjianus*), or closely associated with it and in places the bamboo is extremely dense. The cloud forest consists mainly of a low and dense canopy of trees that are smaller (from 12–20m) than those found at lower levels, but in places there are tall African Pencil Cedars and also **East African Rosewood** (*Hagenia abyssinica*). Because of the high precipitation here the tree branches are often thickly festooned with 'gardens' of ferns, bryophytes, epiphytic orchids and lichens. It is here that you will encounter your first **giant lobelias** (*Lobelia bambuseti* and *L. gibberoa*). Beyond the bamboo and montane forest belts one moves into the heathland with its ericaceous scrub, which includes low scrub but also the **Giant Heath** (*Erica arborea*) that may form dense thickets, as well as the **Sugarbush** (*Protea caffra* subsp. *kilimandscharica*). In the Afro-alpine, mainly above 3,200m, plants are best adapted to withstand the rigours of high-altitude living. It is here one encounters some of the most dramatic of the high-mountain plants, the **giant groundsels** (*Dendrosenecio keniodendron* and *D. keniensis*), **giant lobelias** (including *Lobelia deckenii* and *L. telekii*) and extensive areas of tussock grass. In order to survive freezing, the leaves provide insulation for developing buds and some even produce a thick, sticky substance that serves as a very effective anti-freeze.

Wildlife
Mammals

Savanna Elephant and **Savanna Buffalo** occur throughout, even on to the heathland and subalpine, but in low numbers. In recent years poaching of elephant for their ivory has greatly reduced their numbers. In general, as with all tropical montane zones, game numbers are low and animals are difficult to observe. This is one of only two parks in Kenya where you have a chance of seeing the endangered mountain race of the **Bongo**, although sightings are few and far between. The most commonly observed antelope is the **Bushbuck** (**Imbabala**) and in the heath- and moorland the **Common Duiker**. There is an isolated population of

Mountain Bongo bull

The Rock Hyrax high on Mount Kenya have long coats.

Sykes's Monkey can be found in the forest and bamboo thickets.

Black-fronted Duiker, as well as unknown numbers of **Giant Forest Hog**, **Bushpig** in the forested and bamboo zones, with **Common Eland** mainly on the moorland and subalpine. The most obvious of the primates is the **Guereza (Eastern Black and White Colobus)** and the **Mount Kenya Sykes's Monkey**. The latter occurs in all the forested areas and some troops are approachable, especially around campgrounds, where they can be a nuisance. **Olive Baboon** troops may be encountered pretty much throughout but less so in the subalpine zone. The **Mount Kenya Potto**, a subspecies, lives in the lower-lying forests but is unlikely to be seen and in fact may be extinct. Colonies of the small, tailless **Rock Hyrax** are present, with an endemic subspecies in the glacial moraines of the subalpine and alpine zones. These are somewhat larger than lower living forms and have noticeably longer coats, an adaptation to the cold environment. In the forest areas at night there is a good chance of hearing the blood-chilling calls of the **Southern Tree Hyrax**, which reaches high densities in some parts of the park. On the predator front, **Leopard** occur but are seldom seen, and there are small numbers of **Spotted Hyaena**. In forest clearings, along trails and on the heathlands there are numerous piles of loose earth, which are the creations of one of the most abundant of the mountain mammals, the **Mount Kenya Root-rat**. However, as they seldom venture to the surface you are unlikely to see this fossorial rodent. Another endemic is the **Mount Kenya Mole Shrew**, which occupies the bamboo belt and the adjacent heath- and grassland.

Defassa Waterbuck bull

Hartlaub's Turaco is a common resident in the forests on Mount Kenya.

Birds

Bird diversity is greatest in the forest belt with one of the most sought after being the **Olive Ibis**, which occurs in clearings adjacent to forest streams. The **African Crowned Eagle** may be seen circling over the forest canopy seeking out its mainly monkey prey, with other raptors here including **Ayres's Hawk Eagle, Long Crested Eagle, Augur Buzzard** and the **Cuckoo Falcon**. Birds are not easy to watch in the forested areas but **Scaly Spurfowl** and **Jackson's Spurfowl** are fairly common, as is the **Montane Spurfowl**, which occurs in the grassland and heath above the forest belt. Other forest species to watch out for include **Olive Pigeon, Bronze-naped Pigeon, Hartlaub's Turaco, Red-headed Parrot, Cinnamon-chested Bee-eater, Silvery-cheeked Hornbill** and **Orange Ground Thrush**. A few species are best located around bamboo stands, including **White-starred Robin** and **Abyssinian Crimsonwing**. In more open alpine and subalpine areas the largest raptor is **Verreaux's Eagle**. This is also the home of one of Africa's finest owls, **Mackinder's Eagle-Owl**, which roosts and breeds on the cliffs above the moorlands. Birdlife at these higher altitudes is sparse but one of the highlights is the courtship display of the male **Scarlet-tufted Malachite Sunbird**, flashing his red shoulder patches and spreading his wings. Another denizen of these uplands is the rather dull-coloured **Alpine (Moorland) Chat**.

Reptiles and amphibians

Several reptile species are endemic, or near endemic, to Mount Kenya (not specifically the park). These include **Mount Kenya Hornless Chameleon, Mount Kenya Side-striped Chameleon, Mount Kenya Worm Snake, Kenya Montane Viper** and **Mount Kenya Bush Viper**. The common **Mountain Reed Frog** occurs to about 3,350m on the east of the mountain. There are two near-endemic frogs, **Giant Puddle Frog** (to about 2,000m) and **Mount Kenya Puddle Frog**. A survey up from Chogorio and Sirimon tracks covering zones between 1,700m and 3,800m asl found **Alpine Meadow Lizard** to be common in parts, and **Jackson's Chameleon** occurred up to 3,000m.

WILDLIFE FACTS

- At least 85 mammal species but number could be higher.
- One of two parks that have the endangered Mountain Bongo.
- >300 bird species, including rarities such as Olive Ibis.
- Several endemic or near-endemic reptiles, such as Mount Kenya Bush Viper.
- No definitive list of amphibians.

- Malaria at lower altitudes.
- Weather can change rapidly and hikers and climbers should be prepared.
- Be aware of altitude sickness if you head for the peaks.
- Presence of potentially dangerous species such as Savanna Buffalo and Savanna Elephant.
- Approach tracks to trail heads are poorly maintained and slippery during rain.

Nairobi National Park is under increasing pressure from settlements around the boundary. Here Maasai Ostrich strut across the grasslands.

Lie of the land

Nairobi National Park is situated just 10km south of central Nairobi, and the city's buildings are visible from most parts of the park. It is the only protected area within the Athi-Kapiti ecosystem and makes up just 10%, or 117km², of it. Much of the park lies on a relatively flat plateau with deep, rocky cuts created by the Athi River and its short tributaries. It is fenced on three sides but to the south it is open to the Athi Plains. This is crucial to some of the game species, such as White-bearded Wildebeest and Plains Zebra, which migrate out of the park during the rains. This migration is becoming increasingly broken because of the development on the Athi-Kapiti Plains of farms and erection of fencing and settlements. In the near future it is likely that the entire park will have to be fenced and certain game species will see diminishing numbers, as is already the case.

Brief history

It is known that San peoples had lived in the area for thousands of years before the arrival of first Southern Cushite and then Eastern Cushite peoples about 1,000 years before present, to be followed by Nilotes and various Bantu peoples. This was a process that occurred over much of East Africa. The Maasai were the dominant group in the area when the British colonists arrived and they still occupy parts of the Athi Plains. The British arrived in the late 19th century, whereafter the once-abundant game numbers began to dwindle. In 1946, after the intervention of conservationist Mervyn Cowie, the Nairobi Royal Park was proclaimed,

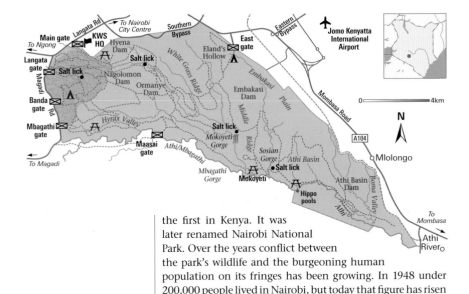

the first in Kenya. It was later renamed Nairobi National Park. Over the years conflict between the park's wildlife and the burgeoning human population on its fringes has been growing. In 1948 under 200,000 people lived in Nairobi, but today that figure has risen to well over 3.5 million!

Geology and landscape

The landscape is dominated by a relatively flat plateau with deep, rocky cuts created by the Athi (Mbagathi) River and several short tributaries. Unfortunately, man-made structures ring the park and are its most obvious landscape features. Most of the rocks and soils in the park are of metamorphic volcanic origin. The park falls in the altitude range of 1,540–1,780m.

Climate

January to March is hot and dry, with April to December generally hot and wet but variable. Average annual rainfall is about 869mm.

Vegetation

Over 90% of the park is dominated by mainly open grassland, which can be divided into short- and long-grassed areas, with scattered **acacias** (*Vachellia* and *Senegalia*). Along watercourses there are denser stands of distinctive species such as **Fever Tree** (*Vachellia xanthophloea*) and other **acacia** species. On higher ground and along watercourses there are small areas of dry forest, including such species as **African Olive (Wild Olive)** (*Olea europaea*), **Orange-leaved Croton** (*Croton dichogamus*), **Silver Oak (Muhugu)** (*Brachylaena*

HIGHLIGHTS

- Easy access from Nairobi and suitable for a day trip.
- Great diversity of game species and birds.
- Reasonably well maintained road network.
- One of the best Kenyan locations to see Hook-lipped Rhinoceros.

huillensis) and **Cape Chestnut** (**Murarachi**) (*Calodendrum capense*). Also along the river valleys and slopes additional trees include **Candelabra Tree** (*Euphorbia candelabrum*), **White Pear** (**Muganyoni**) (*Apodytes dimidiata*), **Mutanga** (*Elaeodendron buchananii*), **Strangler Fig** (*Ficus thonningii*) and **Muthigiu** (*Rhus natalensis*). On the rocky gorge sides a number of species are known only from the vicinity of Nairobi and include the small, cactus-like *Euphorbia brevitorta* that is protected only in the park. More than 500 plant species have been recorded.

Wildlife
Mammals

For such a small park Nairobi has an amazingly diverse mammal fauna with 100 species known to occur. Although Savanna Elephant is absent there is a healthy population of **Hook-lipped Rhinoceros** and a small number of **Common Hippopotamus** are present in pools in the Athi River. The **Square-lipped Rhinoceros** in the park were introduced from South Africa. **Maasai Giraffe** occur, as do good numbers of **Savanna Buffalo**. **Grant's** race of the **Plains Zebra** is present but usually only during the dry season, as is the **Western White-bearded Wildebeest**. These two, and some other species, normally leave the park during the rains but increasing human developments on the Athi Plains are disrupting these movements and in recent years numbers have declined. Apart from the wildebeest,

Grant's Zebra occur in the park.

Maasai Giraffe in Nairobi National Park

- Public campsites.
- Numerous accommodation options in and around Nairobi with Nairobi Tented Camp in the park.
- Picnic sites.
- Walking trails to hippopotamus pools on Athi River.
- Wildlife orphanage.
- Guided drives.
- Fairly good road network but some difficult to negotiate during the rains.

Coke's Hartebeest occur in small numbers.

there is a good complement of antelope species, including **Coke's Hartebeest (Kongoni)**, **Common Eland**, **Bushbuck (Imbabala)**, **Grant's Gazelle**, **Thomson's Gazelle**, **Impala**, **Bohor Reedbuck**, **Common Duiker**, **Klipspringer**, **Steenbok** and **Naivasha Dik-dik**. **Defassa Waterbuck** occur and it is possible that **Chanler's Mountain Reedbuck** may still be present in the Sosian Gorge area. **Common Warthog** is also present. Surprisingly, given its proximity to Nairobi, there is a small population of **Lion**, **Leopard**, **Cheetah** and **Spotted Hyaena**, but as with their prey species they are coming into increasing pressure from human impacts. Both **Black-backed** and **Side-striped jackal** occur, as well as **Serval**, **African Wild Cat** and **Caracal**. The most frequently seen small carnivores include **Dwarf Mongoose** and **Slender Mongoose** but most others are nocturnal. The primates you are likely to see are the **Olive Baboon** and **Vervet Monkey**. The **West African Ground Squirrel** occurs but at low densities and is rather shy, but in bushed areas look out for the **Ochre Bush Squirrel**. Both **Rock Hyrax** and **Yellow-spotted Rock Hyrax** occur in the more broken rocky country but the nocturnal **Southern Tree Hyrax** is restricted to the limited forest areas. Eleven bat species are on record but it is likely that more occur.

Birds

Birdlife in Nairobi National Park is rich and diverse with 529 species at last count occurring, including seasonal migrants, vagrants and occasional visitors. This is an amazing total for such a small park adjacent to a large city. **Maasai Ostrich** are common and in the vicinity of the artificial waterholes **Marabou Stork**, **White-backed** and **Rüppell's vultures** are often present to drink and bathe. Some 45 species of raptor have been recorded but several are Palaearctic visitors

Marabou Storks drinking at a waterhole

and a number are rare vagrants. Although occurring at low densities, the **Bateleur** and **Martial Eagle** are not infrequently seen, with the **Black Kite** one of the most abundant birds of prey. The passage migrant, the **Lesser Kestrel**, has been recorded roosting in the park in the thousands. Two of the most commonly seen gamebirds are the **Yellow-necked Spurfowl** and **Helmeted Guineafowl**. A rare resident along the Athi River is the **African Finfoot** but the **Black Crake** is more commonly observed. Three **bustards** occur on the open grass plains, **Kori**, **White-bellied** and **Hartlaub's**. Also be on the lookout for **Black-faced Sandgrouse** and **Yellow-throated Sandgrouse** on the plains and at waterholes. No less than 10 pigeons and doves are on record, 11 species of cuckoos and coucals, five bee-eaters and six hornbills. Three species of longclaw occur on the grasslands, including the limited-range **Sharpe's Longclaw** and the spectacular **Rosy-breasted Longclaw**, as well as 10 species of lark and pipit. Of the six starling species the **Superb Starling** stands out and is commonly seen around the picnic sites. A species with a limited Kenyan range here is the **Abyssinian Ground Thrush**, as well as **Jackson's Widowbird**, with males displaying over the grassland from March into May.

The Superb Starling is commonly seen around picnic sites.

The Tropical Boubou occurs in the riverine forest.

Reptiles and amphibians

To date some 60 species of reptile and amphibian have been recorded in Nairobi National Park. However, the visitor is only likely to encounter the larger and more obvious species, such as the **Nile Crocodile** and the large **Leopard Tortoise**. A few of the smaller denizens include **Brook's Gecko**, in rocky areas the **Red-headed Rock Agama**, and usually on trees the well-camouflaged **Blue-headed Tree Agama**. **Von Höhnel's Chameleon** is found in mixed bush-grassland, **Variable Skink** occurs widely but the very large **Nile Monitor** is only likely to be seen along the Athi River. Snakes are generally secretive and seldom seen but some of the larger species include **Southern African Rock Python**, **Black-necked Spitting Cobra**, probably also the **Egyptian Cobra** and the **Puff Adder**. The visitor is unlikely to encounter much of the amphibian life but you will certainly hear them during the rains.

- **A relatively low malaria-risk park but it is essential to take precautions.**
- **Campsites are not fenced, so be aware of potentially dangerous species.**

WILDLIFE FACTS

- 100 species of mammal.
- 529 bird species.
- 60 reptile and amphibian species.
- Decreasing numbers of migratory game species such as White-bearded Wildebeest.
- Four of the big five, the exception being the Savanna Elephant.
- 150 butterfly species.

LAKE TURKANA COMPLEX
SIBILOI, CENTRAL ISLAND & SOUTH ISLAND NATIONAL PARKS

Lake Turkana is the fourth-largest saline lake in the world.

Lie of the land

Lake Turkana, previously called Lake Rudolf, has a surface area of about 6,400km², it is 265km long and up to 30km wide, with a depth of 30–90m. It is a chloro-carbonate alkaline giant, the world's fourth-largest saline lake. Because of the colour of its water it is sometimes referred to as the 'Jade Sea' but the Turkana refer to it as *Anam Ka'alakol* ('sea of many fishes') or *Anam a Cheper*. It lies within the Great Rift Valley of north-west Kenya with its northern point entering Ethiopia. Its main feeder is the Omo River, which enters from the north and contributes as much as 90% of its inflow, with additions from the Turkwel and Kerio rivers. The lake has no outflow and water loss is due to evaporation. There are three principal islands, North, Central and South, of which the latter two are national parks. Sibiloi National Park lies on the north-east shore of Lake Turkana and covers 1,574km². This is an arid area of mainly open plains and the highest point is Mount Sibiloi. Sibiloi lies about 800km to the north of Nairobi.

Brief history

More than 100 sites in the Turkana Basin, especially at Koobi Fora, have been found to hold fossils of early hominine remains, including those of *Australopithecus anamensis* dated to about 4 million years before present. Here are also fossils of *Homo rudolfensis* (2 million years before present), *Homo ergaster* (Turkana Boy), *Kenyanthropus platyops* (3.5 million years before

- Far off main circuit and few visitors.
- Great diversity of dryland and shore birds.
- Arid-area mammals such as Gerenuk, Bright's Gazelle, Lesser Kudu and Beisa Oryx but rare.
- Remains of petrified forest in Sibiloi dating back about 7 million years before present.
- Some of the most important paleontological and archaeological sites on Earth.

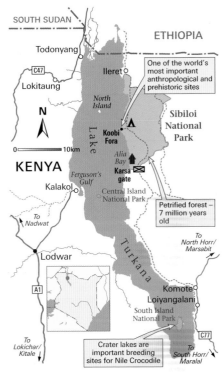

present and known as 'flat-faced man'), as well as early *Homo sapiens*, and the earliest evidence of human warfare between nomadic hunter-gatherers some 10,000 years before present. Over the past few thousand years there were many migrations of diverse peoples into the Turkana area, including Nilotic and Cushitic groups, and today at least 12 different language forms occur in the vicinity of the lake. Depending on conditions the economy has been reliant on fishing, hunting, gathering and animal husbandry. Tribes resident in the area today include the Oromo, Turkana, Borana and Rendille, Molo, Gabbra, Dassanach and Surma, among others. The first Europeans known to 'discover' the lake were Count S. Teleki de Szek and Lt. L.R. Von Höhnel in early 1888, who named it Lake Rudolf in honour of Crown Prince Rudolf of Austria. Sibiloi gained national park status in 1973, South Island in 1983 and Central Island in 1985.

Geology and landscape

Lying within the Great Rift Valley, Lake Turkana is located in a geological area dominated by lavas resulting from volcanic activity from the Quaternary and Tertiary periods. The lavas are mainly of an alkaline form. The lake is the most saline of East Africa's great lakes and it is the largest desert-located lake on Earth and the fourth-largest African lake. Basement rocks in the area are about 522 million years old and the first recorded volcanic activity took place in the late Eocene some 34.8 million years before present at what we know today as the Nabwal Hills to the north-east of the lake. The rocky hills around the lake are made up of extruded basalts. The periodic expulsions of volcanic ash served to preserve over millions of

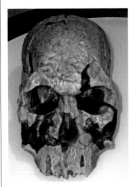

Skull of *Homo rudolfensis*

The dry road to Lake Turkana

years the numerous fossils, such as those at Koobi Fora. It is surmised that water flowed south out of the lake but this was blocked by volcanic action. Within Sibiloi there is an extensive area of petrified (fossilized) forest fragments, which are about 7 million years old and speak of times of more abundant rains. Central Island covers 5km² and is made up of three principal dormant volcanoes and several lesser craters, with its highest point 240m from lake level. Three of the craters contain lakes: Crocodile, Flamingo and Tilapia. South Island still has active volcanic vents that glow at night.

Climate

This is an arid and hot (often to 40°C) area with peak heat from December to March and although June and July are cooler it is rarely cold. From May to September strong, dust-raising winds are normal, especially in the morning and late afternoon but strong wind can be experienced at any time of year. Although the average rainfall is less than 250mm per year, in some areas no, or very little, rain may fall for several years.

Vegetation

Some 367 plant species have been recorded from the overall area, which is located within the Somali-Maasai semi-desert grassland and shrubland zone. Most of the area consists of gravel plains with seasonal grass production during good rains and areas of dwarf shrub and wooded thicket, with a very small area of riparian woodland. In places there are

- Four official campsites (KWS); Koobi Fora (Kenya National Museums).
- Private lodges and camps outside the parks, numbers fluctuate.
- Small museum at Koobi Fora.
- Fishing is allowed with permit.
- Boat hire from Kalokol to visit Central Island and for fishing.
- Poor track network.

stands of **Doum Palms** (*Hyphaene thebaica*), whose fruits form an important food source for several mammal species, including Common Warthog. Important low tree species include **Umbrella Thorn** (*Vachellia tortilis*) and **River Thorn** (*Vachellia elatior*), as well as the **Desert Date** (*Balanites aegyptiaca*). Thickets are formed by **Toothbrush Bush** (*Salvadora persica*) on the mainland as well as on the islands. Incursions by nomadic livestock herders continue to be a problem in this fragile natural community.

Common Hippopotamus

Wildlife
Mammals

Given its arid nature there are no large game herds but there are small populations of **Plains Zebra**, **Common Warthog**, **Tiang**, **Beisa Oryx**, **Gerenuk**, **Bright's Gazelle** (previously Grant's) and **Günther's Dik-dik**. **Common Hippopotamus** occur around the edge of the lake but numbers are not known. Because of poaching, a number of species no longer occur, even seasonally, such as Savanna Elephant, Hook-lipped Rhinoceros and Reticulated Giraffe. It is possible that **Greater Kudu** may still survive in small numbers. **Lion**, **Cheetah** and **Leopard** may still occur but are rarely sighted, although **Spotted** and **Striped hyaenas**, **Black-backed Jackal** and **African Wolf** occur at low densities throughout the area. No comprehensive study of the smaller mammals has been undertaken but **Aardvark** and **Crested Porcupine** are present, as are **White-tailed** and **Slender mongooses**, **Small-spotted Genet**, **Bat-eared Fox** and **Olive Baboon**.

Birds

Apart from being home to resident species associated with the lake and arid land areas, Lake Turkana is an important flyway and stopover for palaearctic migrants. At least 350 bird species have been recorded within the Lake Turkana ecosystem. The **African Skimmer** breeds on some of the islands in low densities. Some of the more interesting species to look out for include the **Fox Kestrel**, **Swallow-tailed Kite** and **Osprey**, as well as **Senegal Stone Curlew**, **Heuglin's Bustard**, **Cream-coloured Courser** and **Curly-crested Helmet Shrike**. During the northern winter large numbers of waders and other migrants enter the area around the lake, especially between March and early May. At times large numbers of Swallow-tailed Kites breed here. **Lesser Flamingos** frequent the island lakes and some of the

WILDLIFE FACTS

- Within the Turkana ecosystem some 350 bird species.
- Very large Nile Crocodile population, one of Africa's largest.
- 49 reptile and just seven amphibian species.
- About 60 species of fish, including several endemics.
- Small museum near park HQ.
- No comprehensive list of mammals.

Lesser Flamingos

shallower lake waters. High fish numbers attract a wide range of piscivorous birds, such as **Great White** and **Pink-backed pelicans**, **White-breasted Cormorant**, **Goliath Heron**, **African Fish Eagle** and **Pied Kingfisher**. Dryland birds are diverse, including the **Arabian Bustard**, which is recorded in very few places in Kenya. Several larks occur, including **Crested Lark**, **Thekla Lark** and **Somali Short-toed Lark**.

Reptiles and amphibians

Lake Turkana is best known for its very large **Nile Crocodile** population, with one estimate of more than 20,000 individuals. At least 49 species of reptile, including 23 lizard and 21 snake species, are known from the eastern side of Lake Turkana, as well as seven amphibian species. Freshwater terrapins include the **Helmeted Terrapin**, **Serrated Hinged Terrapin**, the large (to 90cm) **Nile Soft-shelled Turtle** that occurs only in this lake in Kenya, and the **Lake Turkana Hinged Terrapin** that is endemic here. Being an arid area, it is a gecko hotspot and includes **Somali-Maasai Clawed Gecko, Brook's Gecko, Uniform-scaled Gecko, Prince Ruspoli's Gecko** and **Kenya Dwarf Gecko**. Lizards include the **Tree Skink, Five-lined Skink, Speke's Sand Lizard** and **Southern Long-toed Lizard**. As over much of East Africa, the large, dramatically coloured (male) **Red-headed Rock Agama** is obvious as it perches atop boulders. The largest lizard here is the **Nile Monitor** and it is a major predator of Nile Crocodile eggs. Although most snakes here are harmless or only mildly venomous, a few should be avoided, such as the spectacular **Red Spitting Cobra, Puff Adder** and the **North-east African Carpet Viper**. The last is probably the most abundant dangerous snake in the area. Amphibians are not well represented although this is typical of arid areas, but the **Lugh Toad** is present, as is the apparently endemic **Lake Turkana Toad**. The **Cryptic Sand Frog** is arid-area adapted and adults spend much of their life buried in the soil in between rainy seasons.

The North-east African Carpet Viper is common in the area.

> **!**
> - **This area falls within the malaria zone.**
> - **The area is subject to extreme heat and winds.**
> - **It is extremely isolated and visitors should be well prepared.**
> - **The Nile Crocodile population is large, so keep away from lake edges.**
> - **Be aware that banditry occurs from time to time in general area and approach roads.**

TSAVO EAST & TSAVO WEST
NATIONAL PARKS

Savanna Elephants in Tsavo East are usually coated in red-orange dust due to wallowing and dust-bathing in the area's characteristic red soil.

Lie of the land

Tsavo is divided into two administrative units, Tsavo West and Tsavo East, with the main Mombasa-Nairobi road and railway dividing the two parks. Together the parks cover a total of 20,812km^2, with the larger being Tsavo East at 11,747km^2 and Tsavo West at 9,065km^2. The administrative centre for the East lies in Voi and for the West at Kamboyo close to Mtito Andei. The park lies within what was previously known as Coast Province in the south-east of the country. The southern boundary of Tsavo West lies against the Tanzanian border and in part adjoins Mkomazi National Park in Tanzania. On the northernmost boundary of Tsavo West lies the Chyulu National Park, which feeds water to the Mzima Springs, among others, a major source of water for the city of Mombasa. The East is largely flat, open to thicket country with the Galana River cutting through it. The West is more broken and hilly, and better watered.

Brief history

Prehistoric communities of hunter-gatherer peoples occupied the area from about 100,000 years before present but possibly earlier, where they are known to have occupied rock shelters along the Galana River. It is believed that Kamba people moved south from the southern slopes of Mount Kenya and occupied part of the Tsavo area between 1,500 and 1,000 years before present. These more advanced people had mastered iron production and either drove out, or assimilated, the hunter-gatherers. The dominant Maasai established themselves in the area with their herds and flocks during the course of the 18th century.

- Despite its popularity, large parts not overrun by tourists.
- Kenya's largest Savanna Elephant population.
- Clear waters of Mzima Springs allow excellent views of Common Hippopotamus, Nile Crocodiles and fish.
- Great diversity of game and birdlife.
- Diversity of interesting geological formations.

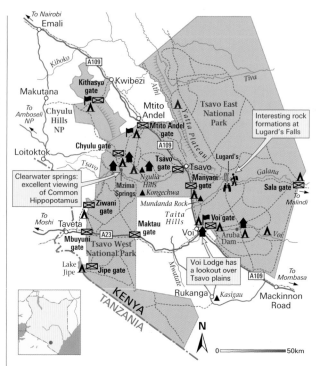

FACILITIES AND ACTIVITIES

- Numerous lodges, tented camps and several public campsites (no facilities).
- Extensive road and track network but poorly maintained.
- Some lodges offer walks with armed guard.
- Game and bird viewing excellent, especially in the East.
- Short walking trail to Mzima Springs.

Tribes living in the area at the time of the park's establishment were the Maasai, Wakamba, Orma, Taita, Giriama and the Duruma. One tribal group, the Waata (Waliangulu), had been hunting elephant in the area and trading the ivory long before the advent of the white man and his conservation plans. To achieve this they used giant bows with a draw-weight of 77kg and poison-tipped arrows.

The first Europeans known to have traversed the area of the Tsavos were the German missionaries Krapf and Rebmann in 1849, the discoverers of Mounts Kilimanjaro and Kenya. Lord Lugard, after whom the Lugard Falls are named, walked along the banks of the Sabaki/Galana rivers, where he is said to have had his finger bitten by a crocodile. Here Joseph Thomson explored in the 1880s and was the first to describe the great Tsavo wilderness. Probably the most noted historical incident here was when two man-eating Lion who had terrorized workers constructing the Mombasa to Nairobi railway were finally shot by Colonel Patterson, immortalized in his book *The Man-eaters of Tsavo*. Tsavo was first gazetted as a park in 1948.

Geology and landscape

The Tsavo ecosystem covers some 43,000km². Western Tsavo is relatively hilly in parts with much of the topography influenced by volcanic activity. There are numerous signs of lava flows and volcanic cones. The well-known Mzima Springs are located here, with the watershed for these crystal clear waters lying in the Chyulu Hills to the north, adjoining the border of the park. Rainwater percolates through the porous volcanic rock and soil, forming underground streams, some of which break the surface at Mzima. The area towards the Tanzanian border and the Mkomazi National Park is relatively flat. Tsavo East is flatter and drier country. To the north of the perennial Galana River lies the Yatta Plateau, one of the largest lava flows on Earth. The lava flowed from the volcano Ol Doinyo Sabuk. The Tsavo River flowing through the West and the Athi River that crosses part of the East have their confluence above the Lugard Falls, and from that point become the Galana River. The Lugard Falls, a series of relatively shallow rapids, at one point has cut a very narrow rocky gorge with some remarkable rock formations. Mudanda Rock, near the Manyani gate, is some 1.5km in length, an inselberg that has formed a natural dam that attracts game, especially Savanna Elephants, during the dry season. Base rocks throughout much of the park consist of granites, gneisses and schists, but to the north the rocks and soils are of more recent volcanic origin. A strong feature, particularly in the East, is the red soil, the reason why such wallowers as Savanna Elephant and Warthog often take on a reddish hue here.

Lugard Falls are actually rapids, which flow over fascinating geological formations.

A view over the dry, flat plains of Tsavo East

Climate

February and March and June to October are generally dry months but recent records indicate this may be changing. Temperatures during the day can be high but evenings are generally mild to cool, with average maximum temperature of 31°C and at night some 20°C. The wet season runs from October into December and late March into May, with November and April being the wettest months. The annual average fall for West is 450mm and the East 250mm. However, rainfall is fairly unpredictable, especially in the east, in both timing and quantity but usually falls in short, heavy showers.

The large fig trees are used as night roosts by Yellow Baboons.

WILDLIFE FACTS

- At least 100 mammal species.
- >430 bird species, including 61 raptors and 23 shrikes; well over 500 in ecosystem.
- Kenya's largest Savanna Elephant population.
- One of the best parks for Lesser Kudu and Gerenuk.

Gerenuk ram

Vegetation

Much of the area is level to undulating open grassland but along the perennial Athi, Tsavo and Galana rivers there are narrow fringes of riverine woodland and thicket that are dominated by **River Acacia** (**Mgunga**) (*Vachellia elatior*) and the **Doum Palm** (*Hyphaene compressa*), as well as stands of the shrub **Suaeda** (*Suaeda monoica*). Much of the northern areas are dominated by *Vachellia-Senegalia-Commiphora* woodland and thicket but to the south of the Galana there are more open grassed areas with thickets. These areas are open as a result of long periods of activity by a large Savanna Elephant population and the impact of frequent fires. Common bushes in the thickets include *Bauhinia*, such as **Msaponi** (*Bauhinia tomentosa*), *Premna* and *Sericocomopsis*, with scattered trees such as **White Gul Mohur** (*Delonix elata*) and *Melia volkensii*. On the Yatta Plateau and elsewhere there are scattered giants, the **Baobab** (*Adansonia digitata*). Vegetation in the West is similar to that in the East but because of higher rainfall thickets tend to be denser, but there are extensive areas of open grassland, especially in the south. Around the Mzima Springs there are stands of **Raphia Palm** (*Raphia farinifera*) and **Wild Date Palm** (*Phoenix reclinata*). In the extreme south-west the park borders on Lake Jipe, which is fed by waters rising on the slopes of Mount Kilimanjaro and the North Pare Mountains in Tanzania. Here are large swamps and extensive reed beds.

Wildlife
Mammals

There are at least 100 mammal species, and it is likely that more could be added as many areas have not been surveyed for their small mammal fauna, especially bats. At one time it was estimated that the **Savanna Elephant** numbered at least 35,000 individuals within the Tsavo ecosystem but by 1976 this had dropped to some 20,000 as a result of poaching and natural attrition due to drought. In 2000 the population plummeted to an estimated 6,000 animals but by 2014 approximately 11,000 were counted. Despite the losses, this is by far the largest population in Kenya and one of the largest surviving in Africa. Tsavo used to be one of the great strongholds of the endangered **Hook-lipped Rhinoceros**. At the end of the Second World War the appropriately named J.A. Hunter shot 1,088 of these rhinos in one year in the Tsavo area at the behest of the colonial government. However, even as late as the early 1970s it was estimated that up to 8,000 rhino survived within the Tsavo ecosystem. Today the Ngulia Rhino Sanctuary in Tsavo West has >70 highly protected animals, with releases elsewhere. **Common Hippopotamus** are best seen at the Mziwa Springs in Tsavo West but **Savanna Buffalo** may be encountered anywhere. The **Grant's** form of the **Plains Zebra** is present, as are the **Maasai Giraffe**, the **Common Warthog** and the **Desert Warthog**. The antelope array is impressive and several species are easier to see here than anywhere else in Kenya. They include **Common Eland, Fringe-eared Beisa Oryx, Lesser Kudu, Bushbuck (Imbabala), Gerenuk, Peters's Gazelle** (split from Grant's Gazelle), **Impala, Common Waterbuck, Bohor Reedbuck**, with **Coke's Hartebeest** north of the Galana River. Smaller antelope include **Common Duiker, Steenbok** and **Kirk's Dik-dik**. The seriously endangered **Hirola (Hunter's Hartebeest)** has been introduced well outside its normal range to the north of the Galana River and is seldom seen. All of the larger predators occur, with good populations of **Lion, Leopard, Cheetah, Spotted** and **Striped hyaenas, African Wolf, Black-backed** and **Side-striped jackal** (mainly in West). **Banded, Dwarf** and **Slender mongooses** are quite commonly observed as they are diurnal. Troops of **Yellow Baboon** are commonly encountered, usually in proximity to the river courses, where large trees grow and provide safe night roosts. The only other primate commonly observed is the black-faced **Vervet Monkey**. Few of the many rodent species are likely to be encountered other than the **Unstriped Ground Squirrel**, but along the sandy tracks look for the small, volcano-like mounds of the unique **Naked Mole-rat**.

There is a good population of Lion, especially in Tsavo East.

Common Warthog

Yellow Baboon troops range across the entire park complex.

Yellow-necked Spurfowl

Rosy-patched Shrike

Northern Red-billed
Hornbill

Birds

The **Maasai Ostrich** occurs, as does the blue-grey-legged **Somali Ostrich**, recognized by some as a species in its own right, the latter mainly to the north of the Galana River. The Mzima Springs, the perennial river courses, dams and Lake Jipe attract a great diversity of water and water-related birds, with 16 species of heron, egret and bittern, as well as 13 duck and goose species. Raptors are extremely well represented, including the **Secretary Bird**, six vulture species, as well as a mix of residents and migrants. Interesting visitors include the **Grasshopper Buzzard, Steppe Buzzard, European Hobby** and the **Sooty Falcon**. The **Red-necked Falcon** is mainly associated with the Tsavo and Galana rivers. The most commonly seen gamebirds include the **Yellow-necked Spurfowl, Helmeted Guineafowl** and the **Vulturine Guineafowl**, as well as **Black-faced Sandgrouse** and **Yellow-throated Sandgrouse**. Although rare, the **African Finfoot** occurs at the Mzima Springs. On the more open plains watch for the **Kori, White-bellied, Buff-crested, Black-bellied** and **Hartlaub's bustards**. The **White-bellied Turaco** (Go-away-bird) is common, as are several **hornbills** including **Eastern Yellow-billed, Northern Red-billed, Grey** and **Von der Decken's**. There are at least eight barbets, including the colourful **D'Arnaud's Barbet**. Some of the most frequently seen species include **Fiscal Shrike, Long-tailed Fiscal, Rosy-patched Shrike, Pied Crow, Superb Starling, White-headed Buffalo Weaver, Black-capped Social Weaver, Red-headed Weaver** and **Red-billed Quelea**. Some of the best birding is to be had in the grounds of the lodges and campgrounds.

Reptiles and amphibians

Nile Crocodiles occur in the Mziwa Springs and along the Galana River, as well is in other watercourses with permanent pools. Of the three land tortoises known from Tsavo, the only one you are likely to encounter is the large **Leopard Tortoise** but at the Mziwa Springs the **Helmeted Terrapin** and **Serrated Hinged Terrapin** are common. If you are staying in one of the lodges you will certainly encounter the **Tropical House Gecko** hunting insects at night around the lights. A number of skinks occur here, including the large, robust **Rainbow Skink** in rocky areas and the **Tree Skink** (to 35cm) in more wooded areas. In rocky areas the **Red-headed Rock Agama** is common, as is **Rüppell's Agama** but this well-camouflaged lizard occupies more open areas. The largest lizards in Tsavo

The male Red-headed Agama is one of the most commonly seen lizards.

are the **White-throated Monitor**, which may reach 1.6m in length, and the **Nile Monitor**, which is present wherever there is permanent water. By far the largest snake is the **Southern African Rock Python** but it is seldom seen, as is the case with all other snake species. Amphibians in Tsavo have not been extensively surveyed but one species, **Sheldrick's Reed Frog**, is known only from Tsavo East and one other locality. You may not see many frogs and toads but if you visit during the rains you will certainly hear the males in mating choruses.

> **!**
> - **Lies within a malaria area.**
> - **Much of the road network only suitable for 4x4 vehicles, or those with high clearance.**
> - **Lodges, tented camps and campsites are not fenced, so be alert for potentially dangerous game.**
> - **Baboons can be a problem in some camps, so do not leave food lying about.**

CHYULU HILLS NATIONAL PARK

Chyulu Hills National Park (471km²), adjoining the north-west boundary of Tsavo West National Park, lies about 190km south-east of Nairobi and 30km south-west of Kibwezi, and is located in Makueni County. The park was gazetted in 1983 to protect the cloud forests. These hills were formed about 1.4 million years ago and are of volcanic origin, composed largely of ash cones and craters, and have a maximum altitude of 2,188m asl. The most recent eruption here was in 1855AD. Although no permanent surface water occurs in the hills rain filters through the porous rock and feeds, among others, the Mzima Springs, as well as the Tsavo and Galana rivers. Some say it takes 20 years for the water to filter through the rocks to the Mzima Springs, others say three years! It also has some of the longest lava tube caves in the world, of which only a few have been explored. The lower levels of the hills are rolling grassland and thicket, with patches of montane

Waterbuck with Chyulu Hills in the background

forest above the 1,800m contour with the appearance of islands in an ocean of grass. Trees here include various figs (*Ficus* spp.), **Lace-leaf** (*Neoboutonia macrocalyx*), **Soccerball Fruit** (*Tabernaemontana stapfiana*), **African Cherry** (*Prunus africana*), **Pillarwood** (*Cassipourea malosana*), **Black Ironwood (Cape Olive)** (*Olea capensis*) and **Red Hot Poker Coral-tree** (*Erythrina abyssinica*). In lower areas stands of mainly **African Pencil Cedar** (*Juniperus procera*) and, especially on the lava flow areas, large numbers of **Itula** (*Commiphora baluensis*). Here also is **Pock Ironwood** (*Chionanthus mildbraedii*) and the most northerly population of **Usambara Yellowwood** (*Podocarpus usambarensis*). In the hills there are 550 plant species, excluding grasses and 37 orchid species, most of which are epiphytes. The mammal fauna is rich but smaller species have not been surveyed. Large game is scarce but includes **Savanna Elephant, Savanna Buffalo, Common Eland, Bushbuck (Imbabala), Chanler's Mountain Reedbuck, Bushpig** and **Warthog**. Several of these species appear seasonally and usually in small numbers. **Lion, Leopard** and **Spotted Hyaena** occur but are considered rare here. Of the birds there are three endemic subspecies of **Shelley's Francolin**, as well as **White-starred Robin** and **Orange Ground Thrush**. Of the rich butterfly fauna, at least four subspecies are endemic to the Chyulu Hills. There are lodges associated with the park as well as public and private campsites, the latter only cleared areas with no facilities. Sadly, these hills are under growing pressure from cattle herders, arsonists and squatters. Hiking is allowed without having to take on an armed guard. An advantage here is that very few people brave the poor roads so it is not unusual to have much of the park to yourself.

SAMBURU, BUFFALO SPRINGS & SHABA NATIONAL RESERVES

Leopard are not uncommonly sighted, especially along the Ewaso Ng'iro River.

Lie of the land

Samburu and Buffalo Springs national reserves cover 104km² and 131km², respectively, with the Ewaso Ng'iro River dividing the two. Shaba extends over 130km² and lies immediately east of Buffalo Springs and also lies along the Ewaso Ng'iro River. The main entry points lie about 340km from Nairobi and around 50km from Isiolo town and are largely lying in the district of the same name. The complex is located within the dry Somali-Maasai biome and has a varied topography, with an altitudinal range of 850–1,250m. Mount Bodech with its great granitic cliffs lies to the north of Shaba and Mount Shaba to its south. Buffalo Springs and Shaba are largely flat to undulating, with Samburu having numerous rock outcrops, or inselbergs, such as Koitogor, Lolkoitoi and Lowa Mara. The Ewaso Ng'iro River, as well as several springs, is the lifeblood of these reserves.

Brief history

Three principal tribal groups inhabit the area around these reserves, the Samburu, Boran and Turkana. The Samburu are closely related to the Maasai and are largely nomadic pastoralists, while the Boran are Cushitic and are the largest Galla-speaking group in Kenya. Apart from cattle, sheep and goats, the Boran also keep large numbers of camels, better adapted to living in this arid environment. The Turkana are Nilo-Hamitic and are relatively recent settlers in this area, having been driven south from the environs of Lake Turkana by years of drought and famine. The first European known to explore the area

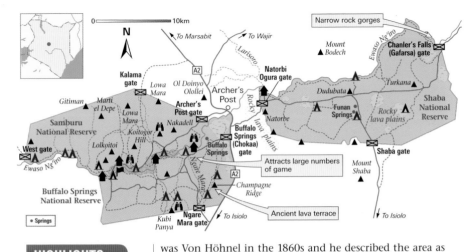

Narrow rock gorges

0 ———— 10km

N

To Marsabit • To Wajir
Larisoro
Mount ▲ Bodech
Ewaso Ng'iro
Chanler's Falls (Gafarsa) gate

Kalama gate
Lowa Mara
Ol Doinyo Ololei
A2
Archer's Post
Natorbi Ogura gate
Dudubata ▲
Turkana ▲

Gitiman
Marti el Depe
Lowa Mara
Archer's Post gate
Rocky lava plains
Natorbe
Funan Springs ▲
Rocky lava plains ▲
Shaba National Reserve

Samburu National Reserve
Koitogor Hill
Nakadell
Buffalo Springs
West gate
Lolkoitoi
Buffalo Springs (Chokaa) gate
Attracts large numbers of game
Shaba gate

Ewaso Ng'iro
Ngare Mara
A2
Mount Shaba ▲
Champagne Ridge
Ancient lava terrace

Buffalo Springs National Reserve

Kubi Panya
Ngare Mara gate
To Isiolo
To Isiolo

• Springs

HIGHLIGHTS

- Diverse landscapes.
- Easiest access to view northern, arid-area fauna.
- The complex is far enough away from main tourist circuits to ensure it is never too crowded.
- Great mammal, bird and reptile diversity.

Ewaso Ng'iro River

was Von Höhnel in the 1860s and he described the area as teeming with game, especially Hook-lipped Rhinoceros and Savanna Buffalo. It was this abundance that attracted many 'white hunters' to the area in the late 19th century and well into the 20th century. The Samburu-Isiolo Game Reserve was established in 1948 and was a sector of the once massive Marsabit National Reserve, which was de-gazetted in 1961. Samburu Game Reserve was established in 1962, Buffalo Springs in 1963, and Shaba proclaimed in 1974. Shaba was the location where Joy Adamson raised and released Penny the Leopard. Joy was murdered here in 1980. At her campsite in the reserve there is a simple plaque in Joy's memory.

Geology and landscape

The Ewaso Ng'iro River is the principal landscape feature of the complex and its name translates as 'River of Brown Water'. Where it flows between Samburu and Buffalo Springs it is relatively wide and meandering but in the east of Shaba it cuts through rocky gorges. Its principal source is in the Aberdares range and after cutting its way through this reserve complex it finds its end point in the Lorian Swamp, a now much degraded wetland. Except during the rains, other rivers do not flow but there are deep pools in the Ngare Mara River. Apart from the rivers, there are a number of springs that form important sources of water to game, especially during the dry season. In Shaba the springs get their waters from underground flow emanating from the Nyambeni Hills. Buffalo Springs are permanent and a year-round source of water. Samburu is dominated by ancient basement complex rocks, such as hornblende and banded biotite gneisses, and schists, with sandy and gravel soils. Buffalo Springs is mainly made up of a gently rolling plain with an ancient lava terrace in the south-east known as Champagne Ridge. The geology is dominated by old lava flows and soils of volcanic origin. The white rocks and light soils around the springs are sedimentary deposits from a lake bed that dates to the Quaternary period. The rocks and soils in Shaba are mainly of volcanic origin but in the vicinity of the inselbergs you will observe lighter-coloured sedimentary soils. The great massifs of Mount Bodech, to the north, and Mount Shaba, to the south, lie on the fringes of the reserve.

Climate

This is an arid, low-rainfall area with an annual average of 350mm recorded at centrally located Archer's Post. Most rain falls in April and May, as well as mid-October to mid-December. Rainfall here, however, is unpredictable and may vary considerably from year to year. The driest periods are June to early October and December to April. For much of the year daytime temperatures are high, with an average maximum of 30°C and average minimum of about 20°C.

Vegetation

Although more than 20 vegetation types have been identified across the three reserves, in the broadest sense just three 'blanket' types can be recognized, namely riverine vegetation, semi-arid scrublands dominated by *Vachellia-Senegalia-Commiphora* bushes and trees, as well as grassland dominated by **Umbrella Thorn** (*Vachellia tortilis*). The riverine forest and thicket is largely absent from Shaba but in Samburu/ Buffalo Springs deep-rooted trees and bushes grow on the rich soils. Two of the most abundant trees are the **Common River Thorn** (*Vachellia elatior*) and the limited-range **Tana River Poplar** (*Populus ilicifolia*). Along the rivers and in the vicinity of the springs the most distinctive is the **Doum Palm** (*Hyphaene compressa*) and it is particularly abundant in Shaba. Smaller bush species along the watercourses include **Henna Bush** (*Lawsonia inermis*), the source of the dye henna, and the large, grey-green-leaved and -fruited **Sodom Apple** (*Calotropis procera*). Thickets of **Toothbrush Bush** (**Mswaki**) (*Salvadora persica*) with their pale green leaves are found throughout. Because of their dense shade they are favoured as lying-up spots for large predators during the day. Large tracts of all three reserves are covered by semi-arid scrub, which consists mainly of three species of thorn tree, **Umbrella Thorn**

FACILITIES AND ACTIVITIES

- There are several lodges and tented camps.
- Some lodges offer guided bush walks.
- Several public and special campsites (often pre-booked by safari operators).
- A fairly extensive network of tracks, generally not well maintained.
- Game viewing and birdwatching.
- No fuel or supplies in the reserves but in Isiolo and Archer's Post.

Tall palms line the river courses.

In places thorned euphorbias form impenetrable barriers.

Beisa Oryx are common.

This is one of the best locations for Gerenuk.

(*Vachellia tortilis*), **Senegal Gum** (*Senegalia senegal*) and **False Umbrella Tree** (*Vachellia reficiens*), with several species of **Paper-bark** (*Commiphora*). Few bushes remain green in the dry season, with the exception of **Mnafisi** (*Boscia coriacea*) and **Grey-leaved Saucer Berry** (*Cordia gharaf*) and a number of succulent species. The **Impala Lily (Desert Rose)**, which resembles a small Baobab, is only obvious when it produces a profusion of delicate pink flowers. Also most obvious when in flower is the **Flame Tree** (*Erythrina melanacantha*) growing mainly in the north of Samburu. On many rock outcrops the **Red-pod Terminalia (Mbarao)** (*Terminalia brownii*) is most visible when bearing masses of its brick-red winged fruits.

Wildlife
Mammals

This is not a reserve area where you will see great game herds but it is rich in species typical of what was previously known as the Northern Territory. Small numbers of **Common Hippopotamus** occur but the Hook-lipped Rhinoceros has long ago been poached from the area. This is one of the best locations to view **Grevy's Zebra, Reticulated Giraffe, Gerenuk, Lesser Kudu** and **Günther's Dik-dik**. It is also home to both the **Common Warthog** and the **Desert Warthog**, the latter being more widespread than previously thought and distinguished by down-turned upper facial warts and ear tips. Several hundred **Savanna Elephant** roam the area in and around the reserves but the main concentrations can be found along the Ewaso Ng'iro River during the dry months. Heavy poaching for ivory, as elsewhere in East Africa, has seen a major reduction in numbers. Apart from Grevy's Zebra, **Plains Zebra** is also present, and is more closely tied to permanent water. **Savanna Buffalo** occur

Grevy's Zebra form small herds.

African Wild Dogs range over vast areas and are rarely seen.

in fairly small numbers and are reliant on areas with permanent water for drinking. Also found are **Impala**, as well as **Common** and **Defassa waterbuck** at the limits of their range here. **Bright's Gazelle** (previously in Grant's Gazelle) is present, as are small numbers of the highly nomadic **Common Eland**, and **Greater Kudu**, mainly in Samburu. **Klipspringer** are seen on rock outcrops, especially in Shaba. All of the major predators occur in the area, including the frequently seen **Lion, Leopard** and **Cheetah**. **Spotted Hyaena** is common but the **Striped Hyaena** is seldom observed. **African Wild Dog (Painted Dog)** range over vast areas and is very rarely seen here. The smaller carnivores the visitor might observe include **African Wolf, Black-backed Jackal, Aardwolf, Serval, Banded Mongoose** and **Common Large-spotted Genet**; the last is nocturnal but frequents lodges and camps. The **Olive Baboon** and **Vervet Monkey** are common and can be a nuisance around lodges and camps. You are unlikely to see many rodent species but the **Unstriped Ground Squirrel** is common and the small mini volcano-like mounds of the **Naked Mole-rat** can be seen along the tracks in sandy soils. No detailed surveys have been undertaken on the small mammals of the area, although 11 bat species are on record.

Although you will not see the unique Naked Mole-rat, you will encounter their small, volcanic cone-like mounds.

WILDLIFE FACTS

- >500 species of plant.
- Potentially more than 100 mammal species should occur.
- Excellent for dryland game, Grevy's Zebra, Gerenuk, Beisa Oryx and Reticulated Giraffe.
- Bird counts vary but >380 species.

Birds

The largest bird here by far is the **Somali Ostrich**, now recognized as a full species. This is one of the best areas in Kenya to see large flocks of **Vulturine Guineafowl**, as well as the more widespread **Helmeted Guineafowl**. **Yellow-necked Spurfowl** is common, as is **Crested Francolin** but the restricted-range

Buff-crested Bustard

The largest member of its group, the Vulturine Guineafowl is relatively common here.

Stone Partridge is only likely to be observed in the rock outcrops. There are many raptors, including six vulture species, most frequently seen being the **White-backed Vulture**. The vultures frequent the principal river where they come to drink and bathe. **Bateleur** and **Martial Eagle** are commonly observed, with **African Fish Eagle** more habitat restricted. In contrast with the giants is the diminutive **Pygmy Falcon**, usually associated with nesting colonies of **Black-capped Social Weavers**. The most frequently observed hornbills include **Eastern Yellow-billed**, **Von der Decken's** and **Northern Red-billed hornbills**. Of the smaller species those commonly encountered include **White-browed Sparrow-Weaver, White-headed Buffalo Weaver, Superb Starling, Golden-breasted Starling** and **Somali Bee-eater**. In the vicinity of the river and springs there is an impressive array, including 11 species of heron and egret, on record and eight species of stork, although only the **Marabou** is permanently resident. The **Orange-bellied Parrot** is resident and usually has nesting holes in Doum Palms. Of the seven barbets present, **D'Arnaud's Barbet** and **Red-fronted Barbet** are fairly common. This is the best location in Kenya to see **Donaldson-Smith's Sparrow-Weaver**.

Reptiles and amphibians

Nile Crocodiles are common along the Ewaso Ng'iro River and are present at some springs. There are some very large individuals along the river. **Pancake Tortoise** occurs in the rock outcrops but you are unlikely to encounter it; the **Serrated Hinged Terrapin**, which can reach a length of 55cm, is found wherever there is permanent water, including at Buffalo Springs. The largest lizard here is the **Nile Monitor**, which may reach a length of 2.5m and is closely tied to water. In rocky areas you cannot fail to see the **Red-headed Rock Agama**, as the brightly coloured males sit in prominent positions. No detailed checklist of snakes exists for the reserves but the attractive **Red Cobra** occurs, as does the **Puff Adder**. The most common venomous snake here is the **North-east African Carpet Viper**, which is aggressive and lethal if bites go untreated. Little is known of the amphibians of this arid area.

- From time to time there are security issues and you are advised to take on a camp guard.
- Baboons can be a major problem in campsites.
- This is a malaria area.
- During the rains some tracks can be difficult, to impossible, to negotiate.
- Facilities in public camps are very basic and minimal.

MAASAI MARA NATIONAL RESERVE

The spectacle of the White-bearded Wildebeest migrating draws thousands of visitors, making this Kenya's most 'gridlocked' park.

Lie of the land

The Maasai Mara lies on the north-eastern edge of the much larger Serengeti National Park in Tanzania. Several areas on the Kenyan side adjoining the reserve are wildlife conservancies and include Mara Naboisha, Mara North, Olare Motorogi, Ol Kinyei, Ol Choro Oiroua, Lemek, Siana, Olderikesi and the Mara Triangle. The reserve is managed by the Narok County Council but the conservancies are a business agreement between the local Maasai landowners and safari operators. The reserve is dominated in the north by the Mara River and its feeder streams, such as the Talek River. Much of the reserve is rolling grassland and open woodland, with bush country in the more hilly east. To the west lies the Esoit Oloololo Escarpment. The reserve is about 280km from Nairobi and covers 1,510km².

Brief history

Modern man has inhabited the Maasai Mara area for at least 2,000 years, based on the discovery of Neolithic sites, including obsidian tools and weapons, in the Lemek Valley just to the north of the reserve. Other remains found indicate that these early inhabitants were livestock keepers. When the first Europeans explored the area they found that the Maasai peoples were living there and had been in the area for at least 200 years. In 1891 the deadly disease rinderpest devastated the Maasai herds, as well as the herds of Wildebeest, Savanna Buffalo and Maasai Giraffe, and many of the Maasai died of starvation and disease. The Maasai in the area belong to three subtribes, the Il-Siria, Il-Purko and Il-Loitai. The massive loss of grazing mammals resulted in much of the area reverting to bush country, which caused the

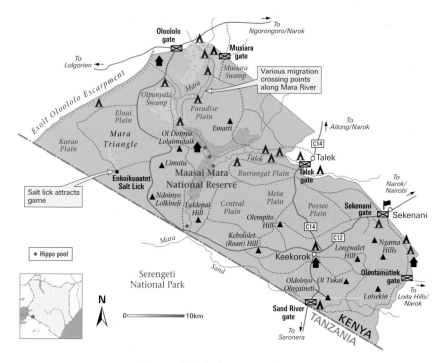

tsetse fly (which carries a disease deadly to cattle) to thrive. In 1948 part of greater Maasai Mara was declared a national game reserve and in 1961 it was placed under the control of the Narok County Council, under whose management it remains to this day. Until fairly recently the growing numbers of Maasai and their cattle were placing unsustainable pressure on the area surrounding the reserve, but the partnership between the people and safari companies has somewhat eased these impacts.

HIGHLIGHTS

- Great diversity of game species and predators.
- Greatest mammal migration on Earth (usually August to mid-October).
- Open terrain makes for easy game viewing.
- Over 450 resident and migratory bird species.

Geology and landscape

The basement rocks in this area are made up of igneous and metamorphic formations that were formed more than 600 million years before present during Precambrian and Cambrian times. These surfaces became heavily eroded and were later covered by volcanic lava and extrusions during the Tertiary period. In some areas the dark volcanic 'cotton soils' make wet-season travel difficult. Much of the reserve consists of flat to gently rolling plains, with the Mara River in the north, isolated inselbergs in the south and more broken hilly country in the east. The low Esoit Oloololo Escarpment in the west breaks the flow of the plains.

The great migration across the plains of the Maasai Mara

Climate

Although rain can fall in any month, the heaviest falls are in December and January and again in April, with an annual average of 1,200mm. There is not a great seasonal temperature fluctuation but the days can be hot, with cooler nights.

Vegetation

The reserve is dominated by open grassland influenced in many areas by a combination of grazing and fire. One of the commonest grasses here and throughout the ecosystem is the nutritious **Red Oat Grass** (*Themeda triandra*). It is on these highly productive pastures that the great herds congregate to feed for part of the year. Scattered across the plains, often in splendid isolation or in small thickets, are several species of acacia thorn-bearing trees. Among the most obvious are the **Whistling Thorn** (*Vachellia drepanolobium*), the **Senegal Gum** (*Senegalia senegal*) and the **Red Acacia** (**Shittah**) (*Vachellia seyal*). Along the watercourses you will encounter the tall and elegant **Fever Tree** (*Vachellia xanthophloea*). Up until just a few decades ago vast tracts of the Maasai Mara area were dominated by dense bushland thickets. However, the combination of elephants feeding and frequent fires have greatly reduced this vegetation type. Isolated thickets still remain on the hills to the east and on some rocky ridges. The **Orange-leaved Croton** (*Croton dichogamus*) usually is

- Great array of lodges, tented camps and campsites in reserve and conservancies.
- Some lodges offer balloon trips over part of the reserve.
- At some conservancies horse riding and escorted game walks are offered.
- Fairly extensive track network but in rains many are difficult to negotiate.

A tree euphorbia stands out on the open grassed plains.

dominant in these thickets. The large and distinctive, cactus-like **Candelabra Tree** (*Euphorbia candelabrum*) grows at a few locations. Scattered along the banks of the Mara River are patches of riverine gallery forest. These patches have a great diversity of tree species but their extent is very limited as a result of elephants feeding and fire. Trees include several species of **fig tree** (*Ficus* spp.), **African Greenheart** (*Warburgia ugandensis*) and the **Wild Date Palm** (*Phoenix reclinata*), as well as **Euclea** (**Mukinyai**) (*Euclea divinorum*) and **Giant Diospyros** (*Diospyros abyssinica*).

Wildlife
Mammals

The reserve is busiest when the great herds move into the reserve from the Serengeti. The **Western White-bearded Wildebeest** move into the Maasai Mara from about July into October but timing varies from year to year. Although the main wildebeest influx is from the Serengeti, a separate population moves into the area southwards from the Loita Plains. These movements are influenced by such factors as timing and quantity of rainfall in different parts of the ecosystem. However, it is not only the wildebeest that take part in this great migration but also large numbers of **Plains Zebra** and **Thomson's Gazelles**. The main attraction for most people at this time is when the great herds cross the Mara River to reach the grass growth in the Mara Triangle. Between November and July the herds return to the Serengeti and the western Ngorongoro. A great diversity of

Game crossing the Mara River are heavily predated by Nile Crocodiles.

WILDLIFE FACTS

- 566 bird species recorded from the Maasai Mara complex, including migrants.
- At least 100 mammal species but bats, rodents and shrews not fully surveyed.
- Best park in Kenya to view large predators, including Lion.
- The greatest ungulate migration on Earth partly plays out here every year.
- No full amphibian and reptile lists but Nile Crocodiles abundant in Mara River.

Common Hippopotamus basking on the bank of the Mara River

game species remain in the Maasai Mara throughout the year, including **Plains Zebra**, **Maasai Giraffe**, **Savanna Buffalo**, some wildebeest, **Topi**, **Coke's Hartebeest**, **Common Eland**, **Impala**, **Grant's Gazelle**, **Thomson's Gazelle** and **Defassa Waterbuck**. **Oribi** are fairly common on the grasslands, as is the **Naivasha Dik-dik** in the thicket country in the east. **Bushbuck (Imbabala)** are largely restricted to the remaining patches of the riverine forest. **Common Hippopotamus** are often sighted and are largely linked to the Mara River and its associated grasslands. This is one of the best conservation areas in Kenya to see **Lion**, **Leopard**, **Cheetah** and **Spotted Hyaena**, but inevitably you are likely to share the viewing with many other safari vehicles. Both **Banded** and **Dwarf mongoose** troops are regularly encountered along river fringes and areas of thicket but not on open grassland. **African Civet** and **Common Large-spotted Genet** are often seen at night around the lodges and tented camps. **African Wolf**, **Side-striped Jackal** and

Topi bull

This is one of the best areas in Kenya to spot Cheetah.

Oribi, here a ram, occur only on the open grassland.

Elephants near Kichwa Tembo Lodge

Guereza Colobus occur only in the restricted area of riverine forest.

Black-backed Jackal occur but only the last is regularly seen. **Savanna Elephant** occurs in relatively small numbers and is usually associated with the area of the Mara River. **Hook-lipped Rhinoceros** used to be common here but intensive poaching has reduced their numbers and the survivors are mainly found in the eastern thickets. Primates include **Olive Baboon, Vervet Monkey, Sykes's (Blue) Monkey, Red-tailed Monkey** and marginally the **Guereza (Black and White Colobus)**, the latter three exclusively tied to the isolated patches of riverine forest. **Unstriped Ground Squirrels** occur but are not common here.

Birds

The birdlife of the Maasai Mara system is amazingly diverse with as many as 566 species, not all centred on the reserve but taking into account the various conservancies around its fringes. The **Maasai Ostrich** is common and the pink-legged and -necked male is distinctive. An impressive 46 species of raptor have been recorded, ranging in size from the **Martial Eagle** and **Secretary Bird** to the tiny **Pygmy Falcon**. More uncommon raptors include **Cuckoo Falcon, Bat Hawk** and **African Goshawk**, all mainly associated with the riverine forest patches. Due to the high density of large predators, numbers of several vulture species and the **Marabou Stork** are relatively high. Also, when the great herds are crossing the Mara River many drown and the carcasses are attended by many of these scavenging birds, often too full to take off easily. Gamebirds to look out for include **Yellow-necked Spurfowl, Crested Francolin** and **Hildebrandt's Francolin** and the common **Helmeted Guineafowl**. There are five bustards with the **Kori Bustard** and **Hartlaub's Bustard** quite commonly sighted but **Black-bellied Bustard** less so. There are five species of turaco, either associated with riverine forest or thicket

Kori Bustard is quite commonly sighted

country: **Schalow's Turaco**, **Ross's Turaco**, **Eastern Grey Plantain-eater**, **White-bellied Go-away-bird** and **Bare-faced Go-away-bird**. Of the hornbills, the large **Southern Ground Hornbill** is mainly seen on the grassed plains but several others are found in the riverine forest, including the very localized **Black and White Casqued Hornbill** and **Crowned Hornbill**, with three other species found in woodland and thicket. The mainly seasonal Musiara Marsh is the only place where the **Rufous-bellied Heron** is known to breed in Kenya, and it also attracts the rare **Madagascar Squacco Heron** from October to May. Up to 13 species of barbet occur in the Maasai Mara, most in association with forest patches along the Mara River but the **Red-fronted Barbet** is usually located in acacia thicket and woodland. Larks, longclaws and pipits are well represented, mainly on the grasslands, including **Yellow-throated**, **Pangani** and **Rosy-breasted longclaws**. At least 18 species of weaver are present, most associated with the riverine areas but the **Buffalo Weaver**, **White-headed Buffalo Weaver** and **White-browed Sparrow-Weaver** are mainly associated with woodland and thicket. As with most parks, some of the best birding is to be had in the grounds of the lodges and camps.

Male Maasai Ostrich in full breeding colours

Reptiles and amphibians

The Mara River is known for its abundance, and large size, of its **Nile Crocodiles**. They are frequently seen sun basking but are at their most active during the migration, when they actively hunt wildebeest, zebra and other game crossing the river. The large **Nile Monitor** lizard also frequents the banks and waters of the Mara River. The **Helmeted Terrapin** also occurs along the river, with the large **Leopard Tortoise** elsewhere. One of the commonest lizards is the **Striped Skink**, which reaches up to 25cm in length and is often seen around the lodges and camps. The brightly coloured and large (to 32cm) **Mwanza Flat-headed Agama** is easy to see and is associated with rocky outcrops. **Rock Pythons** are present but it is not clear whether the species here is the Southern or Central African species. Just 16 species of amphibian are recorded from the area but this is likely to grow as more surveys are undertaken.

Helmeted Terrapin

- Maasai Mara lies in a malaria area.
- This is Kenya's busiest conservation area, particularly during the migration.
- No lodge or camp is fenced, so always be alert for potentially dangerous game.
- Maintenance of access and internal roads is not a priority; especially during the rains mobility can be greatly reduced in areas with cotton soil.

The Golden-rumped Giant Sengi is one of the rare residents in this national park.

Arabuko Sokoke National Park covers a small area (370km²) of the forest reserve of the same name and lies in the north between the towns of Kilifi and Malindi and some 110km north of Mombasa. There is an altitudinal range of 120–450m and an annual rainfall of 900–1,200mm. This forest is the largest remaining block of coastal forest in East Africa. Unfortunately, the forest as a whole comes under considerable human pressures, including illegal logging and poaching, despite the fact that it is considered to be one of the 25 biodiversity hotspots in the world. Arabuko was first protected as a Crown Forest in 1932. The flat eastern sector has sands and clays of Pleistocene origin with red Magarini sands to the west. The forest is made up of three major types, mixed forest in the east that is tall and dense with a diversity of tree species such as **Mgurure** (*Combretum schumannii*), **False Forest Ironplum** (*Drypetes reticulata*), **Pod Mahogany** (*Afzelia quanzensis*) and **Zanzibar Milkwood** (*Manilkara sansibarensis*). More or less through the centre of the forest running north to south is open forest dominated by **Zebra Wood** (*Brachystegia spiciformis*). In the west on the red sands is forest and thicket with tree species such as *Cynometra webberi* and *Manilkara sulcata*, as well as *Oldfieldia somalensis*. Although a small number of **Savanna Elephant** occur, it is the park's numerous smaller species that attract the keen naturalist. These include the endangered **Aders' Duiker**, **Sokoke Bushy-tailed Mongoose**, **Golden-rumped Giant Sengi** and the **African Golden Cat**, which is believed to occur but needs to be confirmed. This forest has been described as the second-most important in Africa for bird conservation, with such rarities as the endemic **Clarke's Weaver**, **Sokoke Scops Owl**, **Fischer's Turaco**, **Spotted Ground Thrush**, **Sokoke Pipit**, **East Coast Akalat**, **Amani Sunbird**, **Scaly Babbler** and **African Pitta**. A total of 230 bird species have been recorded from the forest. It is also an important locality for localized and rare reptiles and amphibians. Reptiles include **Green Keel-bellied Lizard** and **Tropical Girdled Lizard**, and there are at least 36 species of amphibian, including six species of toad and at least nine of reed frog. There is no accommodation in the park but plenty in towns nearby. There are some excellent guides, especially for birding, who will take you on trails for a fee.

HELL'S GATE NATIONAL PARK

The cliffs in Hell's Gate are home to a large colony of Rüppell's Vultures.

Hell's Gate was proclaimed as a national park in 1984. It covers just 68km² and lies almost adjacent to the southern edge of Lake Naivasha. It was named Hell's Gate in 1883 by the explorers Fischer and Thomson. From Nairobi to Naivasha village is just 80km to the north-west, turning on to the Moi South Lake road to the Elsa gate, which takes its name from Elsa, the lioness that was raised by Joy and George Adamson. Her old home lies close to the turnoff to the park. Much of the rugged landscape was formed by volcanic actions and there are still a number of active steam-vents, some of which are tapped for the production of geothermal power. The dominant landform feature in the park is the Ol Njorowa Gorge, the Hell's Gate, with its sheer, towering cliffs and the volcanic plugs known as Central and Fischer's towers. This area receives meagre rainfall (200–700mm), with the principal falls in March and April and November and December, and this is evidenced in the vegetation. Much of the park is rugged and broken with mainly sparse grassland and scattered low trees dominated by several

One of several volcanic plugs located in Hell's Gate National Park

acacia (*Vachellia* and *Senegalia*) species, as well as **Kileleshwa** (*Tarchonanthus camphoratus*), which rarely reaches 6m in height. Game is not abundant but includes small populations of **Plains Zebra, Savanna Buffalo, Common Eland, Coke's Hartebeest, Topi, Impala** and **Naivasha Dik-dik**, among others. Not so readily seen are **Chanler's Mountain Reedbuck** and **Klipspringer**. **Leopard** and **Spotted Hyaena** are present but there are no recent records of Lion. Small carnivores here include the diurnal **Banded Mongoose** and **Dwarf Mongoose** as well as the nocturnal **White-tailed Mongoose** and **Small-spotted Genet**. One of the most frequently observed small mammals is the colonial **Yellow-spotted Rock Hyrax**, which occurs in all rocky situations but is easiest to watch around Fischer's Tower. Several troops of **Olive Baboon** occur in the area. Up to >100 bird species have been listed. The birding highlight is the large numbers of **Rüppell's Vulture** that roost and nest on the gorge cliffs. This is the most accessible roost in East Africa. Other raptors that frequent these cliffs include **Bearded Vulture** (very rare), **Verreaux's Eagle**, **Peregrine Falcon** and **Rock Kestrel**. The largest bird here is the **Maasai Ostrich**. A few others to look for include **Hildebrandt's Francolin**, **Yellow-necked Spurfowl**, **Pectoral-patch Cisticola** and **Golden-breasted Bunting**. No list of reptiles and amphibians has been compiled but the limited-range **Kenya Horned Viper** occurs. There is no accommodation in the park, but there are many options around Lake Naivasha and there are three public campsites with minimal facilities, most with none. Walking, biking and rock climbing are permitted, and there is a limited game-viewing road network.

MOUNT LONGONOT NATIONAL PARK

Mount Longonot's crater is an isolated ecosystem.

Covering just 52km², Mount Longonot National Park protects a recently dormant stratovolcano and its biota, and lies about 60km from Nairobi. The last eruption is believed to have taken place in the 1860s but there are several parasitic cones on the flanks and within the caldera. It is deemed likely that further eruptions could occur. Longonot is said to have taken its name from the Maasai word *Oloonong'ot*, which roughly translated means 'mountains of many spurs'. The caldera is 8×12km and was formed some 21,000 years before present. The gate to the park lies on the 2,150m contour and the summit at 2,776m. There is woodland on the caldera floor, and small numbers of **Plains Zebra**, **Maasai Giraffe**, **Savanna Buffalo** and **Coke's Hartebeest** are present. The only large predator reported is the **Leopard**, but it is not known if any are resident. Little is known of the park's bird, reptile or amphibian life. Access from the gate is by walking trail, and there is a public campsite close to the gate and others deeper in the park.

MARSABIT NATIONAL PARK

The heart-shaped crater of Marsabit

Marsabit, raised from national reserve to national park, covers 1,554km², and the name loosely translates as 'the place of cold'. It has an altitudinal range of 410–1,691m asl. It is a basalt shield volcano with numerous craters known locally as *gofs*. The park lies on the edge of the Chalbi Desert. The tribes in the area surrounding the park include Rendille, Samburu, Borana and Gabbra. Accommodation includes the basic Marsabit Lodge located on the edge of the craterlike Gof Sokorte Dika, a public campsite and a special campsite deeper in the park. Potential visitors should be aware that the park lies 560km from Nairobi and vehicles may be required to travel in convoy because of security risks. Roads leading to and within the park are limited and can become extremely challenging during heavy rain. Poaching, illegal timber cutting and human encroachment are ongoing problems. The crater lakes have been infested by the Nile Cabbage (*Pistia stratiotes*) and the lack of open water has reduced their attractiveness to waterfowl.

Days are generally hot (averaging 28°C) and nights are cool (12°C), becoming colder at higher altitudes. There is a short rainy season, followed by the relatively dry months of January and February, with long rains running from March to May (heaviest in April). Fog is common overnight and into the morning at the higher altitudes.

There is a population of **Savanna Elephant**, **Savanna Buffalo**, **Greater Kudu**, **Bushbuck** (**Imbabala**), with **Peters' Gazelle** (previously a subspecies of Grant's Gazelle), **Beisa Oryx** and **Grevy's Zebra** in the surrounding drier scrub. Game viewing can be challenging. **Olive Baboons** occur throughout, with **Guereza (Black and White Colobus)** in the forests.

Although up to 350 bird species have been recorded, this is for the greater Marsabit area and not just for the park. There are 52 species of raptor, including **Bearded Vulture**, which are said to breed on the cliffs of Gof Bongale, **Mountain Buzzard** and **Peregrine Falcon**. Also here are **Hartlaub's Turaco**, **Somali Bee-eater**, **Somali Courser**, **Somali Crow**, **William's Lark** and **Vulturine Guineafowl**. The **Somali Ostrich** is present on the plains and has recently been recognized as a full species in its own right.

Marsabit has a rich reptile fauna and includes the **Side-striped Chameleon** and **Mount Marsabit Chameleon (Garrara)**, known only from here at about 1,250m.

MOUNT ELGON NATIONAL PARK

Koitobos Peak with moorland in the foreground, Mount Elgon

Mount Elgon straddles the border between Kenya and Uganda, and is a massive solitary shield volcanic mountain believed to be at least 24 million years old – the oldest extinct volcano in East Africa. It is some 80km in diameter and rises over 3,000m above the surrounding plain, with its highest point, Wagagai (4,321m), on the Ugandan side of the border. The other high points are Sudek (4,302m), Koitobos (4,222m), Mubiyi (4,211m) and Masaba (4,161m). Much of the conserved area lies on the Ugandan side (1,110km²) with just 169km² on the Kenya side gazetted as a national park in 1968. Mount Elgon is the main catchment for the Nzoia River, which flows into Lake Victoria, and the Turkwel River, which feeds into Lake Turkana. Annual average rainfall is 2,270mm; rain falls throughout the year, but drier months are June to August and December to March. Vegetation is similar to that on other African equatorial mountains, extending from the lower montane forest with **East African Olive (Black Ironwood)** (*Olea hochstetteri*) and **Navel Fruit** (*Omphalocarpum adolfi-friederici*), with **Yellowwoods** (including *Afrocarpus gracilior*) and bamboo at higher altitudes. Higher up there is **East African Rosewood** (*Hagenia abyssinica*), with **Giant Heath** (*Erica arborea*) and **giant lobelias, giant groundsels** and **everlastings** in the subalpine zone. At least 400 plant species are recorded. Game numbers are low but include **Savanna Elephant** and **Savanna Buffalo**, which penetrate the caves Kitum, Chepnyali and Mackingeny to access natural salts. **Bushbuck (Imbabala)** and **Common Duiker** are the most frequently seen. Primates include the **Guereza, Sykes's (Blue) Monkey** and **Red-tailed Monkey**. Just 42 mammal species have been listed but more smaller species can be expected to occur. At least 244 bird species are known to occur, including **Jackson's Francolin, Bronze-naped Pigeon, Hartlaub's Turaco** and the **Tacazze Sunbird**. Although not fully surveyed, herpetofauna is believed to be rich, with 67 species known, including **Mount Elgon Forest Gecko, Alpine Meadow Skink, Montane Side-striped Chameleon, Von Höhnel's Chameleon** and **Green Bush Viper**. Facilities at the park are limited.

KAKAMEGA FOREST NATIONAL RESERVE

Kakamega Forest is unique in Kenya, as it is the the country's only surviving remnant of the equatorial rainforest. It lies within the counties of Kakamega and Kisumu and within the Lake Victoria Basin. This forest remnant was once a part of the great forests of the Congo Basin. It lies north-west of Nairobi and in close proximity to the Ugandan border. The national reserve covers 45km^2 of the total complex, which extends over some 238km^2, of which about half is degraded. The reserve was gazetted in 1985 and occurs at up to 1,600m asl, although the

Blue Monkey in Kakamega

forested hills Bunyala and Lirhanda rise to 2,060m. The forest has an average annual rainfall of 2,080mm, with the heaviest falls in April and May, and a second peak from September to November. Temperatures are fairly constant, with an average minimum of 11˚C and average maximum of 26˚C. Within the forest there are a number of open glades, and several small streams cut through the reserve. Of the over 380 recorded plant species in the reserve, 150 are trees or bushes and 60 are species of orchid, primarily epiphytes, nine of which occur only here. Trees in the more open areas include **Velvet Bush-willow** (*Combretum molle*), **False Assegai** (*Maesa lanceolata*) and **Dragon's Blood Tree (Haronga)** (*Harungana madagascariensis*), and the forest edge is mostly lined by dense thickets of **Honey Shrub** (*Acanthus polystachyus*). Forest trees mostly have well-buttressed bases and include **Elgon Teak (Elgon Olive)** (*Olea welwitschii*), **White Stinkwood** (*Celtis africana*) and **African Cherry** (*Prunus africana*). Vines and lianas are common. Mammals include **Potto, Olive Baboon, Guereza Colobus, Blue Monkey, Red-tailed Monkey, De Brazza's Monkey, Bushpig, Bushbuck (Imbabala), African Giant Squirrel, Red-legged Sun Squirrel** and a great diversity of small carnivores, but these are rarely seen. This is the only location in Kenya where you are likely to hear the loud honking of the very large male **Hammer-headed Fruit-bat**. Most visitors come here for the birds, some 367 species, including nine species that occur nowhere else in the country, such as **Turner's Eremomela** and **Chapin's Flycatcher**. Other special birds occurring here are **Ross's Turaco, Great Blue Turaco, Eastern Grey Plantain-eater, African Grey Parrot, Blue-headed Bee-eater, Black and White Casqued Hornbill, Bar-tailed Trogon, African Broadbill, Black-headed Paradise Flycatcher, Blue-shouldered Robin-Chat, Blue-throated Brown Sunbird** and **Veillot's Black Weaver**. Reptiles are well represented, with more than 20 snake species, including **Gold's Cobra, Barred Green Snake, Black-lined Green Snake, Jameson's Mamba, Green Bush-viper** and **Rhinoceros Viper**, as well as several gecko and chameleon species. No less than 490 butterfly species occur, as well as the spectacular **Goliath Beetle** and the **African Flower Mantid**. There are campsites and other accommodation options in the area, as well as a network of walking trails, with or without a guide.

SHIMBA HILLS NATIONAL RESERVE

Shimba Hills National Reserve is situated 56km to the south-west of Mombasa and covers an area of 300km². Extending from the reserve's northern boundary is the Mwaluganje Elephant Sanctuary, which serves as a corridor for Savanna Elephants to move between Shimba Hills and Tsavo East. The rest of the reserve is fenced to prevent elephants moving on to adjacent farmland. Shimba first received protection in 1903 as a national forest. This coastal forest is one of the largest surviving blocks in East Africa, but there are also areas of open grassland and woodland. Almost 1,400 plant species have been recorded

Shimba Hills is the only place in Kenya where Sable Antelope occur naturally.

from Shimba and surrounding areas, making up about 20% of all Kenya's plant species. The area is particularly rich in both terrestrial and epiphytic orchids. Rainfall averages 1,213mm per annum, with higher falls in winter than in summer, although rain may fall any time of the year and mist is common. Annual average temperature is 26°C. There is a dense **Savanna Elephant** population of several hundred animals but there is some dispersal out of the reserve to the north-east at times. This is the only conservation area in Kenya with **Sable Antelope** and these are strongly linked to the open grassland areas. **Savanna Buffalo** occur, as do **Bushbuck (Imbabala)**, **Roan Antelope** (introduced) and **Common Warthog**, and there is a small number of **Maasai Giraffe**. **Yellow Baboon** occur, as do **Vervet Monkey**, **Sykes's (Blue) Monkey**, **Angolan Black and White Colobus**, **Thick-tailed Greater Galago** and **Northern Lesser Galago**. **Leopard** are found in the area but are seldom seen and most small carnivores here are nocturnal. However, at night around the Shimba Hill Lodge there is a good chance of seeing **African Civet** and **Common Large-spotted Genet**. Smaller species you may see during the day include **Red Bush Squirrel** (often around the lodge). More than 200 bird species have been recorded, and from late March into early April large numbers of Palaearctic migrants pass through, including **European Golden Oriole** and **European Cuckoo**. Other birds present include **African Crowned Eagle, Red-necked Spurfowl, Kenya Crested Guineafowl, Fischer's Turaco, Trumpeter Hornbill, Silvery-cheeked Hornbill, African Pitta, Pangani Longclaw, East Coast Akalat, Croaking Cisticola, Zanzibar Puff-back Shrike** and **Zanzibar Red Bishop**. An astonishing 35 species of amphibian have been recorded, with several very localized species. Although not as well documented, the reptile inventory is likely high, and includes **Yellow-headed Day Gecko, Speckle-lipped Skink, Bearded Pygmy Chameleon, Spotted Bush Snake, Forest Cobra** and **Green Mamba**. Most people visit for a day from the coastal resorts but there is a lodge in the park, as well as several public campsites.

LAKE BOGORIA NATIONAL RESERVE

Hot-water geysers flank Lake Bogoria, here with the Ngendelel Escarpment as backdrop.

Lake Bogoria National Reserve, managed by the Kenya Wildlife Service, covers 107km² and lies within the Eastern Rift in south-western Kenya, north of Nairobi. The reserve incorporates the lake and a relatively narrow band of land around it. During the colonial period the lake was known as Lake Hannington. It lies in the valley floor with the near sheer wall of the Ngendelel Escarpment rising 600m on the eastern lake shore. The lake is shallow, about 12m, and is rich in sodium, carbonate and bicarbonate ions, with a salinity about twice that of sea water. Only one stream feeds into the lake, the Waseges, which rises on the northern slope of the Aberdares range. The greenish water of the lake has an oily consistency and when the mud is disturbed it gives off a distinctly unpleasant odour. All around the edge of the lake hot steam and water escape from fissures and vents. The lake faces threats from heavy use of agricultural chemicals used along the upper reaches of the Waseges River, as well as siltation. The presence of vast numbers of flamingos, mainly **Lesser Flamingos**, is one of the greatest natural sights, although the timing is hard to predict. Although these colourful birds feed throughout the lake, for drinking and bathing they utilize some of the hot springs, water that may reach a temperature of 50°C. To sit in the reeds just 10 metres away from thousands of flamingos beautifying themselves and slaking their thirst is not only awe-inspiring, but also deafening. Here, not only are the flamingos preyed upon by **Tawny Eagles**, but **African Fish Eagle** have taken to hunting these long-legged waterbirds due to the absence of fish in the lake. Even a few **Olive Baboon** males have got into the act. The official bird list stands at 135 species and includes substantial numbers of **Cape Teal, Yellow-billed Stork** and the nocturnal **Water Stone Curlew**, among others. Large game is not abundant but **Savanna Buffalo, Common Warthog** and **Plains Zebra** occur and it is probably the best location to see the **Greater Kudu**, which is generally scarce elsewhere in Kenya. **Vervet Monkeys** and Olive Baboons can be a nuisance at the campsites. There is a lodge near the northern entrance gate.

UGANDA

Bwindi Impenetrable National Park in south-western Uganda

By African standards, Uganda is a fairly small country, covering 242,554km². It is bounded by South Sudan in the north, Democratic Republic of Congo to the west, Rwanda and Tanzania to the south, with Kenya on its eastern flank. The country is 'sandwiched' between the western and eastern arms of the Great Rift Valley. Much of the country lies at over 1,000m asl. Africa's highest mountain range, the Rwenzoris (the legendary 'Mountains of the Moon'), forms part of its border with DR Congo. This range extends 120km from north to south and averages 48km in width, with its highest point, Mount Margherita, rising to 5,109m. In the south-west the Virunga Volcanoes are the meeting place for the boundaries of Uganda, Rwanda and DR Congo. Lake Victoria, Africa's largest lake, dominates the south-east, while lakes Edward, George and Albert are located in the west. The Victoria Nile exits from Lake Victoria at Jinja, flows into Lake Kyoga and then north-westwards through Murchison Falls National Park to where it joins the Albert Nile. The area to the south of the Nile River is well watered, but the further one moves northward the drier the landscape becomes. Approximately 17% of the country is covered by fresh water.

With the exception of the north-east, which has a distinct dry season, rain can be expected throughout the year. However, there are two discernible rainfall peaks, September to mid-December and March to May. Annual rainfall averages between 1,000mm and 2,000mm but this is exceeded in the montane areas, particularly in the Virungas and Rwenzoris. Forested and mountain areas receive drenching downpours in these seasons and violent thunderstorms are common. Remember though, rain can be expected at any time of year to the south of the Nile. Although the country has an equatorial climate, temperatures in areas are influenced by altitude and proximity to lakes. Overall daily maximum temperatures are in the range of 20°–27°C, minimums 12°–18°C.

The country has a predominantly rural population, and settlement is particularly dense in the south and central areas. There are more than 40 distinct ethnic groups, of which the Baganda, Basoga, Ankole and Toro make up a large percentage of the population in the south, with the Acholi, Karimojong and the Iteso in the north. The first peoples to occupy the area that is now known as Uganda were the nomadic

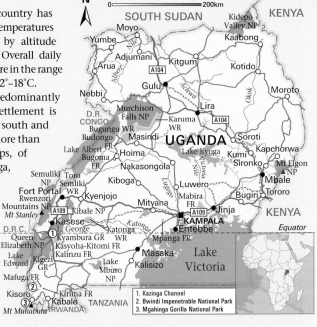

hunter-gatherers, with the first Bantu-speakers moving from West Africa, across the north of Central Africa, into East Africa some 3,000 to 2,000 years before present. The Kingdom of Batembuzi was already well established by 1,000AD to the south of the Nile. There was a succession of kingdoms that evolved into the 19th century, some running concurrently within separate territories, including those of Buganda, Bunyoro, Ankole and Toro. With the arrival of the Arab slave-traders in the middle of the 19th century the Buganda Kingdom was the dominant tribal force. The British took possession in 1892 during the European 'scramble for Africa' and held it until independence in 1962. During the 1970s and 1980s Uganda was under the sway of brutal dictatorship, civil war and invasion.

Uganda has about 25% forest and woodland cover with the most important tropical lowland forests in the south and west. The area to the north of the Nile is dominated by what is known as Sudanian wood- and grassland, with a strong mix of *Vachellia-Senegalia-Brachystegia* tree species.

The British colonial administration set aside a number of conservation areas and today there are 10 national parks, eight wildlife reserves, including Katonga and Toro Semliki (most of which lack proper protection and are not covered here), as well as a number of forest reserves.

More than 6,000 plant species have been recorded from the country, with forest areas being particularly rich in diversity. Some 330 mammal species occur – including critically important populations of Mountain Gorilla and Common Chimpanzee – as well as at least 1,060 bird species, at least eight tortoises and terrapins, 51 lizards, both Nile and Dwarf crocodiles, 105 snakes and 54 amphibian species.

COMMON CHIMPANZEE IN EAST AFRICA

The **Common (Robust) Chimpanzee** occurs in a belt of forest and woodland from Senegal in West Africa to western Tanzania. Up until recently, just four subspecies have been recognized, with *Pan troglodytes schweinfurthii* occurring in forest pockets of western East Africa. However, some scientists believe that these populations should get their own subspecies designation, *P. t. marungensis*. Nearly all of the Chimpanzee populations in the region are isolated, with many forest blocks separated from each other by human settlements and subsistence cultivation. Chimpanzees are not easy to count, but the best estimates for Uganda range from 4,000–5,700, with by far the largest populations in Kibale National Park (± 1,298), Budongo Forest Reserve (± 580), Bugomo Forest Reserve (± 570), Ruwenzori Mountains National Park (± 454), Maramagambo Forest in Queen Elizabeth National Park (± 200) and Bwindi Impenetrable National Park (± 200). The main threats facing Chimpanzees is lack of corridors between forest blocks (which would facilitate interaction between populations), direct hunting (mainly Rwenzoris) for meat for human and dog consumption, and killing of crop-raiding individuals. Snares set for other species often catch Chimpanzees and many, especially in Kibale and Budongo, have lost hands or feet as a result. The only viable Chimpanzee population in Rwanda occurs in the Nyungwe National Park, which adjoins Kibira National Park in Burundi, allowing movement for the ± 700 animals who live there, thus increasing their chances of survival. Conservation levels are much higher in Rwanda than they currently are in Burundi. Only two populations in Tanzania occur in national parks, Gombe Stream and Mahale Mountains, both on the shore of Lake Tanganyika, with the latter home to the largest population in the country. Within the greater Mahale ecosystem beyond the park there are non-protected populations in the Masito-Ugalla areas, as well as Ntakata and Kalobwe forests. The latest estimate for Tanzania is 2,500 Common Chimpanzees, but this may be far too optimistic.

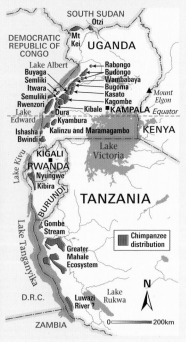

Chimpanzees in Kayumbura Gorge, Uganda

BWINDI IMPENETRABLE NATIONAL PARK

Most people visit Bwindi to see the Gorillas, but many other species occur here.

Lie of the land

Bwindi is located in south-west Uganda on the edge of the Albertine Rift Valley, bordering the Democratic Republic of Congo to the west. The park covers 331km² and is located 29km from the nearest principal town, Kabale. It lies within the highest areas of the Kigezi Highlands, from a minimum of 1,190m asl in the north to 2,607m on Rwamunyonyi Hill at its eastern edge. These highlands are sometimes referred to as Rukiga. The park is composed of rugged and much dissected hills, largely forest covered except for the area of the Mubwindi Swamp. Bwindi is an ecological island ringed by intense cultivation and one of the highest human population densities in Africa.

Brief history

Although no archaeological sites have been located in the park, humans are known to have occupied the region for at least 37,000 years before present. Evidence of first forest clearance dates back some 4,800 years when the area was occupied by Batwa Pygmies, hunter-gatherers still found in areas outside the park today. The first Bantu settlers arrived in the area about 2,000 years ago. The principal tribal groups in the area are the Bachiga, Bafumbira and

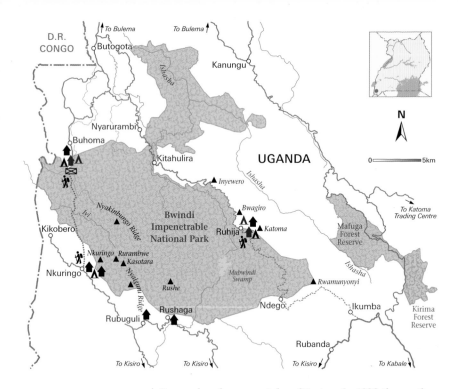

Barwanda, who are mainly cultivators. In 1932 the northern and southern parts of the forest were gazetted as the Kasatora and Kayonza forest reserves, and in 1942 they were amalgamated and named as the Impenetrable Central Crown Forest Reserve. The Batwa were ejected from the forest in 1964.In the same year the reserve gained greater protection, specifically aimed at the Mountain Gorillas, and in 1991 was proclaimed a national park.

Geology and landscape

Bwindi is very rugged and is dominated by steep-sided hills and narrow valleys, especially in the south and south-east. These highlands are an important water catchment: the three tributaries of the Ishasha River rise here and flow into Lake Edward in the north, and the Ndego, Nyamwambo and Shongi rivers course southwards and flow into Lake Mutanda. The 80ha Mubwindi Swamp lies in the southern sector of the park. The highlands were created during the upwarping of the Western Rift Valley, and the underlying rocks belong to the Karagwe-Ankolean system and are mainly phyllites, shales, quartz and quartzite, with some granite outcrops.

HIGHLIGHTS

- Opportunity to trek to habituated Mountain Gorilla groups.
- Great diversity of mammals and birds.
- Many Albertine Rift endemics.

Bwindi Impenetrable Forest National Park is home to some 400 Mountain Gorillas.

FACILITIES AND ACTIVITIES

- Several lodges and camps fringe the park.
- No roads in the park, just hiking trails.
- Guided Mountain Gorilla treks (limited number of permits per day).

Climate

The park has a tropical climate with rainfall peaking in March to May and September to November and averaging 1,130–2,390mm per annum, depending on the location. Average minimum temperatures are 7°–15°C and maximums 20°–28°C.

Vegetation

This is one of the few remaining large expanses of a blend of lowland and montane forest in East Africa. The northern sector of the forest is rich in Guineo-Congolian flora and was a refuge for species during the Pleistocene epoch, which is one of the reasons this forest is so rich in plant and animal species. With more than 200 tree species, Bwindi has few equals in East Africa. The Impenetrable part of its name refers to the dense undergrowth, especially in the valleys, which is impossible to traverse other than by using trails. Of the plus 200 tree species, 12 are known to occur only in Bwindi and include **Tallow Tree** (*Allanblackia kimbiliensis*), *Croton bukobensis, Grewia midbraedii*

Bwindi is rich in plant species and has dense undergrowth.

A young Mountain Gorilla

and *Strombosiopsis tetrandra*. Other tree species include **Brown Mahogany** (*Lovoa swynnertonii*), **Red Stinkwood** (*Prunus africana*), *Newtonia buchananii*, **Chewstick** (*Symphonia globulifera*) and several **Yellowwood** types (*Podocarpus* spp.). At lower levels, **Guinea Plum** (*Parinari excelsa*) is common, as is *Chrysophyllum gorungosanum* around the 2,200m contour.

Wildlife
Mammals

Most visitors come to spend time with the habituated **Mountain Gorillas** at Bwindi, which is home to some 400 of these endangered apes. They differ from the Mountain Gorillas in the nearby Virungas in that they have shorter coats, live at lower altitudes and include much more fruit in their diet and may be more closely related to the Eastern Lowland Gorilla. Of the 120 mammals recorded in Bwindi, 14 are primates, including **Common (Robust) Chimpanzee**, **L'Hoest's Monkey**, **Guereza (Black and White Colobus)**, **Red-tailed Monkey**, **Blue Monkey**, **Vervet Monkey** and **Olive Baboon**. There are also a number of nocturnal primates, including the **Potto, Spectacled Lesser Galago, Thomas's Dwarf Galago** and **Demidoff's Dwarf Galago**. A few **Savanna Elephant** are believed to survive here, and **Giant Forest Hog, Bushpig**

L'Hoest's Monkey is one of 14 species of primate known to occur in Bwindi.

and **Bushbuck** are still found widely. Three duiker species occur, **Yellow-backed**, **Black-fronted** and **Weyns's duikers**. Small mammal species number 67, including rodents, shrews and bats.

Birds

There are 348 bird species recorded, including 70 of the Albertine Rift endemics, with 14 species known only from Bwindi and a few neighbouring forests in Uganda. Some of the specials include **Dwarf Honeyguide**, **African Green Broadbill**, **Lagden's Bushshrike**, **Kivu Ground Thrush**, **Oberlander's Ground Thrush**, **Grauer's Rush Warbler**, **Chaplin's Flycatcher** and **Dusky Crimsonwing**. The forest is home to other rarities, including **Fraser's Eagle-Owl**, **White-bellied Robin-Chat**, **Yellow-eyed Black Flycatcher**, **Montane Double-collared Sunbird** and **Dusky Twinspot**. As with birding in any forest, one needs patience and an experienced guide. Although birding is good throughout the year, during the heaviest rain periods roads and park trails become muddy and difficult to negotiate. Migratory birds are present November into April.

Reptiles and amphibians

There are 14 snake species recorded from Bwindi, nine of which are endemic, or near endemic, in this park. A few of the more restricted species include the **Pale-headed Forest Snake**, **Günther's Green Tree Snake**, **Jameson's Mamba**, **Rhinoceros Viper** and **Great Lakes Bush Viper**. Although lizards are not particularly diverse here there are six known species of chameleon, such as **Montane Side-striped**, **Rwenzori Three-horned**, **Rwenzori Side-striped** and **Boulenger's Pygmy chameleons**, the last reaching a length of just 8cm and living mainly on the forest floor. Of the 27 amphibian species, 11 are Albertine Rift endemics, of which six are considered to be rare because of limited range, including **Western Rift Leaf-folding Frog** and **Ahl's Reed Frog**. The **White-snouted Reed Frog** is known only from Bwindi and a few other locations nearby.

> **!**
> * **Lies in a malaria area.**
> * **There are only walking trails in the park, which are mostly steep and slippery.**
> * **Limited number of gorilla tracking permits issued daily.**

WILDLIFE FACTS

* 120 mammal species.
* Home to almost half the world's Mountain Gorilla population.
* 348 bird species.
* 34 reptiles and 27 amphibian species.
* >1,000 plant species, including >200 trees and >100 ferns.
* >220 butterfly species; three species only in Bwindi; eight Albertine Rift endemics.

Lagden's Bushshrike

Jameson's Mamba

A habituated chimp in Kibale National Park

Lie of the land

Kibale lies within the districts of Kabarole and Kamwenge and is located some 320km from Kampala, with Fort Portal the nearest town. To the south it adjoins Queen Elizabeth National Park, forming a long corridor for wildlife migration. The park covers 795km^2 and has an altitudinal range of 1,100–1,590m asl. The park incorporates extensive areas of mature tropical rainforest, swamp, thicket, grassland and secondary forest.

Brief history

Kibale was established as a forest reserve in 1932, was later extended to the border of Queen Elizabeth National Park, and raised to national park status in 1993. The principal tribes in the area are the Batoro and the Bakiga, who utilize the park (legally and illegally) for resources. The Batoro are native to the region and trace their heritage back to the Toro Kingdom but the Bakiga are relative newcomers. Signs of human utilization of the area of the park, even the old forest, probably date back to the advent of the first humans in the area and accelerated as populations grew. Today the park is ringed by settlements and a growing human population.

Geology and landscape

The rocks of Kibale were formed during the Pre-Cambrian times and are therefore strongly folded and metamorphosed. Overlying these are rocks of the Toro system, which have formed prominent ridges of quartzites intruded by mainly gneiss and granites. Most of the park has red ferralitic soils – mainly sandy clay loams in the north and clay loams in the south. The park is at its highest in the north and lowest in the south where it descends to the Albertine Rift Valley floor.

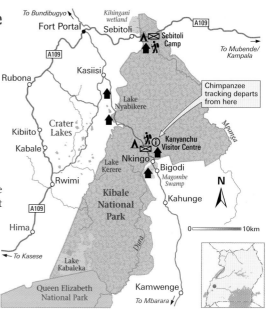

Climate

The north of Kibale has an average annual rainfall of 1,100–1,600mm, with the principal falls in March to May and September to November, but rain should be expected in every month. Higher falls are experienced in the north of the park. The driest month, January, receives an average of 51mm of rain. There are no temperature extremes, with a 24-hour average of 19.9°C in March and 18.6°C in July.

Lowland tropical rainforest

HIGHLIGHTS

- Opportunity to track habituated Common Chimpanzees.
- Great diversity of plants, mammals, birds, reptiles, amphibians and butterflies.
- Network of walking trails – guide/ranger required in park, but not along the main road and in fringing areas.
- Guided night walks in some areas.

Pollia condensata occurs in forested regions.

FACILITIES AND ACTIVITIES

- A variety of accommodation options, including lodges and campsites, mainly fringing the park.
- Walking trails inside and outside the park; guides are required inside and recommended outside.
- Chimpanzee tracking of habituated groups.
- Birdwatching.

Vegetation

Kibale is classified as a transitional lowland-montane moist forest. The moist tropical forest areas and woodland within the park have 351 species of tree including **Mobola Plum** (*Parinari curatellifolia*), **Uganda Ironwood** (**Muhimbi**) (*Cynometra alexandri*), *Cordia millenii*, **'African Mahogany'** (*Entandrophragma angolense*), **Brown Mahogany** (*Lovoa swynnertonii*), **Newtonia** (*Newtonia buchananii*), **Strombosia** (*Strombosia scheffleri*), **Guinea Plum** (*Parinari excelsa*) and **Barkcloth Fig** (*Ficus natalensis*). The park's vegetation is 58% forested area, 15% grassland (mostly located in the south), and a mix of bushland, forest undergoing regeneration (after past human activity) and exotic plantations on the periphery. In some valley bottoms there are swamps and swamp-supported forest.

Wildlife
Mammals

Apart from the large **Common Chimpanzee** population, probably the largest in East Africa, other primates include **Olive Baboon**, **Uganda Mangabey**, **Ugandan Red Colobus**, **L'Hoest's Monkey**, **Red-tailed Monkey**, **Blue Monkey** and **Guereza** (**Black and White Colobus**). The chimpanzees, at least 1,200, have been the focus of studies since the 1980s, including one particularly large group of some 200 individuals. **Vervet Monkeys** occur on forest margins and in wooded grasslands. Nocturnal primates include **Potto**, **Demidoff's Dwarf Galago** and **Spectacled Lesser Galago**. **Savanna Elephant** move between Kibale and the adjoining Queen Elizabeth National Park, so numbers fluctuate and they are rarely encountered, likewise with the **Savanna Buffalo**. Although both are sometimes referred to as forest races, this apparently is not the case. Both **Giant Forest Hog** and **Bushpig** occur, with **Common Warthog** in bush and

Ugandan Red Colobus

grassed areas, as do **Bushbuck, Sitatunga** and **Blue Duiker**. Although **Harvey's Red Duiker** has been listed, it seems more likely that it is **Weyns's Duiker**, which is known to occur in a number of other west Ugandan forests. Most carnivores are secretive and seldom seen but the park is home to **Leopard, African Golden Cat, Serval, Side-striped Jackal, African Civet, African Palm Civet, Servaline Genet** and seven species of mongoose, including **Alexander's Cusimanse**. **Lion** occasionally enter the area but none are apparently resident. Seven species of squirrel have been recorded, as well as **Lord Derby's Anomalure**. Very little work has been undertaken on the smaller rodents, shrews and bats of Kibale.

WILDLIFE FACTS

- 13 primate species, including more than 1,200 Common Chimpanzees.
- At least 70 mammal species (excluding most smaller species).
- 375 bird species.
- 47 reptile and 28 amphibian species.
- 250 butterfly species.
- 229 tree species.

Birds

To date 375 species of bird have been recorded, including the endemic **Kibale Ground Thrush**, as well as localized **Olive Long-tailed Cuckoo, Western Tinkerbird, African** and **Green-breasted pittas, African Grey Parrot, Afep Pigeon, White-naped Pigeon, Red-chested Owlet, Dusky Crimsonwing, Black-capped Apalis, Blue-headed Sunbird, Purple-breasted Sunbird, Black Bee-eater, Blue-breasted Kingfisher, Scaly-breasted Illadopsis, Brown Illadopsis**, and the principal monkey predator, the **African Crowned Eagle**. In addition to forests, the swamps and southern savanna areas are also good birding locations.

Reptiles and amphibians

Kibale has a rich herpetofauna with 15 lizard, 32 snake and 28 amphibian species currently known. Several chameleon species are known to occur, including the **Ituri Forest Chameleon, Ituri Chameleon, Montane Side-striped Chameleon** and **Boulenger's Pygmy Chameleon**. Lizards are not particularly common within the forest but the most conspicuous are **Multi-scaled Forest Lizard** and **Sparse-scaled Forest Lizard**, which are rather slender, reach a length of 20cm and forage in the leaf litter. Wherever there are suitable trees the large **Blue-headed Tree Agama** is common, as is the **Striped Skink**. By far the largest snake is the **Central African Rock Python**.

!
- **Malaria is ever present.**
- **During heavy rain the trails can be heavy going.**
- **Strict rules apply when chimpanzee tracking.**

Black and White Casqued Hornbill

Common Reed Frog

MURCHISON FALLS NATIONAL PARK

Murchison Falls on the Victoria Nile

Lie of the land

Murchison Falls National Park is Uganda's largest conservation area, covering 3,893km², and lies at the northern tip of the Albertine Rift Valley, within north-west Uganda. It adjoins the north-eastern shore of Lake Albert, and the Victoria Nile traverses the park from east to west for 115km, before pouring its waters into the lake. The Bugungu (501km²) and Karuma (678km²) wildlife refuges act as buffers to the south, with the Budongo Forest Reserve (591km²) adjoining Bugungu. As a unit this is now called the Murchison Falls Conservation Area, straddling the districts of Buliisa, Nwoya, Kiryandongo and Masindi. Southern Murchison lies about 305km from Kampala, but can be accessed via several gates.

Brief history

Little is recorded of the early history and pre-history of the area but by as early as 1,000AD the area of the present park fell under the control of the Batembuzi Kingdom, in what is today the Bunyoro District. John Speke and James Grant were the first Europeans to enter the area of Lake Albert in 1862. However, in March 1864 Sir Samuel and Lady Florence Baker were the first Europeans to discover the falls, which they named in honour of Sir Roderick Murchison, then president of the Royal Geographical Society. Between 1907 and 1912 the colonial authorities evacuated most of the inhabitants of this area due to sleeping sickness spread by tsetse flies. In 1910 the area south of the Nile River was proclaimed as the Bunyoro Game Reserve,

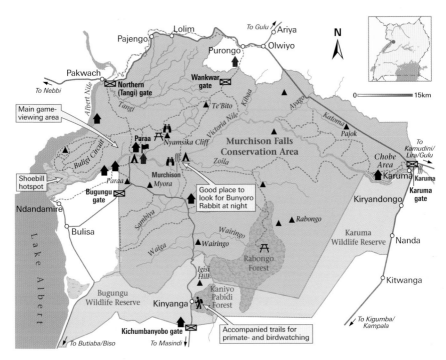

which was expanded in 1928 to include the Gulu District. The conservation area was raised to national park status in 1952 and became one of the top tourist destinations in East Africa. During the 1970s and 1980s, a time of civil war and lawlessness, game numbers were decimated, but with the return of peace things stabilized and game numbers are once again substantial.

Geology and landscape

The Victoria Nile roughly divides the park in half. Before it confluences with Lake Albert it enters a narrow cleft through which its waters foam and thunder – this is the Murchison Falls. The falls are just 43m high as the river rages over the Rift Valley escarpment. The Albert Nile forms the north-west boundary of the park. The altitudinal range is 619m where the Victoria Nile enters Lake Albert, to 1,292m at Rabongo Hill. Much of the park is flat to undulating once one moves away from the river.

Climate

The area of Murchison Falls is tropical and hot with distinct rainy and dry seasons. Temperatures are fairly uniform throughout the year with day temperatures of about 30°C

HIGHLIGHTS

- The Victoria Nile and Murchison Falls, as well as Karuma Falls, Chobe.
- Being able to walk with an armed escort at various points within the park.
- Common Chimpanzee tracking in Kaniyo Pabidi Forest in the south.
- Good game viewing and excellent birding.

FACILITIES AND ACTIVITIES

- Several lodges and campsites.
- Track network for game viewing.
- Accompanied walking trails in Kaniyo and Rabongo forests, and at Nile and lake confluence.
- Birdwatching.
- Hot-air balloon flights.
- Launch trips.
- Fishing (with permit) below Murchison Falls.
- Common Chimpanzee tracking at Kaniyo Pabidi.

and an average of some 18°C at night. The rains appear in March through to November, peaking in October, with the dry season from December into February, although some rain may fall in these months. Rainfall is usually in the form of torrential downpours accompanied by thunderstorms.

Vegetation

The vegetation of Murchison Falls National Park can be broadly divided into grassland, and in some areas with **Borassus Palms** (*Borassus aethiopum*), and extensive areas of open to closed woodland. The latter occurs particularly in the north-west, north-east and south and includes a great diversity of tree/bush species such as **Muyati** (*Terminalia glaucescens*) and **African Mesquite** (*Prosopis africana*). There are areas of thicket and bushland to the west of the falls and fringing the wetlands of the Victoria Nile/Lake Albert delta. There are extensive areas of new and recovering forest growth mainly in parts of the south-east, and major areas of tropical high forest at Rabongo and on the south-west border to the Budongo Forest. Tree diversity is great and includes **White Nongo (False Thorn)** (*Albizia glaberrima*), *Caloncoba crepiniana*, **Giant Diospyros** (*Diospyros abyssinica*), **Mumuli** (*Holoptelea grandis*), **Uganda Ironwood** (*Cynometra alexandri*) and **Poison Devil's Pepper Tree** (*Rauvolfia vomitoria*). Much of the park boundary is ringed by subsistence farmland, where natural vegetation has been destroyed. The swamps in the Victoria Nile/Lake Albert delta have extensive areas of **Papyrus** (*Cyperus papyrus*) and reeds.

Uganda Kob in Murchison Falls National Park

Wildlife
Mammals

This area is extremely rich in mammals, including big game such as **Savanna Elephant** (a recovering population of about 1,500), **Common Hippopotamus, Savanna Buffalo** and the largest population of the so-called **Rothschild's Giraffe** surviving within its range. There are substantial numbers of **Jackson's (Lelwel) Hartebeest, Uganda Kob, Bohor Reedbuck, Defassa Waterbuck, Oribi, Common Duiker, Weyns's Duiker, Blue Duiker** and **Bushbuck.** Possibly Uganda's only population of the **Red-flanked Duiker** is known to occur in Bugungu Wildlife Reserve. **Common Chimpanzee** are present in at least two forest blocks, as are **Guereza (Black and White Colobus), Red-tailed Monkey** and in open woodland **Patas Monkey,** as well as **Tantalus Monkey** and troops of **Olive Baboon.** Nocturnal primates include the forest-dwelling **Potto, Thomas's Dwarf Galago,** possibly also **Demidoff's Dwarf Galago,** and in the woodland the **Northern Lesser Galago.** Both **Common Warthog** and **Bushpig** occur, but only the former is regularly seen. **Lion** are fairly frequently seen but the **Leopard** less so and **Serval** are not uncommon on the grasslands. **Spotted Hyaena** and **Side-striped Jackal** occur throughout. **African Civet, Servaline Genet, Common Large-spotted Genet** and **African Palm Civet** are all present but tend to be separated by habitat preferences. **Honey Badger** occur but are seldom seen, although the diurnal **Banded Mongoose** and **Slender Mongoose** are commonly observed. There are several other mongoose species,

Sausage Tree

Defassa Waterbuck bull

Jackson's (Lelwel) Hartebeest

WILDLIFE FACTS

(within the Murchison system)

- 144 mammal species.
- Largest population of Rothschild's Giraffe.
- 556 bird species, including Shoebill.
- 51 reptiles.
- 45 amphibians.
- 755 plant species, including 145 different trees.

Butterflies on buffalo dung

Mole Cricket at its burrow

Shoebill sub-adult

such as **Jackson's Mongoose**, **Slender Mongoose** and **Water Mongoose**. **Aardvark** occur throughout but are seldom seen. The rare **Giant Pangolin** and **Ground Pangolin** occur, as does the arboreal forest-dwelling **White-bellied Forest Pangolin**. The smaller creatures are very well represented and if you are camping above the falls you have a good chance of spotting the localized **Bunyoro Rabbit** if you scan the area with a torch at night. No less than 27 bat species, 15 of shrew and 16 mice and rats are known to call Murchison home.

Birds

Bird diversity here is one of the highest of any African conservation area, with 556 species recorded so far. Many avid birders visit to see one of Africa's most iconic species, the powder-grey, massively billed **Shoebill**. The best chance of seeing this bird is during the dry season (January to March). Although sightings can never be guaranteed, a launch trip to the delta area where the Victoria Nile enters Lake Albert gives you the best chance you have. Other water-associated birds are abundant and diverse, and include **Goliath Heron**, **Woolly-necked Stork**, **African Openbill Stork** and **Glossy Ibis**. Raptors are represented by 45 species, of which the most frequently seen along the river and towards Lake Albert is the **African Fish Eagle**. **African Skimmer** is quite frequently seen but not when the river is flooding, and **White-winged Black Tern** at times is quite abundant in the vicinity of the lake and delta. This is a bee-eater hotspot with 10 species recorded, although a few are seasonal migrants. These include **Northern**

Carmine, Blue-breasted, Swallow-tailed, Cinnamon-chested and Red-throated bee-eaters. **Abyssinian Ground Hornbill** is quite frequently seen and this is one of the best locations in East Africa to observe this species. In the forest areas the **Black and White Casqued Hornbill** and **Crowned Hornbill** are quite common. Eleven species of swallow and martin have been recorded, at least 17 shrikes, including limited-range **Emin's Shrike, Papyrus Gonolek** and **Yellow-billed Shrike**. Other specials to seek out here include **Nahan's Francolin, Ituri Batis, Orange Weaver, Puvel's Illadopsis, Bronze-tailed Starling** and **Beautiful Sunbird**. The **Bat Hawk** may be seen at dusk hunting bats emerging from Baker's View at the top of the falls.

Abyssinian Ground Hornbill

Reptiles and amphibians

51 species of reptile and 14 amphibians have been recorded within the Murchison Falls Protected Area. The **Nile Crocodile** is abundant in the rivers and lake, with particularly large specimens below the falls. Chelonians include **Bell's Hinged Tortoise, Helmeted Terrapin, African Soft-shelled Turtle, Congo Hinged Terrapin, Adanson's Hinged Terrapin** and probably **Williams's Hinged Terrapin**. At lodges you will find the **Tropical House Gecko** hunting around lights at night and during the day the large **Striped Skink**. In rocky areas, such as along the Victoria Nile, you are likely to see the widespread **Red-headed Rock Agama**. Three fairly large chameleons occur in the area, the **Slender Chameleon** and **Smooth Chameleon** in woodland and the **Ituri Chameleon** in forest. The large **Nile Monitor** is common along the Nile and in the delta. By far the largest snake here is the **Central African Rock Python**, which may reach a length in excess of 6m. There is a great diversity of harmless, or mildly venomous, snake species but on the more serious level are the **Boomslang, Egyptian Cobra, Forest Cobra, Black-necked Spitting Cobra, Jameson's Mamba, Forest Night Adder, Puff Adder** and **Gaboon Viper**. The arboreal **Green Bush Viper** occurs in the Budongo Forest. The amphibian fauna is diverse but the best that most visitors can hope for is to hear the mating calls of males during the breeding season.

Colourful Swallow-tailed Bee-eaters

Nile Crocodile

- This is a high-risk malaria area.
- Tsetse flies are present and there is a small risk of contracting sleeping sickness.
- Lodges and camps are not fenced, so be alert for potentially dangerous game.
- Nile Crocodiles are ever present so keep a good distance from water edges.

One of the crater lakes in Queen Elizabeth National Park

Lie of the land

This park straddles the equator, and lies in south-western Uganda. In the south-west it shares a common border with *Parc National des Virungas* in the Democratic Republic of Congo, to the north with the Kibale Forest National Park and to the east with the Kyambura and Kigezi game reserves. Part of Lake Edward is incorporated in the park, as well as much of Lake George. It covers 1,978km² and is mostly flat to rolling savanna, with the lakes linked by the Kazinga Channel, but in the north there is a system of explosion craters. Rarely, on a clear day away to the north-west one may catch a glimpse of the Rwenzori Mountains but they are usually shrouded in cloud. However, across Lake Edward the Mitumba Mountains in DR Congo usually reveal themselves. Queen Elizabeth National Park lies about 400km from Kampala.

Brief history

It is known that humans lived in and around the area of the present-day park for many thousands of years. Certainly the first inhabitants were hunter-gatherers but by about 5,000 years before present they began to settle, keep livestock, and started to work iron into tools, weapons and ornaments. In 1889 the explorer Stanley found the area to be quite heavily populated, with a settlement of at least 2,000 at the Katwe salt works. This settlement still forms an inhabited enclave within the central sector of the park and salt is still 'harvested' here by evaporation and excavation of rock salt. During the 1890s rinderpest, a disease that decimates cattle and game species such as buffalo, swept through the area. Soon the area became suitable habitat for the tsetse fly, which transmits sleeping sickness in humans. Many people died, others left the area, and the colonial authorities removed the remainder.

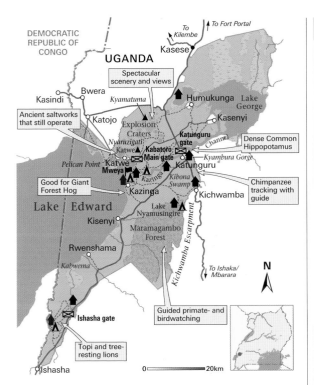

Map labels:
DEMOCRATIC REPUBLIC OF CONGO
UGANDA
To Kilembe
To Fort Portal
Kasese
Spectacular scenery and views
Kasindi
Bwera
Kyamatuma
Humukunga
Lake George
Ancient saltworks that still operate
Katojo
Kasenyi
Explosion Craters
Katunguru gate
Nyaruzigati
Katwe
Kabatoro
Main gate
Channel
Dense Common Hippopotamus
Kyambura Gorge
Pelican Point
Katwe
Mweya
Katunguru
Good for Giant Forest Hog
Kazinga
Kibona Swamp
Kichwamba
Chimpanzee tracking with guide
Lake Edward
Kisenyi
Lake Nyamusingire
Maramagambo Forest
Kichwamba Escarpment
Rwenshama
Kabwema
To Ishaka/ Mbarara
N
Guided primate- and birdwatching
Ishasha gate
Topi and tree-resting lions
Ishasha
0 ———— 20km

HIGHLIGHTS

- Uganda's most accessible major park.
- Good game viewing with specials such as Giant Forest Hog and Uganda Kob.
- Some of most diverse birdwatching in East Africa.
- Boat trips on Kazinga Channel.
- Common Chimpanzee tracking in the challenging Kyambura River Gorge.

Caldera in Queen Elizabeth National Park

Saltworks at Lake Katwe, an ancient Ugandan site

Game populations increased dramatically from that time on and in 1952 the area was proclaimed as the Kazinga National Park. Following a visit by the British monarch in 1954, the park was named the Queen Elizabeth National Park. Confusingly, the dictator Idi Amin renamed the park Ruwenzori during his brutal hold on power.

Geology and landscape

The two lakes, George and Edward, with their linking 33km Kazinga Channel, are dominant features in the park. Much of the park is flat to gently undulating with an altitudinal range of 910m at the lakes to 1,390m in the vicinity of the explosion craters to the north of the Kazinga Channel. To the north-west the Rwenzori Mountain range rises to over 5,000m asl. In the east the park is bordered by the Kichwamba escarpment and to the south the Virunga Volcanoes. The only significant river in the park is the Ishasha, which forms the border with the Democratic Republic of Congo in the far south. The deep, forested Kyambura Gorge lies in the north-east. The park lies

- Several lodges and campsites.
- Fairly extensive road/ track network but most difficult after heavy rain.
- Boat tours on Kazinga Channel.
- Chimpanzee tracking in Kyambura Gorge with permit.
- Guided walks in Maramagambo Forest.
- Lion and Leopard tracking.
- Balloon safaris.

within the western arm of the Great Rift Valley, formed over a period of about 10 million years and continuing, through upheavals of the Earth's crust. Lake George drains into Lake Edward, which in turn flows out via the Semliki River into Lake Albert and finally into the Nile. Approximately 1 million years before present during the early Pleistocene much of the area was covered by a great lake but volcanic upheaval that formed the Virunga Volcanoes resulted in Lakes Edward and Kivu being separated. The explosion craters to the north of Katwe were only formed some 10,000 years before present.

Climate

Rain can be expected at any time of the year but there are two peaks, March to May and September to November. Rainfall is regionally variable, with the headquarters at Mweya receiving about 750–1,250mm at the foot of the Kichwamba escarpment in the Maramagambo Forest. Average annual minimum temperature is 18°C, with a maximum average of 28°C. There is little monthly or seasonal variation.

Vegetation

The park lies in the convergence area of two great biomes, the forests of Central Africa and the savanna grasslands of East Africa. The dominant vegetation types are grassland, woody thickets, forest and swamps but scientists recognize more than 50 distinct plant communities within these. There are extensive areas of both short and long grassland and species here are fire-tolerant because of frequent burning. Common grass species include **Red Grass** (*Themeda triandra*) in drier areas and **Sword Grass** (*Imperata cylindrica*) in areas that are seasonally inundated. Throughout the park are islands of thickets scattered in the grassland. These thickets are dominated by an evergreen, rambling shrub **Woolly Caper Bush** (*Capparis tomentosa*), and include many other species, such as the cactus-like **Candelabra Tree** (*Euphorbia candelabrum*). You will see another tree euphorbia growing on the slopes of the Kazinga Channel, *Euphorbia dawei*, which is similar but has a more compact crown and shorter branches. With the great decline in Savanna Elephant numbers, there has been an increase in acacia trees, especially **Paperbark Thorn** (*Vachellia sieberiana*) in the vicinity of Ishasha and the area south of the Kazinga Channel. The main species in the crater area to the north is **Red Thorn** (*Vachellia gerrardii*). On the slopes in the crater area you will notice the silver-grey-leaved **African Olive** (*Olea europaea* subsp. *cuspidata*). Another tree that stands out in the Ishasha

Tree Euphorbia with creeper

area is **Sycamore Fig** (*Ficus sycomorus*), whose horizontal branches are used as a retreat by the Lion in the area. The lake fringes and associated swamps are dominated by **Papyrus** (*Cyperus papyrus*) and **Hippo Grass** (*Vossia cuspidata*). Apart from the thin line of forest along the Kyambura River Gorge, by far the largest block, covering 280km², is the Maramagambo Forest. One of the commonest trees in its middle and lower reaches is the **Giant Diospyros** (*Diospyros abyssinica*), which may reach a height of 30m, or more. Closer to the escarpment floor **Uganda Ironwood** (**Muhimbi**) (*Cynometra alexandri*) is dominant where rainfall is at its highest.

Wildlife
Mammals

There is a great diversity of mammal species in the park but two stand out because of sheer numbers, the **Common Hippopotamus** and the **Uganda Kob**. **Savanna Elephants** were decimated during the years of turmoil in Uganda but it is estimated they are now back to about 3,000 individuals but not entirely tied to the park. They may be encountered anywhere in the park but there are some seasonal movements to favoured feeding grounds. **Savanna Buffalo** are common but by far the most abundant ungulate is the Uganda Kob, which inhabits the open flat to rolling grasslands and gathers in large numbers in the dry season. **Topi** are found only in the southern Ishasha grasslands but the **Defassa Waterbuck** occurs throughout except in the forests. **Bushbuck** (**Imbabala**) are common especially in association with the thickets and forest fringes. The semi-aquatic **Sitatunga** is rarely seen and is apparently mainly centred on the papyrus swamps that fringe Lake George. Other antelope include **Bohor Reedbuck, Common Duiker, Yellow-backed Duiker, Weyns's Duiker** and **Blue Duiker**. The pigs are represented by **Common Warthog, Bushpig** and the **Giant Forest Hog**, the last quite commonly seen. Predators are well represented, with **Lion** (such as the famous tree 'roosters' around Ishasha), **Leopard, Serval, Spotted Hyaena, Side-striped Jackal, African Civet, Palm Civet** (forest only), **Common Large-spotted Genet** and six mongoose species, of which the social and diurnal **Banded Mongoose** is most frequently seen. Primates include **Common Chimpanzee** with troops in Kyambura Gorge and Maramagambo Forest, the latter also home to **L'Hoest's Monkey, Red-tailed Monkey, Blue Monkey, Eastern Red Colobus, Guereza** (**Black and White Colobus**), **Potto, Northern Lesser Galago** (woodland)

Thickets in Queen Elizabeth National Park

Uganda Kob ram

Leopard is one of a number of predator species in the park.

WILDLIFE FACTS

- 95 mammal species.
- Habituated Common Chimpanzees.
- Best place in region to see Giant Forest Hog.
- Large Common Hippopotamus population.
- 612 bird species, including 54 different raptors.
- 34 reptile species, of which 20 are snakes.
- At least 35 amphibian species.

Ugandan Helmeted Guineafowl

and **Demidoff's Dwarf Galago**. In more open woodland you may encounter troops of **Olive Baboon** and **Vervet Monkey**. Ant and termite-eating mammals include the **Aardvark, Giant Pangolin** and **White-bellied Tree Pangolin**. At least 14 bat species occur, including a large colony of **Egyptian Fruit-bats** in a cave in the Maramagambo Forest. This roost can be visited with a guide. Rodents are well represented, including the **North African Porcupine, African Brush-tailed Porcupine** (forest) and **Greater Cane-rat**. Several squirrel species occur and at least 20 different mice and rats.

Birds

To date 612 bird species, including 54 raptors, have been recorded from the park. It is likely more species await discovery, especially within the poorly explored Maramagambo Forest. Probably top of the list for many birders would be the **Shoebill Stork**, which frequents the papyrus swamp fringing Lake George. Of other water-orientated birds there are 16 species of heron and egret, including **Black Heron, Goliath Heron** and **Purple Heron**, as well as eight different storks, with **Marabou Stork** common around the fishing villages. There are 18 species of duck and goose, several of which are seasonal Palaearctic migrants. Few parks in the region can match the diversity of birds of prey. **African Fish Eagle** is commonly seen and heard, especially around the lakes and along the Kazinga Channel, with **African Crowned Eagle** associated with the forested areas. You are likely to encounter **Long-crested Eagle, Martial Eagle, Tawny Eagle** and **Red-necked Falcon** in the more open grassed woodland areas. Over the lakes and channel huge numbers of **swallows, martins** and **White-winged Black Terns** hawk for lake flies. **Red-necked Spurfowl** and **Helmeted Guineafowl** are commonly associated with thicket-patched grassland. There are 12 doves and pigeons present and five species of turaco, the most impressive of which is the **Great Blue Turaco**, easiest to see in the riverine woodland along the Ishasha. The **African Grey Parrot** is associated with the forest. In the park you will also find eight species of owl, including the **Red-chested Owlet**, six species of nightjar and no less than 12 kingfisher species, not all of which are water orientated. Of the seven species of bee-eater, the **Black Bee-eater** is known only from the Maramagambo Forest. The very range-restricted **White-thighed Hornbill** occurs, as does the large **Black and White Casqued Hornbill**. Weavers and weaver-related species are represented by 28 species.

Reptiles and amphibians

Martial Eagle

The **Nile Crocodile** is common wherever there is suitable habitat but the **Dwarf Crocodile** is known only from streams feeding into Lake George. The large **Nile Monitor** lizard is common around lakes, channel and rivers. The **Forest Hinged Tortoise** is said to occur, as well as **Helmeted Terrapin** and **Williams's Hinged Terrapin**, with possibly **Bell's Hinged Tortoise** in the savanna areas. Around the lodges at night you are likely to see the **Tropical House Gecko**. Both the **Striped Skink** and **Speckle-lipped Skink** are common, as is the large **Blue-headed Tree Agama**. At least eight chameleon species are likely to occur, including the **Smooth Chameleon, Rwenzori Side-striped Chameleon** and the **Ituri Chameleon**. The largest snake by far here is the **Central African Rock Python**, with other species of snake including **Smyth's Water Snake, Emerald Snake, Blanding's Tree Snake, Forest Vine Snake, Forest Cobra, Gold's Tree Cobra** and **Jameson's Mamba**. Both the large **Gaboon** and **Rhinoceros vipers** occur in forest and woodland. One small viper, the green **Acuminate Bush Viper**, is known only from the Kyambura Game Reserve close to Lake George. The amphibian fauna is rich, with at least 35 species.

Cameroon Toad

 • The park lies within a malaria area.
• Lodges and camps are not fenced, so be alert for potentially dangerous game, especially hippos.
• Roads and tracks are difficult to negotiate after heavy rain.

African Giant Snail

RWENZORI MOUNTAINS NATIONAL PARK

View of Lake Bujuku, Rwenzori Mountains National Park, during ascent to Elena Hut

Lie of the land

The Rwenzori Mountains, the fabled 'Mountains of the Moon', lie in western Uganda straddling the border of the Democratic Republic of Congo. The range is 120km long and up to 65km wide and rises to 5,109m asl on Mount Stanley's Margherita Peak. The park lies within the Albertine Rift, a section of the Western Rift Valley, with the Virunga National Park sharing the international boundary. Rwenzori Mountains National Park covers 996km², of which 70% is located above the 2,500m contour. It lies in part within Bundibugyo, Kabarole and Kasese districts, within 25km of the town of Kasese, which in turn lies some 437km west of Kampala. These are the only mountains in Uganda that have glaciers and permanent snow.

Brief history

These legendary mountains are shrouded in clouds and mist for much of the time but the first documented sighting of these elusive peaks was made in 1876 by Sir Henry Stanley. He revisited the area in 1888 and was lucky to see the snow and ice-capped peaks. In 1889 he returned and one of his expedition members, W.G. Stairs, climbed above the 3,000m contour in the direction of Mount Emin. Several explorers and naturalists subsequently explored the range but it was only in 1906 that the Duke of Abruzzi expedition scaled most of the major peaks and compiled detailed maps of the Rwenzoris. The first complete traverse of the six major peaks had to wait until 1975 when a Polish team succeeded in just 17 days. The principal tribes ringing the Rwenzoris are the Bakonjo and Amba, who have settled the area for more than 300 years and up to an altitude of 2,200m asl. Their cultivations have created an isolated montane island of the Rwenzoris on the Ugandan flanks of the range. Sadly, this is the case with many African conservation areas!

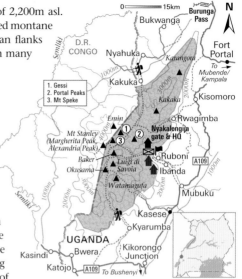

Geology and landscape

During the Miocene, some 10 million years before present, the area where the range now stands was a vast plain that sloped westwards. At this time there was considerable tectonic movement that caused major rifting, resulting in volcanic activity, faulting and uplifting. The uplift of the underlying Precambrian rocks resulted in the birth of the Rwenzori range. From that point on the watershed divided with streams flowing both eastwards and westwards. Much of the rock structures are igneous or metamorphic, with gneisses dominating and amphibolite obvious in the central area. There are hot springs at three locations. Glaciation in the past was much more extensive than it is today. The glacier-gouged valley at Mubuku-Bujuku and great lateral moraines can be observed on the valley's north slope. Other large moraine deposits are present in valleys of the Lamya, Ruanoli, Nyamagasani and Nyamwamba. The glaciers one sees today are a mere shadow of their former glory. At the centre of the park are six peaks, three of which still carry small glaciers, Mounts Stanley (Africa's third-highest peak), Alexandria, Speke, Emin, Gessi and Luigi di Savoia.

Climate

There are two main rainy periods, mid-March to May and September to mid-December, with the heaviest falls between the 2,000m and 3,000m contours. Throughout the year mist can be expected and may be present for hours, days or weeks at a time. The mountains are best for the early risers, as best clarity can be expected between 02h00 and 07h00. The mountains have a chilly and wet climate with daytime temperatures of between 10°C and 15°C, with nights being much colder. The best times to hike these mountains is considered to be June to August and December to February, but the chances of rain and snow are still high.

HIGHLIGHTS

• The opportunity to hike in pristine mountains.
• Home to numerous Albertine Rift endemics.
• Dense stands of afro-alpine plants.
• Only one of three mountains in Africa with receding glaciers.

Margherita Peak

Vegetation

Although the botanical structures of the Rwenzoris are similar to that on other high African mountains, the vegetation is denser and more luxuriant because of its higher rainfall. Up to 2,200m asl the natural vegetation has given way to numerous cultivated plots, but above this one enters the montane forest. This forest has an open and broken canopy which allows many smaller plants to thrive. The more common trees include **Boarwood** (*Symphonia globulifera*), **East African Yellowwood** (*Afrocarpus gracilior*) and a giant **Tree Fern** (*Cyathea deckenii*). Large areas in the clearings are carpeted with beds of **Bracken** (*Pteridium aquilinum*) and other ferns and shrubs. From about the 2,500m contour one enters the realm of the **African Mountain Bamboo** (*Oldeania alpina*) and the **giant heathers** (*Philippia benguelensis* and *P. johnstonii*). Here there are also very dense stands of the shrub *Mimulopsis elliotii* and small numbers of the **Giant Lobelia** (*Lobelia gibberoa*). Between 3,000m and 4,000m contours there are numerous giant heathers, many of which are draped with the grey-green, string-like lichen **Old Man's Beard** (*Usnea* spp.), as are tree branches, a strong indication of the abundant moisture. A few tree species also grow here, including the **East African Rosewood** (*Hagenia abyssinica*), *Rapanea rhododendroides*, several species of tree-form **St John's Wort** (*Hypericum* spp.), and the **Tree Groundsel** (*Dendrosenecio erici-rosenii*) and several other related species. Towards the higher altitudes there are extensive areas of bogs with various moss species carpeting the ground, as well as low **everlastings** (*Helichrysum* spp.), **Tussock Grass** (*Carex runsorrensis*) and scattered **Giant Lobelia** (*Lobelia bequaertii*). Above 4,000m one enters the alpine zone, which has bushy thickets of the everlasting *Helichrysum stuhlmannii* and forests of *Dendrosenecio adnivalis*, especially in the narrow valleys.

Lower Bigo Bog at 3,400m in the Ruwenzoris

Wildlife
Mammals

Large mammals are rare and although a few **Savanna Elephant** and **Buffalo** still occur, they are seldom seen. Poaching of most larger species is a major ongoing problem. **Bushbuck** occur, as do **Yellow-backed Duiker, Black-fronted Duiker** and **Rwenzori Red Duiker. Giant Forest Hog** and **Bushpig** are present but seldom seen. Primates include the **Common (Robust) Chimpanzee** (none are habituated), the widespread **Blue Monkey**, the western race of the **Guereza (Black and**

FACILITIES AND ACTIVITIES

- Mountaineering and trail network.
- Basic mountain huts.
- Walking trails at lower levels.
- Guides and porters.
- Bird and primate watching at lower levels.

White Colobus) and the more localized **L'Hoest's Monkey.** **Leopard** are present but scarce and **African Golden Cat** is said to occur. One of the few mammals you are likely to see is the **Southern Tree Hyrax,** which lives in both the forest zone and among rocks above the forest. Several species are known to occur only in these mountains, or the central Albertine Rift, namely the semi-aquatic **Rwenzori Otter-shrew, Rwenzori Shrew** and **Rwenzori Sun Squirrel,** among others.

WILDLIFE FACTS

- 70 mammal species, including endemics and near endemics.
- 217 species of bird.
- 34 reptile species, nine endemic.
- 28 amphibian species, many endemic or near endemic.

Birds

Of the 217 species of bird recorded in the park, 18 are Albertine Rift restricted-range specials, and 60 of the 86 Afro-montane biome species are present. These include **Rwenzori Turaco, Bamboo Warbler, Golden-winged Sunbird, Scarlet-tufted Malachite Sunbird** and **Stuhlmann's Double-collared Olive-back.** Other species include **Handsome Francolin, Archer's Robin-Chat, Montane Masked Apalis, Rwenzori Batis, Rwenzori Hill Babbler** and **Mountain Sooty Boubou.** Birding is not easy here but a determined birder should be able to produce a good tally over a few days.

Reptiles and amphibians

Reptiles and amphibians are not easy to observe but there is great diversity and a number of species that occur only here, or also in adjoining areas of the Albertine Rift. Among other species here are the **Montane Side-striped Chameleon,** which may occur up to 2,800m asl, and the **Rwenzori Three-horned Chameleon,** which occurs in trees and bushes up to 2,800m. The altitude record is taken by the **Rwenzori Side-striped Chameleon,** which has been recorded up to the 4,000m contour on various mountains. **Carpenter's Chameleon** is known only from the Rwenzoris. The **Strange-horned Chameleon** is another large endemic. Although the area is probably fairly rich in snake species, they are seldom seen and most seldom occur above 2,000m asl. Amphibians are unlikely to be encountered here, especially above 2,000m, but the **Albertine Rift Tree Frog** that is present has been recorded in the Virungas at 4,000m asl.

Rwenzori Turaco

A male Jackson's Three-horned Chameleon

- **Areas surrounding the Rwenzoris hold a high risk for malaria.**
- **To attempt the ascents one must be physically fit and healthy; rescue chances are poor.**
- **Be prepared for adverse conditions, including altitude sickness.**
- **Rain, fog and snow frequent; visibility often poor.**

MGAHINGA GORILLA NATIONAL PARK

The peak of Mount Sabyinyo in Mgahinga

Mgahinga is located at the south-west tip of Uganda, in the Kisoro District, some 540km south-west of Kampala. It lies within the Virunga Mountains in the Albertine Rift Valley and adjoins the Volcanoes National Park in Rwanda and Virunga National Park in the Democratic Republic of Congo. Despite being the country's smallest national park (33.7km²), it encompasses in part three of the eight volcanoes in the range – Muhabura, Gahinga and Sabyinyo – and lies in an altitudinal range of between 2,227m and 4,127m asl. The British colonial authority proclaimed it as a game reserve in 1930 and it was gazetted as a national park in 1991. Much of the park is covered by woodland with only a remnant of pure Afro-montane forest remaining, with a belt of **African Alpine Bamboo** (*Oldeania alpina*) between the western boundary and the lower slopes of Sabyinyo and Gahinga. Beyond this lies the stratification of typical East African Afro-alpine mountains, with *Hagenia* and *Hypericum*, then **giant heath**, or **ericaceous belt**, above which one encounters the giant *Dendrosenecio* and *Lobelia* species. Although only 76 mammal species are on record, it is likely that at least another 20 smaller species occur within the cross-border park. Most visitors come to see the **Mountain Gorillas** but there is only one habituated troop, which occasionally crosses into Rwanda, making it less reliable than Bwindi to the north. Apparently the habituated group has remained within the park for three years but this could change. It is best to visit the park during the drier months of June to August, and December to January, when trails are easier to negotiate. There is a habituated troop of the rare **Golden Monkey**, sometimes regarded as a subspecies of Blue Monkey but now believed to be a full species. Small numbers of **Savanna Elephant** and **Savanna Buffalo** occur, as well as **Giant Forest Hog, Black-fronted Duiker, Bushbuck, Leopard, Spotted Hyaena, Side-striped Jackal, Serval** and **African Golden Cat**. No detailed surveys have been undertaken. Over 185 bird species have been recorded from the trans-frontier area and it is likely all, or most, are present in Mgahinga. A number of reptiles and amphibians are endemic to the Albertine Rift. No in-depth survey has been undertaken, but the herpetofauna for Mgahinga is probably similar to that of nearby Bwindi.

SEMULIKI NATIONAL PARK

One of the hot springs at Semuliki

Semuliki, covering just 219km², lies in Bundibugyo District of western Uganda and is separated from the Democratic Republic of Congo by the Semliki River, with the Rwenzori Mountains to the south-east and Lake Albert to the north. It was proclaimed as a national park in 1993 due to its importance as one of the richest floral and faunal locations in Africa. It is a continuation of the tropical lowland Ituri Forest in neighbouring DR Congo and has most species in common. The park consists of mainly flat to slightly undulating plains, with an altitudinal range of just 90m. Rain falls throughout the year but peaks March to May and September to December, with an annual average of 1,250mm, and large areas are subject to regular flooding. There are two hot springs that attract wildlife to the mineral salts they produce. The canopy forest averages 30m in height and is dominated by trees of the genus *Cynometra*, especially the **Uganda Ironwood (Muhimbi)** (*C. alexandri*). Although the forest dominates the landscape, there are small areas of grassland, swamps and stands of **Borassus Palm**. Of the >60 mammal species recorded here, 11 occur only here or at one other site in East Africa, including **Water Chevrotain, Bates's Pygmy Antelope, Long-tailed Tree Pangolin, Lesser Anomalure** and **Zenker's Pygmy Flying Anomalure. Savanna Elephant** and **Forest Buffalo** occur but are seldom seen. **Common Hippopotamus** and **Red River Hog** are present. Primates include **Common Chimpanzee, Olive Baboon, De Brazza's Monkey, Red-tailed Monkey, Dent's Monkey, Blue Monkey, Potto** and **Thomas's Dwarf Galago**. Most visitors come here for the birds (over 440 species), of which several do not occur elsewhere in East Africa, including **Long-tailed Hawk, Congo Serpent Eagle, Lyre-tailed Honeyguide, Black-wattled Hornbill, Piping Hornbill, Red-billed Dwarf Hornbill, White-crested Hornbill, Nkulengu Rail, African Piculet, Maxwell's Black Weaver** and **Red-bellied Malimbe**. Reptiles and amphibians are equally diverse. The nearby Toro-Semliki Wildlife Reserve covers 548km² and has a total of 69 mammal species (including **Uganda Kob**), 435 birds, 33 reptiles and 13 amphibian species. In Semuliki there are campsites and bandas, accompanied walking trails, in Toro-Semliki there is a lodge and campsites. In the grounds of the lodge the extremely rare **Pousarge's Mongoose** is occasionally sighted.

Savanna Elephant is one of the 86 mammals species found at Kidepo.

Kidepo is Uganda's third-largest national park at 1,442km², and most remote, lying between 600km and 840km north-east of Kampala, depending on the route. Most visitors fly into the park but driving is feasible. In the north the park borders on South Sudan and lies close to the Kenyan border in the north-east. The area was occupied by pastoralist Ik and Dodoth people, subgroups of the Karimojong. It was proclaimed as a game reserve in 1958, and in 1962 as a national park. The park consists of two major valley systems, the Kidepo and Narus, along which seasonal rivers flow. There is an altitudinal range of 910–2,749m asl, with the Nyangea-Napore hill range in the north-west and to the south of the Kidepo Valley the Morungola range. To the north-east across the South Sudan border lies Mount Lotuke. Rains fall April to October, with an annual average of 800mm. Permanent water during the dry season occurs only in the Narus Valley and the Kanangarok hot spring in the north. There are four major vegetation types, open savanna grassland with scattered **acacias**, savanna woodland, bushland, and forest patches on the higher hill slopes. On ridgelines the slender-trunked **Borassus Palms** are obvious, with almost 700 plant species recorded. Of the 86 mammals species occurring, about a third occur in no other Ugandan national park, such as **Greater Kudu, Lesser Kudu, Bright's Gazelle, Chandler's Mountain Reedbuck, Günther's Dik-dik, Klipspringer, Cheetah, Striped Hyaena** and **Aardwolf.** Heavy poaching, mainly cross border, has extirpated some species and reduced others. **Savanna Elephant, Savanna Buffalo, Plains Zebra, Lelwel Hartebeest, Defassa Waterbuck, Lion, Leopard, Side-striped Jackal** and **Black-backed Jackal** occur. The bird list stands at an impressive 475 species, of which 58 species are birds of prey, with 14 raptors occurring nowhere else in Uganda. **Nile Crocodiles** occur only in a few pools along the Narus River. Precautions should be taken against malaria and tsetse flies are present. If you are self-drive you should first check on the road conditions and security situation.

LAKE MBURO NATIONAL PARK

Grant's Zebra in Lake Mburo National Park

Lake Mburo covers just 260km² and is located in Kiruhura District in south-west Uganda, 240km west of Kampala. There are five lakes in the park, of which Lake Mburo is by far the largest. There is a mix of grassed and lightly wooded plains, wooded rocky hills, forest at Rubanga, and wetlands. The area first received protection as a controlled hunting area in 1935 and was raised to national park status in 1982. The local people are pastoralists and run large herds of the massively horned Ankole cattle, which sometimes enter the park. This is the only park where you will see

Wattled plover on eggs

Impala, with other game including **Plains Zebra, Rothschild's Giraffe, Savanna Buffalo, Common Eland, Topi, Defassa Waterbuck, Bushbuck, Sitatunga, Common Duiker, Bohor Reedbuck, Klipspringer, Oribi** and **Common Warthog**. Predators include **Leopard, Serval, Spotted Hyaena** and troops of social **Banded Mongoose**, with **Water Mongoose** associated with the wetlands. Troops of **Olive Baboon** and **Vervet Monkey** occur, as well as nocturnal **Northern Lesser Galago**. More than 310 bird species are on record, including papyrus specials **Papyrus Gonolek, Papyrus Yellow Warbler** and **Blue-headed Coucal**. Shoebill may be present but they are considered to be rare here. This is the only place you have a chance to see both the **Southern Ground Hornbill** and **Abyssinian Ground Hornbill**, although the latter is not resident. There are lodges and campsites, and activities include guided walks, boat trips on Lake Mburo and game drives on the track network.

The subalpine zone of Mount Elgon

Mount Elgon, or Masaba, as it is known to the local people, is a remnant of a vast extinct shield volcano that first erupted about 24 million years before present. The last major eruption took place some 10 million years ago. During the Pleistocene mighty glaciers crushed down from its summit to about the 3,500m contour, creating the deeply cut Suam Gorge and the many small lakes on the crater floor. Here also are hot springs. Its highest peak is the jagged Wagagai, which rises to 4,321m asl. The park, proclaimed in 1993, covers 1,145km² and borders on the Mount Elgon park in neighbouring Kenya. Average annual rainfall is 1,270mm, with the driest periods being June to August and December to March. The vegetation, as with other high mountains in East Africa, has four distinct and merging altitudinal belts with forest at the lowest level, a bamboo zone, subalpine or heath zone and the Afro-alpine region. Two species of **giant groundsel** (*Dendrosenecio barbatipes* and *D. elgonensis*) are endemic to the mountain. Small numbers of **Savanna Elephant** move freely across the international boundary and are seldom seen. **Savanna Buffalo, Bushbuck, Black-fronted Duiker, Common Duiker** and **Bushpig** occur. Small numbers of **Leopard** and **Spotted Hyaena** are present, as are **Southern Tree Hyrax**. Here also are **Olive Baboon, Guereza (Black and White Colobus), Blue Monkey, De Brazza's Monkey** and **Red-tailed Monkey**. In general game is rather shy, in part due to heavy poaching in the past and some disturbance that continues today. The bird list stands at 305 species, including **Jackson's Francolin, Hartlaub's Turaco, Ross's Turaco, Eastern Bronze-naped Pigeon, Black and White Casqued Hornbill, African Crowned Eagle** and **Tacazze Sunbird**. The visitors that venture here come for climbing, hiking and birdwatching.

RWANDA

Mountain Gorilla in the Virungas

Rwanda is a small (26,338km²), landlocked country and is bordered by the Democratic Republic of Congo, Uganda, Tanzania and Burundi. Mountains dominate central and western Rwanda and are part of the Albertine Rift mountains, with rolling hills giving way to plains, swamps and lakes in the east. Rwanda has one of the highest human population densities in Africa, most of whom are involved in subsistence farming. Most people remember Rwanda for its shocking recent history when almost one million were killed during the genocide. However, today the country is peaceful. Compared with many other African countries, Rwanda has an enviable recent conservation record. Here we will just give a brief overview of its top three national parks, Akagera, Nyungwe and Volcanoes.

AKAGERA NATIONAL PARK

Akagera National Park has many wetlands.

Savanna Buffalo and Cattle Egret

Akagera, covering 1,122km², is one of the region's largest protected wetlands and is the only area in Rwanda that still has large numbers of plains game, albeit much of it reintroduced in recent years. The park landscape includes rolling hills, grassed and wooded plains and swamp-fringed lakes. The park takes its name from the Akagera River that flows along the eastern border and feeds into numerous small lakes, including the largest, Ihema. Game species include **Savanna Elephant, Common Hippopotamus, Hook-lipped Rhinoceros** (20 recently reintroduced), **Plains Zebra, Maasai Giraffe, Savanna Buffalo, Roan Antelope, Common Eland, Defassa Waterbuck, Topi, Impala, Bushbuck, Bohor Reedbuck, Oribi, Bushbuck** and **Common Duiker**. **Lion** were recently reintroduced but **Leopard, Spotted Hyaena, Serval** and **Side-striped Jackal** also occur. Troops of **Olive Baboon** and **Vervet Monkey** are commonly seen but **Blue Monkey** are less conspicuous. An amazing 525 bird species have been recorded here, including the **Shoebill, Grey Crowned Crane, Papyrus Gonolek, Grey-backed Fiscal, Red-faced Barbet, Bennett's Woodpecker, White-headed Chat** and **White-winged Warbler**. Although only 23 reptile and nine amphibian species have been recorded, this list is likely to be more extensive. There is a lodge in the park, as well as campsites.

NYUNGWE NATIONAL PARK

L'hoest's Monkey is one of a number of primate species in the park.

Proclaimed as a national park in 2004, Nyungwe covers 1,020km² and is located in the south-west of Rwanda towards the border with Burundi. This is the largest swathe of surviving high-altitude montane tropical forest in the region, it rises to 2,950m asl and lies in the Albertine Rift. Much of the park is circled by tea plantations. Apart from its extremely high biodiversity, it is also a very important water catchment area, contributing flows to both the Congo and Nile rivers. The latest checklists document the presence of 1,050 plant species, which includes some 200 orchid species, 96 mammals (63 are rodents and bats), 310 bird species and 38 different reptiles. The primate fauna is particularly rich and totals 13 species, with a substantial population of **Common Chimpanzee** (of which two groups are partially habituated to humans), **Angolan Black and White Colobus, Owl-faced Monkey, L'Hoest's Monkey, Blue Monkey, Dent's Monkey, Red-tailed Monkey, Grey-cheeked Mangabey, Vervet Monkey, Potto** and **Spectacled Lesser Galago**. Several troops of monkey and colobus are habituated to human presence. Three species of duiker occur, **Yellow-backed, Black-fronted** and **Weyns's duikers**. Both the **Giant Forest Hog** and **Bushpig** are present, as are small numbers of **Leopard, Serval, African Golden Cat, African Civet, Servaline Genet** and **Southern Tree Hyrax**. There are also six species of tree squirrel, including the **African Giant Squirrel**. The bird diversity is great, with a number of specials, such as **Hartlaub's Duck, Cassin's Hawk Eagle, Handsome Francolin**, three species of **flufftail, African Grey Parrot, Great Blue Turaco, Rwenzori Turaco, Black-billed Turaco, Fraser's Eagle-Owl, Albertine Owlet, Blue-breasted Kingfisher, Black and White Casqued Hornbill, Montane Oriole, Red-collared Mountain Babbler, Snowy-headed Robin-Chat, Kungwe Apalis, Grauer's Warbler, Lagden's Bushshrike** and **Rockefeller's Sunbird**. There are several walking trails, lodges and campsites. There is also a short tree canopy walkway.

More than half of the world's Mountain Gorillas occur in this park.

The Volcanoes National Park is located in north-west Rwanda, covers an area of 125km², and forms part of the Virunga conservation area that extends into the Democratic Republic of Congo and Uganda. The park was gazetted in 1925 to protect the endangered Mountain Gorilla and encompasses five of the Virunga volcanoes – Karisimbi, Bisoke, Muhabura, Gahinga and Sabyinyo. The vegetation strata are similar to those on other high East African mountains, with lower montane forest, but much of this has been lost to subsistence agriculture. There is a belt of **African Alpine Bamboo** from between the 2,500m and 3,200m contour, and from 2,600m to 3,600m an extensive area of **East African Rosewood** woodland. From 3,500m one starts to encounter the subalpine species such as the **giant lobelias** and **senecios**, extending to tussock grassland. This is the park where naturalist Dian Fossey (*Gorillas in the Mist*) undertook her research on the **Mountain Gorilla**, now one of Rwanda's greatest tourist attractions. The park holds more than half of the world's population of these large primates, more than 400 individuals, and 12 groups have been habituated to allow visitors to spend time with them in the wild. Apart from the gorillas, more than 70 mammal species occur, including the localized **Golden Monkey**. Small numbers of **Savanna Elephant** and **Savanna Buffalo** occur but they move freely across borders. **Bushbuck** are relatively common, as is the **Black-fronted Duiker**, with predators represented only by smaller species, including **Spotted Hyaena**, **Side-striped Jackal**, **Slender Mongoose**, **Serval** and **African Golden Cat**. **Carruthers's Rope Squirrel** is an Albertine Rift endemic that is quite common in forested and recovering woodland areas. Some 178 bird species have been recorded, of which 13 species and 16 subspecies are known only from the Virungas and Rwenzoris. Some of the species include **African Green Broadbill, Lagden's Bushshrike, Kivu Ground Thrush, Archer's Ground Robin, Dusky Crimsonwing, Rwenzori Turaco, Rwenzori Double-collared Sunbird, Rwenzori Batis** and **Strange Weaver**. Although reptile and amphibian diversity is great across the Virunga Volcanoes complex, little work has been done specifically on this park. There is a trail network for accompanied gorilla and Golden Monkey viewing, and several lodge and camping options on the fringes of the park.

Golden Monkey

RIFT VALLEYS AND VOLCANOES

There are two principal rift valleys in East Africa, the Eastern Rift Valley and the Western Rift Valley. The longer Eastern Rift Valley extends from Eritrea southwards through Kenya and Tanzania, to Malawi and Mozambique. The Western Rift Valley, more commonly known as the Albertine Rift, has all of the great lakes except Lake Victoria, which lies between the two rifts. The Albertine Rift is also flanked by some of Africa's highest mountain ranges, the Virungas, Mitumba and Rwenzoris. The lakes in the Albertine Rift, including Tanganyika, Kivu, Edward and Albert, are freshwater lakes. However, in the Eastern Rift some are freshwater but many are shallow, with no outlets and have high mineral contents, including lakes Magadi, Bogoria and Nakuru. The two rifts merge in south-western Tanzania and cut south together and incorporate Lake Nyasa (Malawi). Extinct, dormant and active volcanoes abound in East Africa and are associated with the two rift valleys. There are 22 volcanoes in Kenya, nine in Tanzania and seven in Uganda. Within the Virungas (in the Albertine Rift, on the borders of Uganda, Rwanda and the Democratic Republic of Congo) there are eight volcanoes, of which Nyamuragira and Nyiragongo are still potently active. The best-known East African volcanoes, Kilimanjaro and Kenya, are extinct. The most active Tanzanian volcano is Ol Doinyo Lengai, lying 160km west of Kilimanjaro and rising to 2,878m. It is unique in that it is the only one that produces natrocarbonatite lava. In recent times it has erupted on several occasions, most recently in 2013.

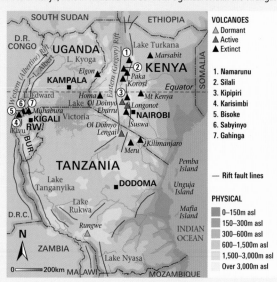

IDENTIFICATION GUIDE

Small-eared or Northern Greater Galago

Thick-tailed or Large-eared Greater Galago

Olive Baboon

Yellow Baboon

Vervet Monkey

Blue Monkey

Sykes's Monkey

Patas Monkey

Red-tailed Monkey

Zanzibar Red Colobus

Guereza or Black and White Colobus

Angolan Black and White Colobus

Common Chimpanzee

Mountain Gorilla

Grevy's Zebra

Plains or Grant's Zebra

Common Hippopotamus

Hook-lipped or Black Rhinoceros

Square-lipped or White Rhinoceros

Desert Warthog

Common Warthog

Bushpig

Giant Forest Hog

African or Savanna Buffalo

Rothschild's Giraffe

Maasai Giraffe

Reticulated Giraffe

Common Eland

Eastern Bongo bull

Lesser Kudu ram

Greater Kudu bull

Bushbuck or Imbabala ram

Beisa Oryx

Roan Antelope

Sable Antelope bull and cow

Defassa Waterbuck

Common Waterbuck cow and young

Uganda Kob rams

Puku ram

Bohor Reedbuck

Southern Reedbuck

Chanler's Mountain Reedbuck

Coke's Hartebeest

Lichtenstein's Hartebeest

Jackson's or Lelwel Hartebeest

Topi bull

Western White-bearded
Wildebeest

Impala ram

Gerenuk ram

Bright's Gazelle

Thomson's Gazelle

Grant's Gazelle

Suni ram

Oribi ram

Steenbok ram

Sharpe's Grysbok ewe

Klipspringer ram

Naivasha Dik-dik

Ugogo Dik-dik

Günther's Dik-dik

Common Duiker

Ader's Duiker

Natal Red Duiker

Blue Duiker

Savanna Elephant

Bat-eared Fox

Black-backed Jackal

Side-striped Jackal

African Wolf

African Wild Dog

Zorilla or Striped Polecat

Honey Badger or Ratel

African Civet

Small-spotted Genet

Common Large-spotted Genet

Slender Mongoose

Banded Mongoose

Dwarf Mongoose

White-tailed Mongoose

Spotted Hyaena

Striped Hyaena

Aardwolf

Cheetah

Lion

Leopard

Serval

Caracal

Yellow-spotted Rock Hyrax

Rock Hyrax

Aardvark

Ground Pangolin

White-bellied Hedgehog

Cape Hare

Savanna Hare

Springhare

Unstriped Ground Squirrel

North African Porcupine

Golden-rumped Sengi

Little Grebe

White-breasted
Cormorant

Reed Cormorant

African Darter

Hamerkop

Grey Heron

Purple Heron

Goliath Heron

Black-headed Heron

Great White Heron

Western Reef Heron

Green-backed Heron

Black-crowned Night
Heron

Cattle Egret

Greater Flamingo

Lesser Flamingo

African Spoonbill

Hadeda Ibis

Sacred Ibis

Glossy Ibis

Pink-backed Pelican

Great White Pelican

Shoebill Stork

Marabou Stork

Saddle-billed Stork

African Openbill Stork

Woolly-necked Stork

Abdim's Stork

European White Stork

Yellow-billed Wood Stork

Knob-billed Duck male

White-faced Whistling Duck

Fulvous Whistling Duck

Cape Teal

Red-billed Teal

Egyptian Goose

Spurwing Goose

Black Kite

African Fish Eagle

Egyptian Vulture

Bearded Vulture

Bearded Vulture

Lappet-faced Vulture   Palmnut Vulture   Rüppell's Vulture   White-backed Vulture

Hooded Vulture   Black-breasted Snake-Eagle   African Harrier Hawk or Gymnogene   Eastern Chanting Goshawk

Augur Buzzard   Bateleur   African Crowned Eagle   African Crowned Eagle

Crested Eagle   Martial Eagle   Verreaux's Eagle   Tawny Eagle

Pygmy Falcon

Lanner Falcon

Greater Kestrel

Rock Kestrel

Helmeted Guineafowl

Crested Guineafowl

Kenya Crested
Guineafowl

Vulturine Guineafowl

Crested Francolin

Coqui Francolin

Yellow-necked
Spurfowl

Jackson's Spurfowl

Red-necked Spurfowl

Black Crake

Common Moorhen   Purple Swamphen   African Finfoot   Grey Crowned Crane

Buff-crested Bustard   Black-bellied Bustard   Kori Bustard

Northern White-bellied   African Jacana   Crab Plover   Spotted Stone Curlew
Bustard

Water Stone Curlew   Red-winged Pratincole

Temminck's Courser

Double-banded Courser

Brown-breasted Plover

Three-banded Plover

Blacksmith Lapwing

Spur-winged Lapwing

Long-toed Lapwing

Crowned Lapwing

Wattled Lapwing

Painted Snipe

Avocet

Black-winged Stilt

Sooty Gull

Grey-headed Gull

Swift Tern

African Skimmer

Black-faced
Sandgrouse

Green Pigeon

Olive Pigeon

Speckled Pigeon

Mourning Dove

Laughing or Palm Dove

Namaqua Dove

Cape Turtle Dove

Emerald-spotted Wood Dove   Red-eyed Dove

Red-fronted or
Jardine's Parrot

African Grey Parrot

Fischer's Lovebird

Purple-crested Turaco

Schalow's Turaco

White-crested Turaco

Ross's Turaco

Hartlaub's Turaco

White-bellied Go-
away-bird or Turaco

Green Malkoha

White-browed Coucal

Black Coucal

African Wood Owl

African Scops Owl

African White-faced Scops Owl

Giant or Verreaux's Eagle-Owl

Spotted Eagle-Owl

African Hoopoe

Speckled Mousebird

Woodland Kingfisher

Giant Kingfisher

Mangrove Kingfisher

Half-collared Kingfisher

Pied Kingfisher

Pied Kingfisher

Blue-breasted
Kingfisher

Purple Roller

European Roller

Lilac-breasted Roller

Little Bee-eater

Swallow-tailed Bee-
eater

White-fronted Bee-
eater

European Bee-eater

Southern Carmine
Bee-eater

Somali Ostrich

Masaai Ostrich

Secretarybird

Southern Ground
Hornbill

Abyssinian Ground
Hornbill

Crowned Hornbill

Black and White Casqued Hornbill

Northern Red-billed Hornbill

Trumpeter Hornbill

Von der Decken's Hornbill male

Von der Decken's Hornbill female

Silvery-cheeked Hornbill

Grey Hornbill

Double-toothed Barbet

Red and Yellow Barbet

Crested Barbet

Black-collared Barbet

D'Arnaud's Barbet

Golden-tailed
Woodpecker

Greater Striped
Swallow

Barn Swallow

Wire-tailed Swallow

Red-breasted Swallow

Cape Wagtail

Pink-throated
Longclaw

Fork-tailed Drongo

White-necked Raven

Black-headed Oriole

Arrow-marked Babbler

Dark-capped or Black-
eyed Bulbul

Groundscraper Thrush

Kurrichane Thrush

Mountain Thrush

White-browed
Robin-Chat

Snowy-crowned
Robin-Chat

Cape Robin-Chat

Mocking Chat

Familiar Chat

Capped Wheatear

Chinspot Batis

Red-backed Shrike

Taita Fiscal

African Paradise
Flycatcher

Long-tailed Fiscal

Common Fiscal

Magpie Shrike

Rosy-patched Shrike

White Helmet-Shrike

Tropical Boubou

Black-headed Gonolek

Violet-backed Starling

Lesser Blue-eared
Glossy Starling

Golden-breasted
Starling

Superb Starling

Red-winged Starling

Fischer's Starling

Wattled Starling

Yellow-billed Oxpecker

Red-billed Oxpecker

Grey-headed Sparrow

White-headed Buffalo Weaver

Red-billed Buffalo Weaver

White-browed Sparrow-Weaver

Red-headed Weaver

Chestnut Weaver

Lesser Masked Weaver

Southern Masked Weaver

Thick-billed Weaver

Village Weaver

Yellow Weaver

Red-billed Quelea

Green-winged Ptylia

Southern Bishop

White-winged Widowbird

Paradise Whydah

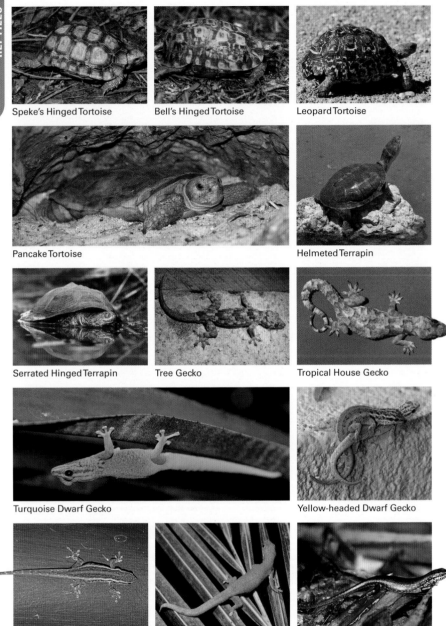

Speke's Hinged Tortoise

Bell's Hinged Tortoise

Leopard Tortoise

Pancake Tortoise

Helmeted Terrapin

Serrated Hinged Terrapin

Tree Gecko

Tropical House Gecko

Turquoise Dwarf Gecko

Yellow-headed Dwarf Gecko

Cape Dwarf Gecko

Dull-green Day Gecko

Speckle-lipped Skink

Tree Skink

Striped Skink

Great Plated Lizard

Red-headed Rock Agama male

Mwanza Flat-headed Agama

Blue-headed Tree Agama

Flap-necked Chameleon (two colour variations)

Von Höhnel's Chameleon

Giant One-horned Chameleon

White-throated Savanna Monitor

Nile Monitor

Nile Crocodile

Southern African Rock Python

Brown House Snake

Boomslang male

Bark Snake

Common Egg-eater

Egyptian Cobra

Mozambique Spitting Cobra

Red Spitting Cobra

Green Mamba

Black Mamba

Gaboon Viper

Rhinoceros Viper

Puff Adder

Common Squeaker

Flat-backed Toad

Morara Forest Toad

Guttural Toad

Red Toad

Bocage's Tree Frog

Fornasini's Spiny Reed Frog

Mountain Reed Frog

Tinker Reed Frog

Common Reed Frog

Kivu Reed Frog

Senegal Kassina

Angolan River Frog

Common Ornate Frog

Southern Foam-nest Frog

Natal Puddle Frog

African Giant Bullfrog

Mascarene Ridged Frog

Banded Rubber Frog

Doum Palms

Raffia Palms

Lala Palm

Borassus Palm

Wild Date Palms

Wild Date Palm

African Tulip Tree

African Tulip Tree flowers, pods

Baobab wet season

Baobab dry season

Cape Ash fruits and leaves

Sickle Bush flowers

Sickle Bush

Tree Euphorbia

Hagenia

Hagenia flower clusters

East African Yellowwood

East African Yellowwood detail

Wild Mango

Weeping Wattle flowers

Waterberry

Waterberry fruits

Quinine Tree

Quinine Tree fruit and leaves

Red Mahogany

Red Mahogany fruit on ground

Fried Egg Tree flower

Wild Teak

Wild Teak fruits

Leadwood

Leadwood bark

Paperbark Thorn flowers

Umbrella Thorn

Whistling Thorn

Fever Tree

Knob Thorn bark

Ana Tree flowers

Broom Cluster Fig

Broom Cluster Fig fruits

Common Cluster Fig buttressed trunk

Common Cluster Fig

Strangler Fig roots

Strangler Fig

Rock Fig aggressive roots

Knobbly Fig fruits

Wild Gardenia

Neat's Foot Bauhinia flower

Vernonia

African Pencil Cedar

African Pencil Cedar detail

African Pencil Cedar

Paperbark typical bark

Large-fruited Combretum

Pod Mahogany pods, leaves

Pod Mahogany seed pod

Screw Pine fruits

Screw Pine

Screw Pine

Marula

Marula fruits and leaves

Wooden Banana

Mutondo pods and leaves

Tamarind

Tamarind fruits

Msasa pods and leaves

Monkey Orange fruit, leaves

Sausage Tree

Sausage Tree flower

Sausage Tree fruits

Black Mangrove

Toothbrush Tree

Red Mangrove

Sand Olive

Desert Rose or Impala Lily

Desert Rose flower

Forest Fever Tree fruit, leaves

Natal Mahogany fruits, seeds

Apple-leaf Tree

Apple-leaf Tree pods

Cape Chestnut flowers

PHOTOGRAPHIC CREDITS

Key: b = bottom, l = left, m = middle, r = right, t = top

AI = Africa Image Library; AVZ = Ariadne van Zandbergen; AW = Alan Weaving; DSB = Daryl and Sharna Balfour; IOA = Images of Africa; JC = John Carlyon; ND = Nigel Dennis; SS = Shutterstock.com; WC = Wikimedia Commons

INTRODUCTION: p6: DSB/IOA; **p9**: DSB/IOA; **p10**: paula french/SS; **p12**: Travel Stock/SS; **p13**: andBeyond.com/ Stevie Mann

TANZANIA: p14: andBeyond.com/Stevie Mann; **p16**: GUDKOV ANDREY/SS; **p17**: DSB/IOA; **p24**: AVZ/AI; **p27 t**: Ikiwaner/WC, GFDL 1.2; **p27 b**: DSB/IOA; **p28**: ND/IOA; **p29**: Gillian Black; **p32**: AW; **p38**: Vadim Petrakov/SS; **p39**: Walter Mittelholzer/ETH-Bibliothek/WC, public domain; **p40**: Avatar_023/SS; **p41 t**: Alexander Chizhenok/SS; **p41 b both**: ND/IOA; **p47**: Peter Blackwell/IOA; **p49 t**: AVZ/AI; **p49 b**: ND/IOA; **p58**: JC; **p65 m**: JC; **p79**: S. Brøgger-Jansen; **p83**: User: (WT-shared) Digr at wts wikivoyage/WC, CC BY-SA 3.0; **p84**: BBM Explorer/www.bbmexplorer.com/ WC, CC BY-SA 2.0; **p85**: Panii/WC, CC BY-SA 3.0; **p86**: Laika ac/WC, CC BY-SA 2.0; **p87 t**: Peter Blackwell/IOA; **p88**: Peter Blackwell/IOA; **p92 t**: DSB/IOA; **p92 m**: ND/IOA; **p92 b**: DSB/IOA; **p93 m**: Roger de la Harpe/IOA; **p93 b**: Ludmila Yilmaz/SS; **p94**: Lara Tranter; **p95**: Jojona/WC, CC BY-SA 4.0; **p96**: AVZ/AI; **p97**: AVZ/AI; **p99**: AVZ/AI

KENYA: p100: Gail Johnson/SS; **p102**: DSB/IOA; **p103**: Tomas Hulik/SS; **p105 m**: Lenka Krejcova/SS; **p106 b**: Victor Lapaev/SS; **p107 t**: huang jenhung/SS; **p107 m**: Merrittimages/WC, CC BY-SA 4.0; **p109**: Gil.K/SS; **p111**: DSB/IOA; **p113 t**: Serge Vero/SS; **p115**: alanf/SS; **p117 t**: ND/IOA; **p119 t**: Vorobyev Dmitry/SS; **p120**: AVZ/AI; **p122 br**: Tristan Kyle Bruce/SS; **p123**: Lanz von Horsten/IOA; **p124 b**: ND/IOA; **p125**: Chris 73/WC, CC BY-SA 3.0; **p126**: Mehmet Karatay/WC, CC BY-SA 3.0; **p127 t**: Josski at Dutch Wikipedia/WC, public domain; **p129 tl**: Chris 73/WC, CC BY-SA 3.0; **p131**: mbrand85/SS; **p133 b**: mbrand85/SS; **p136**: Martin Harvey/AfriPics; **p137**: Durova/WC, CC BY-SA 4.0; **p138**: Byelikova Oksana/SS; **p139**: Andrew Banister/IOA; **p140 t**: DSB/IOA; **p140 b**: TimVickers/WC, public domain; **p141**: kyslynskyyhal/SS; **p145 bl**: DSB/IOA; **p147**: Bernard DUPONT/WC, CC BY-SA 2.0; **p148**: DSB/IOA; **p149**: MicheleB/SS; **p153 t**: MicheleB/SS; **p155**: GUDKOV ANDREY/SS; **p157**: Circumnavigation/SS; **p158 b**: andBeyond.com; **p159 bl**: ND/IOA; **p160 tl**: Alexandr Junek Imaging/SS; **p160 tr**: andBeyond.com/Stevie Mann; **p160 b**: DSB/IOA; **p162**: Marius Dobilas/SS; **p164**: TheLearningPhotographer/SS; **p165**: EXPLORER/SS; **p166**: Ronaldcameron/WC, CC BY-SA 4.0; **p167**: Matthias Bohnen/WC, CC BY-SA 4.0

UGANDA: p170: Travel Stock/SS; **p172**: andBeyond.com /Andrew Schoeman; **p173**: Duncan Wright/WC, CC BY-SA 3.0 htt; **p175 t**: GUDKOV ANDREY/SS; **p175 b**: Radek Borovka//SS; **p176 t**: H. v. Rompaey; **p176 b**: Charlesjsharp/ Sharp Photography/WC, CC BY-SA 4.0; **p177 t**: Jukka Jantunen//SS; **p177 b**: Heiko Kiera/SS; **p178**: Dror Feitelson/WC, CC BY-SA 3.0; **p180 t**: Juliano Costa/WC, CC BY-SA 3.0; **p180 b**: Charlesjsharp/Sharp Photography/WC, CC BY-SA 4.0; **p181 t**: JC; **p182**: Delmas Lehman/SS; **p184**: JC; **p185**: JC; **p186 b**: JC; **p187**: JC; **p188**: edeantoine/SS; **p192 b**: JC; **p193 t**: Andrew Bannister/IOA; **p194**: Albert Backer/WC, CC BY-SA 4.0; **p195**: By Albert Backer/WC, CC BY-SA 3.0; **p196**: Manuel Werner/WC, CC BY-SA 2.5; **p197 t**: feathercollector/SS; **p197 b**: Mark Dudley Photography/SS; **p198**: Guswen/WC, CC BY-SA 3.0; **p199**: Radek Borovka/SS; **p200**: Alberto Loyo/SS; **p201 t**: Robert Haasmann/SS; **p202**: Monika Hrdinova/SS

RWANDA: p203: andBeyond.com; **p204 t**: Louis Dewame/WC, CC BY 3.0; **p204 b**: Tetyana Dotsenko/SS; **p205**: Mr. Meijer/SS; **p206**: Charlesjsharp/Sharp Photography/WC, CC BY-SA 4.0; **p207**: Charlesjsharp/Sharp Photography/WC, CC BY-SA 4.0

IDENTIFICATION GUIDE: p208: DSB/IOA; **p209 top row l**: Ltshears/WC, CC BY-SA 3.0; **p209 bottom row l**: M. Boddicker; **p209 bottom row m**: H. v. Rompaey; **p210 2nd row m**: Bastiaan Boon; **p210 3rd row l**: I. Gaigher/Lajuma; **p210 3rd row m**: Bastiaan Boon; **p212 top row l**: DSB/IOA; **p213 top row r**: JC; **p213 2nd row r**: JC; **p213 bottom row m**: JC; **p213 bottom row r**: JC; **p214 2nd row l**: I. Gaigher/Lajuma; **p214 2nd row m**: JC; **p214 2nd row r**: JC;

p214 3rd row l: JC; p214 4th row l: JC; p214 4th row r: M. Jongbloed; p215 3rd row r: W. Poduschka; p215 4th row m: JC; p215 bottom row r: K. Rudloff; p216 top row l: JC; p217 top row l: ND/IOA; p217 2nd row r: JC; p218 third row r: ND/IOA; p218 bottom row r: JC; p219 top row l: ND/IOA; p219 3rd row r: JC; p223 2nd row l: ND/IOA; p224 bottom row mr: AW; p225 top row l: AW; p225 top row r: JC; p225 2nd row l: JC; p225 3rd row m: JC; p225 bottom row l: AW; p225 bottom row mr: ND/IOA; p226 3rd row ml: ND/IOA; p226 3rd row r: Nicor/WC, CC BY-SA 3.0; p227 3rd row r: Peter Blackwell/IOA; p227 bottom row r: JC; p228 top row ml: JC; p228 top row r: JC; p228 3rd row l: JC; p228 3rd row ml: John Kessy/WC, CC BY-SA 2.0; p238 bottom row l: ND/IOA; p229 2nd row l: SandyCole/WC, CC BY-SA 3.0; p229 3rd row mr: JC; p229 3rd row r: JC; p230 2nd row ml: JC; p230 2nd row mr: JC; p230 bottom row r: Albert Froneman/IOA; p231 2nd row l: JC; p231 3rd row mr: AW; p231 4th row l: Albert Froneman/IOA; p232 3rd row l: ND/IOA; p234 2nd row l: Richard Boycott; p234 3rd row l: Johan Marais; p234 3rd row ml: Richard Boycott; p238 2nd row m: Roger de la Harpe/IOA; p238 bottom row m: David Casto/WC, public domain; p238 bottom row r: Dwergenpaartje/WC, CC BY-SA 4.0; p239 top row l and m: Forest and Kim Starr

SUGGESTED FURTHER READING

Channing, A. & Howell, K.M. 2006. *Amphibians of East Africa*. Cornell University Press, New York.

Dharani, N. 2011. *Field Guide to Common Trees and Shrubs of East Africa*. Struik Nature, Cape Town.

Estes, R.D. 2012. *The Behaviour Guide to African Mammals*. University of California Press, Berkeley.

Martins, D.J. 2014. *Pocket Guide: Insects of East Africa*. Struik Nature, Cape Town.

Spawls, S. *et al*. 2006. *Reptiles and Amphibians of East Africa*. Princeton University Press, Princeton.

Stevenson, T. & Fanshawe, J. 2006. *Birds of East Africa*. Princeton University Press, Princeton.

Stuart, C. & Stuart, M. 2009. *Pocket Guide: Mammals of East Africa*. Struik Nature, Cape Town.

Stuart, C. & Stuart, M. 2013. *A Field Guide to the Tracks and Signs of Southern, Central and East African Wildlife*. Struik Nature, Cape Town.

Stuart, C. & Stuart, M. 2017. *Stuarts' Field Guide to the Larger Mammals of Africa*. Struik Nature, Cape Town.

USEFUL CONTACTS

Kenya Forest Service **www.kenyaforestservice.org**
Kenya Wildlife Service **www.kws.go.ke**
Tanzania Forest Reserves **www.tfs.go.tz/services/category/forest-reserves**
Tanzania National Parks **www.tanzaniaparks.go.tz**
Uganda National Forestry Authority **www.nfa.org.ug/index.php/products-services/eco-tourism**
Uganda Wildlife Authority **www.ugandawildlife.org**